it's a STITCH

21 Patchwork Quilt Projects with an Eye on Tradition

Edited by Karen Bolesta

RODALE

Printed in the United States of America

Rodale Inc. makes every effort to use acid-free ∞, recycled paper ♲.

The quilt projects in this book were originally published in the Classic American Quilt Collection series, published by Rodale Inc.

Contributing Writer: Laurie Edwards Baker
Illustrations by: Mario Ferro and Jackie Walsh (pages 4–9, 12–19, 40–47, 50–55, 68–71, 82–87, 90–95, 98–103, 106–111, 114–120, 140–147, 168–171); Sandy Freeman (pages 30–37, 58–65, 74–79, 132–137, 160–165, 174–181); Charles Metz (pages 22–26, 114–120, 124–129, 150–157)

Photographs by Mitch Mandel/Rodale Images (pages 2, 10, 20, 28, 38, 48, 56, 66, 72, 80, 88, 96, 104, 112, 122, 130, 138, 148, 158, 166, 172); John Hamel (pages 20, 122, 148); Kurt Wilson (pages 88, 104)

The Amish Easter Baskets quilt by Elsie Vredenburg and photograph appear courtesy of the Collection of the Museum of the American Quilter's Society (MAQS), Paducah, Kentucky.

Library of Congress Cataloging-in-Publication Data

It's a stitch : 21 patchwork quilt projects with an eye on tradition / edited by Karen Bolesta.
    p.   cm.
  ISBN 1–57954–914–4 paperback
    1. Patchwork—Patterns. 2. Quilting—Patterns. 3. Patchwork quilts. I. Bolesta, Karen.
  TT835.I86 2004
  746.46—dc22
                                                 2003069341

Distributed to the book trade by St. Martin's Press

2 4 6 8 10 9 7 5 3 1   paperback

WE **INSPIRE** AND **ENABLE** PEOPLE TO IMPROVE
THEIR LIVES AND THE WORLD AROUND THEM

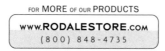

FOR MORE OF OUR PRODUCTS
WWW.RODALESTORE.COM
(800) 848-4735

Contents

Introduction

Quilting really is a stitch, isn't it? Who else but a quilter could have so much fun rummaging through piles of fabric and dreaming the day away thinking about the design possibilities?

Who else could find joy in a small spool of metallic thread and excitement in a funny-looking gadget called a darning foot? Who else thinks cutting up fabric and sewing it back together again is cause for celebration?

Who else gets a thrill out of a pile of quilt blocks, then gets an even greater thrill by sewing together row after row of those quilt blocks into a large, and often unmanageable, quilt top?

Who else relishes sitting upright in a chair for months, making tens of thousands of tiny hand-quilting stitches just so a quilt can have an heirloom feel?

Who else finds immense pleasure in pinning and hand-sewing a binding and in making tightly mitered binding corners and a nearly invisible seam join where the binding ends meet?

Who else but a quilter understands the sense of accomplishment you get when you hang a completed wallhanging and the edges don't ripple?

Who else spends days or weeks waxing poetic about the quilt's label and finds just the right words to express the love that went into the quilt?

A quilter does, that's who! And we quilters are having a stitch doing it! From the very first moment you step into a fabric store to buy yardage for a new project to the last stitch you put in the binding, you're celebrating your creativity and your unique ability to combine colors and textures into a work of art.

Sure there are bumps along the way, such as discovering that your ¼-inch seam allowance is a little too generous or that you've sewn a row on upside down, but the sense of joy and accomplishment at the sight of your finished quilt is a feel-good, giddy, positively wonderful moment. It's a stitch, in fact!

It's a Stitch
Projects

Barn Raising Pinwheels

Skill Level: Easy

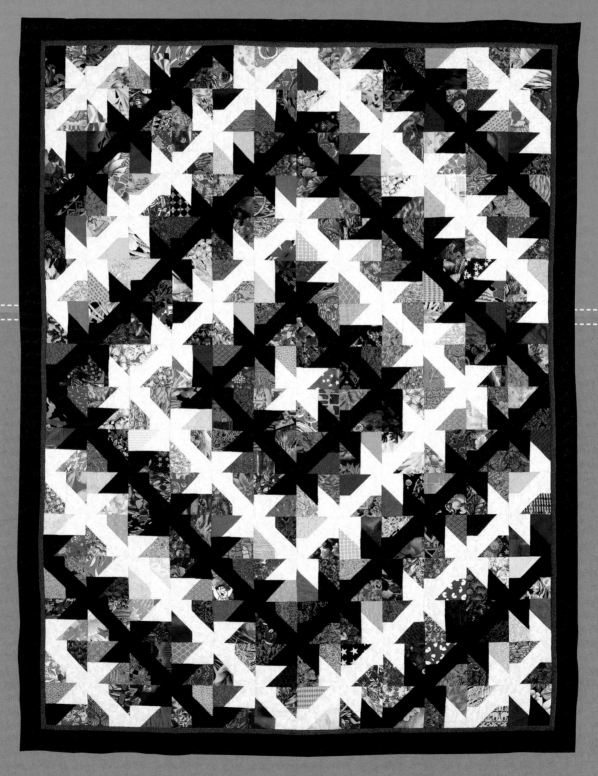

*E*asy enough for a confident beginner, this dynamic double-size quilt offers a bold design that looks harder to piece than it actually is. Pinwheel blocks with dark and light centers are arranged in a barn raising–style setting to create lots of movement, so the viewer's eyes can't help but travel about the quilt top examining the many scraps of fabric. Quiltmaker Barbara Berliner obviously has a sense of humor, having included fabrics with cartoon characters, sneakers, holiday themes, tropical birds, and a guitar along with more traditional florals and prints.

Before You Begin

The blocks in this machine-pieced quilt go together quickly. At first glance, the design appears complex because of the jagged barn raising setting, but just two block variations are used in the quilt. Blocks have only straight seams, and no setting in is required. The completed blocks are simply rotated to achieve the medallion-style effect.

Choosing Fabrics

In the quilt shown, a light gray print and a black print were used for the rows of diagonal pinwheels. These neutral fabrics are surrounded by scraps of vibrant medium to medium-dark fabrics. The scrap fabrics range from bright florals to juvenile prints (there's even one containing Fred Flintstone!). This quilt would work equally well featuring any two contrasting fabrics for the pinwheels, such as red and white or forest green and tan, with

scraps that are bold or subdued. The most critical design element is that the color value of the scraps be medium to dark.

To create your own color

scheme for this quilt, photocopy the **Color Plan** on page 210, and use colored pencils, crayons, or markers to fill in the blocks until you are satisfied with the design.

Quilt Sizes

	Double (shown)	King
Finished Quilt Size	80½" × 104½"	104½" × 104½"
Number of Blocks	48	64
Finished Block Size	12"	12"

Materials

Fabric	Double	King
Black print	2⅜ yards	3⅛ yards
Light gray print	2⅜ yards	3⅛ yards
Assorted medium prints	4⅝ yards	6⅛ yards
Dark blue	½ yard	⅝ yard
Black	1⅛ yards	1⅛ yards
Backing	7⅝ yards	9⅝ yards
Batting	89" × 113"	113" × 113"
Binding	¾ yard	⅞ yard

NOTE: *Yardages are based on 44/45-inch-wide fabrics that are at least 42 inches wide after preshrinking.*

3

Cutting Chart

Fabric	Used For	Strip Width	Number to Cut Double	Number to Cut King	Second Cut Piece	Number to Cut Double	Number to Cut King
Black print	Pinwheels	3½"	20	26	A	192	256
Light gray print	Pinwheels	3½"	20	26	A	192	256
Medium prints	Pinwheels	3½"	40	52	A	384	512
Dark blue	Inner border	1½"	10	11			
Black	Outer border	3½"	10	11			

Cutting

Make a durable template from pattern piece A on page 8—one that will hold up as you cut all the pieces for your quilt from it. For more information about making and using templates, see page 186.

While a template is required for this project, all sides of the pattern piece are straight, which allows you to use your rotary cutter. The Cutting Chart lists the number of strips and their width to cut from the dark and light fabrics, followed by the number of A pieces to cut from those strips. After cutting strips with your rotary-cutting equipment, tape the A template to the underside of a see-through rotary ruler. Align the longest side of the template with the 45 degree line on your ruler, and position the diagonal edge of the template flush with the edge of the ruler, as shown in **Diagram 1.** Then place the template over your fabric strip, as shown, and simply make the final diagonal cut for each A piece. This rotary shortcut will save you from tracing hundreds of A pieces on the black and gray fabrics.

All measurements include ¼-inch seam allowances. Refer to the Cutting Chart for the number of pieces to cut from each fabric.

Note: Cut and piece one sample block before cutting all the fabric for the quilt.

Sew Easy

The rotary ruler/template method described in "Cutting" can speed up cutting all of the bright print A pieces, too. If you use scraps, you won't have long strips of fabric, but you can still stack a few scraps, cut the layers into 3½-inch-wide strips (even if they are short), and then tape your A template to the ruler as described. You may not be able to cut a dozen A pieces from one set of strips, but even if you cut one or two pieces, you'll save time because your scrap fabrics are layered for quick rotary cutting.

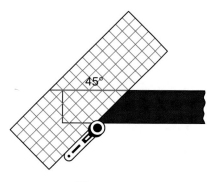

Diagram 1

Piecing the Blocks

Two block variations are used in this quilt to give the light and dark diamond effect in the quilt setting. One block has light gray print pinwheels in the center, and the other has black print pinwheel centers. The placement of the medium prints is the same in both block variations, as shown in the **Block Diagram.**

Gray
Pinwheel

Black
Pinwheel

Block Diagram

Gray Pinwheel Blocks

Step 1. For one gray Pinwheel block, you'll need six light gray A pieces, two black A pieces, and eight medium print A pieces. Lay out the fabric into four groups, each containing four pieces, as shown in **Diagram 2A.**

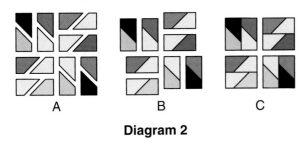

A B C

Diagram 2

Step 2. Sew each pair of A pieces together along the diagonal edges, as shown in **2B.** Press the seam allowances toward the darker fabric in each pair.

Sew Quick

Assembly line piecing can be used to make piecing this quilt top quick and easy. Instead of laying out all your pieces individually, start by sewing each light gray piece to a print piece along the diagonal edge. Keep feeding pairs of light gray and print A pieces through your machine. Then sew each black piece to a print piece along the diagonal edge in the same assembly line manner. When you lay out your pieces, you'll already have Step 2 (above) completed!

Step 3. Sew the two pairs in each quadrant together, as shown in **2C.** Press the seam allowances to one side.

Step 4. Sew the four units together to complete the block. Don't press the seam allowances yet. Repeat until you've assembled the total number of gray Pinwheel blocks required for your quilt size.

Black Pinwheel Blocks

For one black Pinwheel block, you'll need six black A pieces, two light gray A pieces, and eight medium print A pieces. In this block, the gray and black pieces are in opposite positions from the light Pinwheel blocks, as shown in **Diagram 3.** Sew these blocks together in the same manner as the gray blocks. Make the total number of black Pinwheel blocks required for your quilt size. Do not press the seams yet.

Diagram 3

Assembling the Quilt Top

Step 1. Following the assembly diagrams on pages 6–7, use a design wall or other flat surface to arrange the quilt blocks for your size quilt into horizontal rows. Press the center seams of adjacent blocks in opposite directions so you can more easily align them for sewing.

Step 2. Sew the blocks in each row together. Press all seams in adjoining rows in opposite directions, then sew the rows together, matching seams carefully. Press the quilt top.

Attaching the Mitered Borders

All the action in this quilt is contained within a mitered double border. You will need to sew the

Double-Size Assembly Diagram

dark blue strips to the black strips for each edge of the quilt first, then add them to the quilt top as a single unit, mitering the corners.

Step 1. To determine the length for the side borders, measure the quilt top vertically, taking the measurement through the center of the quilt. To this measurement, add two times the finished width of the border (4 inches × 2 = 8 inches), plus 5 inches. This is the length you will need to make the two side borders. In the same manner, measure the quilt top horizontally through the center and calculate the length of the top and bottom borders.

Step 2. Sew the 1½-inch-wide dark blue border strips together end to end to make strips of the lengths calculated in Step 1. Repeat with the 3½-

inch-wide black border strips. Keep the side border strips separate from those for the top and bottom of the quilt.

Step 3. Working with the side borders first, pin and sew a dark blue border strip and a black border strip together, as shown in **Diagram 4.** Press the seams toward the black border. Repeat with the remaining side border strips. In the same manner, pin and sew the top and bottom border strips together into two units. Press the seams toward the blue border.

Diagram 4

Step 4. Pin and sew the four border units to the quilt top, making sure the narrow blue border is flush with the quilt's edges. Refer to page 204 for instructions on adding borders with mitered corners. When preparing the miters, be sure to match the seams of the strips in adjacent borders, as shown in the **Quilt Diagram** on page 8.

Quilting and Finishing

Step 1. Mark the quilt top for quilting, if desired. The quilt shown was machine quilted in the ditch around each piece. A simple scallop design was used in the outer border as a nice relief from all of the jagged edges in the patchwork.

Step 2. Regardless of which quilt size you've chosen to make, the backing will have to be pieced. For either quilt, cut the backing fabric crosswise into three equal pieces, and trim the selvages. Cut a 35-inch-wide segment from the entire length of two pieces. Sew a narrow segment to each side of the wide piece, as shown in **Diagram 5.**

Step 3. Layer the quilt top, batting, and backing; baste the layers together. Quilt as desired.

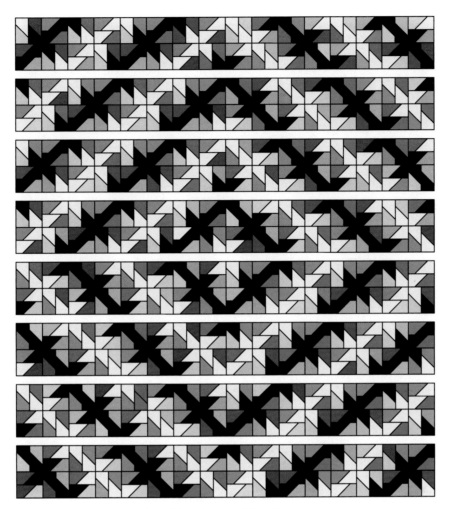

King-Size Assembly Diagram

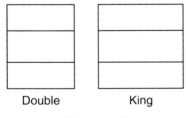

Double   King

Diagram 5

Step 4. Referring to the directions on page 206, make and attach double-fold binding. In the quilt shown, the binding is the same fabric as the outer border. To calculate the amount of binding needed for your quilt size, add the length of the four sides of the quilt plus 9 inches. The total is the approximate number of inches of binding you will need.

King   Double   King

Quilt Diagram

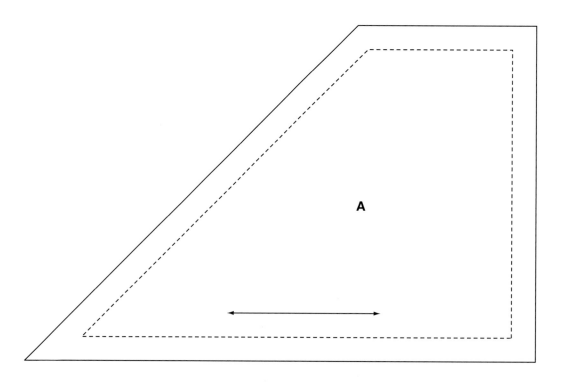

A

12 Steps to Stash Reduction

(Or, How to Use Up What You've Got So You Can Buy More)

Is every closet in your house harboring yards of fabric? Do you hide newly acquired purchases from your loved ones? Should you buy stock in a storage container company? Quilters are known for their love of fabric, so if you've answered yes to any of the above questions, maybe it's time to slow down on the buying and speed up on the stitching. Making changes isn't easy, but these suggestions could take you step-by-step to a more manageable and less cluttered workspace.

1. Take your name off all quilt shop and fabric store mailing lists. That includes e-mail lists. Knowledge of a sale will only tempt you.

2. When you're tempted to go shopping, visit your stash. You're sure to find something you forgot you had. It will almost be like having something new. Realizing the sheer magnitude of what you own may deter you from buying more.

3. While you're visiting your long lost "friends," weed out pieces that no longer appeal to you. You could also donate unused yardage to an organization that makes charity quilts, or you could give yardage to a new quilter.

4. Organize your stash so you know what you own. Store it so it is visible and accessible. Knowing what you have and being able to find it will create all sorts of inspiration.

5. Sort through your patterns and find two or three you'd like to make. Match up the patterns with fabric from your stash, and bundle everything together as projects-in-waiting. Having projects ready to go keeps you thinking in the right direction. (And be sure to repeat as necessary.)

6. Finish projects you've started.

7. If you need something to complete a project, send someone else to the fabric store to get it. You know you have friends who would love to help out.

8. If you find that you must go to a fabric store, make a list of the items that you need before entering the premises. Stick to your list.

9. Give yourself a nonfabric reward for every five pieces you use from your stash. How about a massage or a manicure?

10. Your stash probably includes stacks of magazines. Periodically go through them, tearing out what you'll use and passing along or recycling the rest of the pile. Then, stop buying them. Get all the benefits without the storage problems by checking them out of your local library or borrowing them from a friend.

11. Just use gray thread. It goes with everything. Every quilter could use fewer tangled spools.

12. Save your fabric receipts. Nothing hurts like the truth.

Rose Rings

Skill Level: Challenging

$\mathcal{Q}$uiltmaker Susan Stein combined her mastery of curved piecing, machine quilting, and three-dimensional appliqué into a striking wallhanging. The interlocking Wedding Rings adorned with another symbol of love—the rose—make this a quilt that no true romantic can resist. In addition to the appliqué, machine stipple quilting provides further visual interest to the quilt.

Before You Begin

This quilt is an intricate combination of pieced Wedding Rings and appliqué. We have provided yardage requirements and cutting instructions for two sizes, the wallhanging pictured and a queen-size quilt. Because the three-dimensional appliqué is added after the entire quilt top is pieced, we have not given specific numbers of flower pieces to cut for the queen size. You may prefer to add flowers and vines just around the outer rings so you won't have to maneuver your way to the center of the quilt top to appliqué. Or you may want the challenge of appliquéing across the entire surface. Therefore, we have provided guidelines for yardage and cutting, but we'll leave the specifics up to you.

Read through the entire project directions before beginning, and refer to "Quiltmaking Basics," beginning on page 191, if you need additional information on sewing curved seams.

You will need to make both Wedding Ring templates and flower templates for this quilt. Use templates A, B, C, D, and E on page 18 to piece the quilt top. The flower templates are on page 19. For more information on making and using templates, see page 186 in "Quiltmaking Basics."

Quilt Sizes

	Wallhanging (shown)	Queen
Finished Quilt Size	39" × 48½"	96" × 105½"
Finished Ring Size	15"	15"
Number of Rings	12	90
Number of Pieced Arcs	62	398

Materials

Fabric	Wallhanging	Queen
Beige	1½ yards	9⅞ yards
Tan	½ yard	1¼ yards
Taupe	⅓ yard	2 yards
Brown	1¼ yards	3½ yards
Pink	⅜ yard	1¼ yards
Rose	⅓ yard	2 yards
Maroon	1¾ yards	4½ yards
Mauve	½ yard	2½ yards
Dark mauve	⅓ yard	2 yards
Rose print	⅓ yard	¾ yard
Backing	2¾ yards	8¾ yards
Batting	46" × 56"	103" × 113"
Binding	½ yard	⅞ yard

NOTE: *Yardages are based on 44/45-inch-wide fabrics that are at least 42 inches wide after preshrinking.*

Cutting Chart

Fabric	Used For	Piece	Number of Pieces	
			Wallhanging	Queen
Beige	Background	A	12	90
	Melons	B	31	199
Tan	Connecting diamonds	C	31	199
Pink	Connecting diamonds	C	31	199
Rose	Arcs	D	62	398
Maroon	Arcs	E	62	398
Mauve	Arcs	E	62	398
Dark mauve	Arcs	E	62	398
Brown	Arcs	E	62	398
Taupe	Arcs	D reverse	62	398

Fabric	Used For	Strip Width	Number of Strips	
			Wallhanging	Queen
Maroon	Borders	6"	4	10

NOTE: *You will also need to cut the flower pieces from a variety of fabrics, including the rose print, using the patterns on page 19. Each pattern piece indicates the number of pieces to cut from each fabric for the wallhanging-size quilt. See "Appliquéing the Flowers" on page 14 for more details.*

Choosing Fabrics

The quiltmaker selected solid hand-dyed fabrics for her quilt. The surface of the quilt changes from shades of rose to greenish tans, with an occasional splash of light pink to brighten the quilt. Only one print was used to add detail to the petals of the three-dimensional roses. This print was also used for the quilt binding.

You can buy commercially dyed fabrics in the same color range or in another color scheme. Look for complementary colors in muted shades if you want to achieve the soft mood of this quilt.

If you prefer to use hand-dyed fabrics but don't have access to them in your area, shop online or substitute tone-on-tone prints.

Cutting

All measurements include ¼-inch seam allowances. Referring to the Cutting Chart, cut the required number of pieces for your quilt size. For the floral appliqué for the wallhanging, you will find the number of pieces to cut from each fabric listed on the individual pattern pieces.

You will also need to cut 1⅛-inch-wide bias strips from the brown fabric to make the vines. The bias strips should be about 20 inches long. For the wallhanging, you will need about 15 bias strips. The number needed for the queen-size quilt will depend on whether you appliqué just around the edges or across the entire quilt top. If you appliqué the entire top, you will need about sixty 20-inch bias strips. If you appliqué only the outer edges, you will need about 25 bias strips.

Note: Cut and piece one sample block before cutting all of the fabric for the quilt.

Piecing the Arcs

Step 1. Stack the D, D reverse, and E pieces in separate piles, according to color. Begin each pieced arc with a rose D. To the right of it, sew a maroon E, then a mauve E, a dark mauve E, and a brown E; end with a taupe D reverse piece. As you sew, be sure pieces are oriented so that curves arch in the same direction, so your finished arc looks like the one in **Diagram 1**. Gently press seams to one side, taking care not to stretch the unit. Repeat, assembling all the arcs required for your quilt.

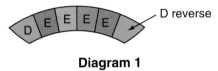

Diagram 1

Step 2. Center and sew one pieced arc to one side of each B melon, as shown in **Diagram 2**. For more detailed information on assembling the curved pieces common to most Wedding Ring quilts, refer to page 191 in "Quiltmaking Basics." Press the seams toward the melon. You will use half of the pieced arcs for this step.

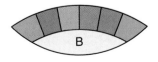

Diagram 2

Step 3. Sew a tan C piece to the light rose D end of the remaining arcs. Sew a pink C piece to

the taupe D reverse piece at the opposite end of each arc, as shown in **Diagram 3**. Gently press the seams in the same direction as the other seams in the arc.

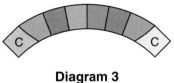

Diagram 3

Step 4. Center and sew these longer pieced arcs to the arc/melon units, as shown in **Diagram 4**. Press all seams toward the melons.

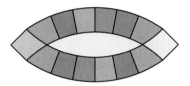

Diagram 4

Assembling the Quilt Top

Step 1. Use a design wall or other flat surface to lay out the completed arc/melon units and the A background pieces in rows, as shown in the **Partial Assembly Diagram**. Note that the orientation of arc/melon units changes from row to row, so refer to the diagram or the photograph on page 10 for directional placement of the pink and tan tips of the arc/melon units.

Partial Assembly Diagram

For the wallhanging, you will have four horizontal rows of three rings each. For the queen-size quilt, you will have ten horizontal rows of nine rings each.

Step 2. Sew the units into horizontal rows. You will need to start and stop stitching ¼ inch from each end of the arcs as you attach them to the beige background pieces. Refer to page 192 in "Quiltmaking Basics" for more details on piecing curves.

Step 3. The assembled rings are appliquéd to a preassembled border unit. For the wallhanging, trim two of the 6-inch-wide maroon strips to 37½ inches for the side borders and trim the others to 39 inches for the top and bottom borders. For the queen-size quilt, you will first need to piece the strips together. Then cut two 94½-inch borders for the sides and two 105½-inch borders for the top and bottom.

Step 4. Beginning at any corner, sew a side border to a top or bottom border, placing the right sides together and aligning the outer edges. Repeat to assemble the border unit shown in **Diagram 5.** Press the seams open.

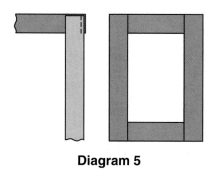

Diagram 5

Step 5. Center the completed quilt top on the border unit. Pin or baste the rings in place, then hand or machine appliqué the outer ring edges to the border, turning under the edges of rings as you work. See the **Wallhanging Diagram.** Refer to page 201 for details on the freezer paper method that can be used for this step. When the appliqué is complete, trim the excess border fabric from beneath the rings to eliminate bulk.

Appliquéing the Flowers

To plan the position of the roses, buds, and leaves, refer to the photo on page 10, or make photocopies of the **Color Plan** on page 216 and sketch in flowers and vines until you are happy with your layout. Making extra bias vine will give you more flexibility to experiment with the design in progress.

Making the Bias Vines

The vine winding through the rings of this quilt appears to be continuous. However, since there are so many junctions of leaves, blossoms, and buds, you can use shorter, easier-to-handle lengths, then hide their raw edges under the appliquéd shapes. We recommend you use a ¼-inch bias bar to make these long, narrow stems.

Step 1. Cut 1⅛-inch-wide bias strips from the brown fabric. Each strip should be at least 20 inches long so you can position graceful curves between appliquéd pieces on your quilt.

Step 2. Fold the strip in half lengthwise, with *wrong* sides together. Press lightly to hold the edges of the fabric together as you stitch. To avoid stretching, do not move the iron back and forth—use an up-and-down motion. Sew the raw edges together using a ¼-inch seam allowance. Trim the seam allowance to approximately ⅛ inch.

Step 3. Insert a ¼-inch bias bar into the tube you've just created, turning the tube slightly to center the seam along the flat edge of the bar. Press the seam allowance to one side, dampening the fabric with water or a bit of spray starch to achieve crisp edges. Trim the seam allowance a bit more if it is too bulky.

Step 4. Flip the tube over, and check to be sure that the seam will be hidden when the strip is appliquéd to the quilt. When you are satisfied with the appearance, press the top side of the tube and remove the bias bar. If your vines are particularly long, you will have to slide the bias bar along the inside of the fabric tube to press the entire length before removing the bar.

Wallhanging Diagram

Step 5. Position the stems as shown in the photograph on page 10 or as determined by your own design. Make sure junctions with raw edges will be hidden by leaves, buds, or blossoms. You can appliqué the stems to the quilt now or after all other designs have been added.

Making the Roses and Leaves

Step 1. For each rose, you will need one background F piece from the rose print fabric. Use the technique of your choice to prepare these pieces for appliqué, referring to page 200 in "Quiltmaking Basics" for more information on appliqué.

Step 2. Each rose also requires two two-sided G petals and three two-sided H petals. Place your petal fabrics (rose print and maroon) *right* sides together, then make two tracings of template G and three tracings of template H onto the wrong side of the lightest fabric. Be sure to leave at least ¼ inch between tracings for seam allowances. Do not cut out the shapes yet.

Step 3. To avoid shifting, press the two petal fabrics together or use a few pins to hold them in place. Machine stitch through both fabrics, sewing directly on the marked lines and backstitching at the beginning and end of seams. Be sure to leave an opening at the bottom of each piece, as indicated on the templates. Cut out all shapes approximately ⅛ inch from the stitching, then clip into the curves. Turn the petals right side out and smooth the seams. Gather the petals slightly with a basting stitch along the open edges. Secure the threads.

Step 4. For the center of each rose, you will need to make a rosebud using template I. The quilt shown has rosebuds cut from a variety of the quilt fabrics. Trace your required number of rosebuds onto your selected fabrics and cut them out. Fold each circle in half, with *wrong* sides together.

Make another fold across the straight folded edge, as shown in **Diagram 6,** angling the fold so that the right edge is folded under more than the left edge. With the second fold away from you, fold each side of the half circle diagonally toward the middle, overlapping the sides. Pin to keep the folds in place. Gather the bottom of the bud, using a basting stitch and pulling the threads tight. Secure the threads.

Fold circle in half.

Fold top edge.

Fold sides toward center. Gather this lower edge.

Diagram 6

Step 5. Pin or baste the flower background in place on the quilt, then appliqué it. Position two G petals, darker fabric face up, with their upper edges slightly below the top of the flower background, then tack them to the background at their bases. Center a rosebud between the two petals, tacking it to the background at its base. When tacking the bud and petals in place, do not let your needle come through the top layers of fabric. See **Diagram 7.**

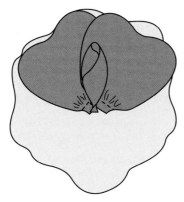

Diagram 7

Step 6. Position an H petal beneath the bud and sew it in place along its base. Position one of the remaining H petals to the lower left of the bud. Tuck under the lower unfinished petal edges and appliqué the petal in place, leaving the top edge free. Repeat with the last H petal, positioning it to the lower right of the bud. See **Diagram 8.** Fold down the top edges of petals as desired, taking more tacking stitches through the back layer of fabric to hold petals in place as necessary.

Note: Edges that will be overlapped by another piece of fabric should not be turned under, as this will just add bulk to your roses. Take as many stitches in the bottom layers of petals as necessary to secure them before adding outer layers.

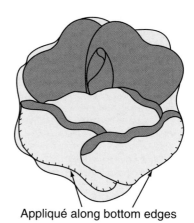

Appliqué along bottom edges

Diagram 8

Step 7. Repeat Steps 1 through 6 for the remaining roses.

Step 8. Use the technique of your choice to prepare the J and K leaves for appliqué. Arrange leaves as desired and appliqué to the quilt top.

Step 9. Make the rosebuds as described in Step 4. Position and secure the buds to the quilt top. Use template L and the method of your choice to prepare the calyxes (bases) for appliqué. Position them over the lower portions of the buds, as shown in **Diagram 9**, and appliqué them. For extra dimension, you can stuff the lower half of the calyxes with a bit of batting.

Diagram 9

Quilting and Finishing

Step 1. Mark the quilt top for quilting. The quilt shown was machine stipple quilted within the melons and ring backgrounds; the rings were also quilted in the ditch. A line was quilted along the center of the leaves to give them depth and a more natural appearance. Clusters of leaves on vines were quilted in the borders. You can use appliqué templates J and K to trace the leaf

shapes, or you can make a variety of your own leaves.

Step 2. Regardless of which quilt size you've chosen to make, the backing will have to be pieced. For the wallhanging, cut the backing fabric into two equal lengths, and trim the selvages. From one length, cut two 8-inch-wide panels. Sew a narrow panel to each side of the full-width panel, as shown in **Diagram 10**. Press the seams open.

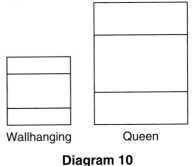

Wallhanging   Queen

Diagram 10

Step 3. For the queen-size quilt, cut the backing fabric into three equal lengths, and trim the selvages. Cut a 37-inch-wide panel from two of the lengths, and sew one to each side of the remaining full-width panel, as shown. Press the seams open.

Step 4. Layer the backing, batting, and quilt top, and baste. Quilt as desired.

Step 5. Make and attach double-fold binding, referring to page 206 in "Quiltmaking Basics" for more information. To calculate the amount of binding needed for the quilt size you are making, add the length of the four sides of the quilt plus 9 inches.

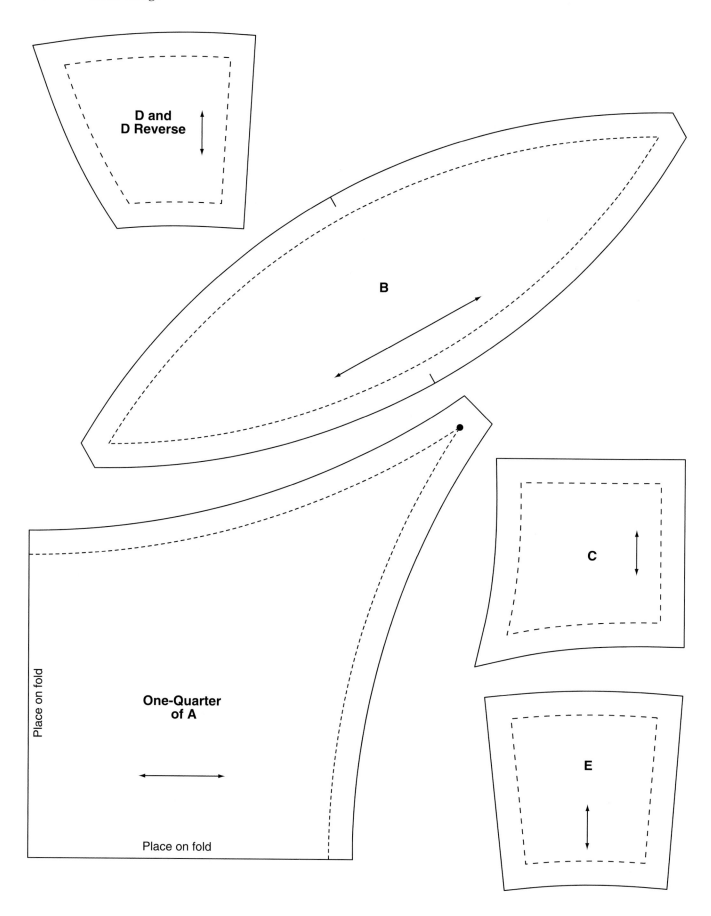

**D and
D Reverse**

B

**One-Quarter
of A**

Place on fold

Place on fold

C

E

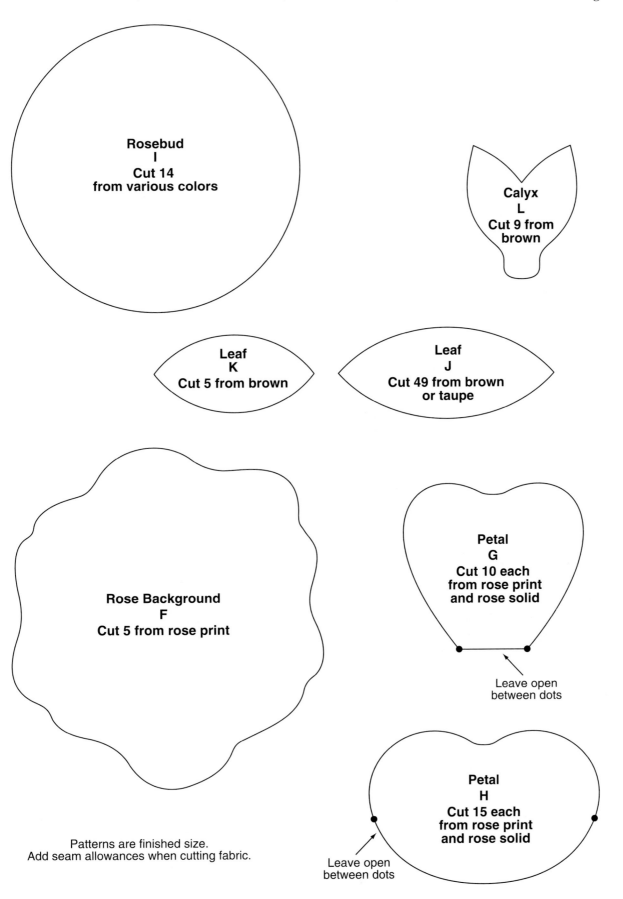

Rosebud
I
Cut 14
from various colors

Calyx
L
Cut 9 from
brown

Leaf
K
Cut 5 from brown

Leaf
J
Cut 49 from brown
or taupe

Rose Background
F
Cut 5 from rose print

Petal
G
Cut 10 each
from rose print
and rose solid

Leave open
between dots

Petal
H
Cut 15 each
from rose print
and rose solid

Leave open
between dots

Patterns are finished size.
Add seam allowances when cutting fabric.

Barn Raising

Skill Level: Easy

$\mathcal{B}$old, colors in a traditional setting make up Mark Stratton's striking king-size quilt. The dramatic interplay of colors creates an almost three-dimensional effect, making it easy to imagine the beams of a barn, which give the setting its name. Surprisingly subtle visual effects are created by six color variations of the basic block.

Before You Begin

The directions for this quilt are written using the chain piecing technique, although the foundation method would work equally well. Read through the general construction directions in "Quiltmaking Basics," beginning on page 197, to become familiar with the technique. All of the logs are cut to length, then the blocks are pieced in assembly line fashion. If you prefer to use the foundation method, prepare a foundation for each block using the pattern on page 26. The pattern given is reduced in size and must be enlarged 150 percent before tracing. See page 186 in "Quiltmaking Basics" for details on enlarging patterns.

Choosing Fabrics

Although at first glance this quilt appears to consist of simple half-light and half-dark blocks, it actually has a very complex, yet subtle, color arrangement. If you study the photo, you'll notice that the quiltmaker rearranged the placement of the fabrics to get six different color variations. **Diagram 1** on page 22 illustrates the six different blocks.

Quilt Size

Finished Quilt Size	115½" × 115½"
Finished Block Size	10"
Number of Blocks	100

NOTE: *Because specific color and value placement is critical to the overall design of this quilt, no variations in size or layout are provided.*

Materials

Fabric	Amount
Navy blue	5¼ yards
Royal blue	1¾ yards
Medium purple	2½ yards
Light teal	3 yards
Medium teal	1½ yards
Dark teal	1½ yards
Rose pink	⅝ yard
Backing	10¾ yards
Batting	120" × 120"
Binding	1½ yards

NOTE: *Yardages are based on 44/45-inch-wide fabrics that are at least 42 inches wide after preshrinking.*

If you wish to create your own unique color scheme, photocopy the **Color Plan** on page 214, and use crayons or colored pencils to experiment with different color arrangements.

Note: There are actually two different medium purple fabrics used in the quilt, but they are so close in value that we have treated them as one fabric in the Materials list and Cutting Chart. The same is true for the light teal. If you choose to purchase two different fabrics in each color, make sure they are similar in color and value.

21

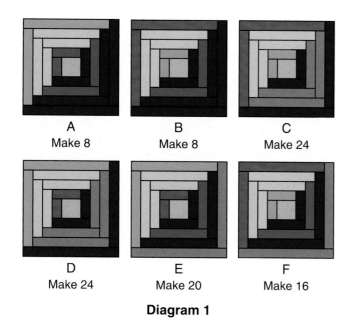

A
Make 8

B
Make 8

C
Make 24

D
Make 24

E
Make 20

F
Make 16

Diagram 1

Cutting

All measurements include ¼-inch seam allowances. Referring to the Cutting Chart, cut strips in the width needed, then cut the strips into logs. Cut all strips across the fabric width (crosswise grain). You may find it helpful to pin a number label to each group of logs as you cut them. **Note:** Cut and piece one block before cutting all the pieces for the quilt.

Piecing the First Block

Start on page 194 of "Quiltmaking Basics" and read through the directions for foundation

Sew Easy

You could simplify the quilt's construction by using just two block variations throughout instead of the six different blocks used in the original. Use Block A to give you the dark center and corners, and choose any one of Blocks C through F to complete the design.

piecing. Piece a sample block first; it will allow you to become acquainted with the technique and to double-check the accuracy of your seam allowances. Cut enough logs for one sample block, and use the **Block Diagram** and the **Fabric Key** as guides to piecing order.

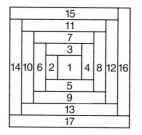

Block Diagram

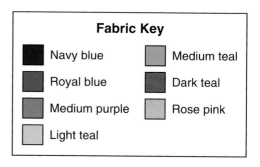

Fabric Key

Navy blue   Medium teal

Royal blue   Dark teal

Medium purple   Rose pink

Light teal

Step 1. Place a log 2 right sides together with a center piece 1, aligning the edges. Stitch the pieces together using a ¼-inch seam. Open out the pieces, as shown in **Diagram 2A**, and press the seam allowance toward log 2. Always press the seam allowance toward the log you have just added.

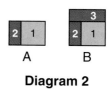

A   B

Diagram 2

Step 2. Place a log 3 right sides together with the pieced segment, aligning the edges. Stitch the pieces together. Open out the pieces and press the seam allowance toward log 3. See **2B**.

Step 3. Sew a log 4 to the right side of the pieced segment, as shown in **Diagram 3A**, and

Cutting Chart

Fabric	Strip Width	Number of Strips	Piece	Length	Number Needed
Navy blue	5½"	11	Border		
	1½"	74	4	3½"	100
			5	4½"	100
			12	7½"	52
			13	8½"	52
			16	9½"	64
			17	10½"	64
Royal blue	2½"	10	Border		
	1½"	17	8	5½"	52
			9	6½"	52
Medium purple	1½"	53	8	5½"	48
			9	6½"	48
			12	7½"	48
			13	8½"	48
			16	9½"	36
			17	10½"	100
Light teal	1½"	65	6	4½"	100
			7	5½"	100
			10	6½"	100
			11	7½"	100
Medium teal	1½"	31	2	2½"	48
			3	3½"	48
			14	8½"	52
			15	9½"	52
Dark teal	1½"	31	2	2½"	52
			3	3½"	52
			14	8½"	48
			15	9½"	48
Rose pink	2½"	6	1	2½"	100

press. Sew a log 5 to the bottom of the segment and press. See **3B.**

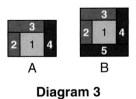

Diagram 3

Step 4. Continue to add logs in numerical order until all 17 logs have been added. The completed block should measure 10½ inches square. If it does, you have established an accurate ¼-inch seam allowance and are pressing seams carefully. If the block measures a different size, double-check your seam allowances. If you need more practice, make another sample block before continuing.

Piecing the Remaining Blocks

Chain piecing can help speed up the block assembly process. Instead of making an individual block from start to finish, perform one step at a time on all the blocks. The easiest way to organize your sewing for this quilt is to make all the blocks for variation A, then move on to variation B, and so on.

Step 1. Cut and stack all the logs for block variation A, placing them in numerical order near your sewing machine. Stitch a log 2 to a center piece 1 as described previously. Without removing the stitched pair from the sewing machine, feed a second pair under the presser foot and sew them together. Continue sewing until all remaining center sections are pieced. See **Diagram 4.**

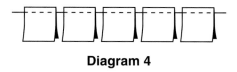

Diagram 4

Step 2. Cut the stitched segments apart. Press each seam allowance toward log 2.

Step 3. In the same manner, add log 3 to all of the blocks. Cut the segments apart and press each seam allowance toward log 3. Continue adding logs in numerical order until all of the variation A blocks are completed.

Step 4. Repeat Steps 1 through 3 for the five remaining block variations, completing each type before moving on to the next.

Assembling the Quilt Top

Step 1. The blocks are arranged in ten rows, each containing ten blocks. Referring to **Diagram 5,** the **Quilt Diagram,** and the photo on page 20, carefully lay out the blocks. **Diagram 5** shows the correct placement of the blocks in the layout, while the **Quilt Diagram** and the photo illustrate the correct orientation. Check to make sure the blocks are turned the right way.

A	D	C	F	E	E	F	C	D	A
D	C	F	E	D	D	E	F	C	D
C	F	E	D	C	C	D	E	F	C
F	E	D	C	B	B	C	D	E	F
E	D	C	B	A	A	B	C	D	E
E	D	C	B	A	A	B	C	D	E
F	E	D	C	B	B	C	D	E	F
C	F	E	D	C	C	D	E	F	C
D	C	F	E	D	D	E	F	C	D
A	D	C	F	E	E	F	C	D	A

Diagram 5

Step 2. Sew the blocks into rows, pressing the seam allowances in opposite directions from row to row.

Step 3. Join the rows, carefully matching seams where blocks meet. If you pressed the seams in opposite directions, the seams should fit tightly against each other, helping you to achieve a perfect match. Press seam allowances where rows are joined.

Adding the Borders

Step 1. To make the narrow inner border, sew eight of the 2½-inch-wide royal blue strips together in pairs. Cut the remaining two strips in half, and sew one half to each of the four long strips.

Step 2. Measure the quilt from top to bottom, taking the measurement through the vertical center of the quilt, not at the sides. Cut two of the long strips to this length.

Step 3. Fold one strip in half crosswise and crease. Unfold it and position it right side down along one edge of the quilt top, with the crease at the horizontal midpoint. Pin at the midpoint and ends first, then along the length of the entire side, easing in fullness if necessary. Sew the border to the quilt top using a ¼-inch seam allowance. Press the seam allowance toward the border. Repeat on the opposite side.

Step 4. Measure the width of the quilt, taking the measurement through the horizontal center of

Quilt Diagram

the quilt and including the side borders. Cut the remaining two royal blue strips to this length.

Step 5. In the same manner as for the side borders, position and pin a strip along one end of the quilt top, easing in fullness if necessary. Stitch, using a ¼-inch seam allowance. Press the seam toward the border. Repeat on the opposite end.

Step 6. Use the 5½-inch-wide navy blue strips for the wide outer border. The side borders consist of two and a half strips each, while the top and bottom borders consist of three strips each. Add the borders to the quilt top in the same manner as for the inner borders.

Quilting and Finishing

Step 1. Mark the quilt top for quilting. The quilt shown was quilted with diagonal lines in the inner border and garlands of hearts in the outer border. The blocks are quilted in the ditch.

Step 2. The backing should be approximately 125 inches square. Cut the 10¾-yard piece of backing fabric into three equal segments, and trim the selvages. Sew the panels together lengthwise and press the seams open.

Step 3. Layer the backing, batting, and quilt top; baste the layers together. Quilt as desired.

Step 4. Referring to the directions on page 206 in "Quiltmaking Basics," use the binding fabric to make double-fold binding. The quilt shown is finished with ¾-inch-wide binding. If you wish to make your binding this wide, cut the binding strips 4½ inches wide, and attach the binding to the quilt using a ¾-inch seam. You will need approximately 475 inches of binding.

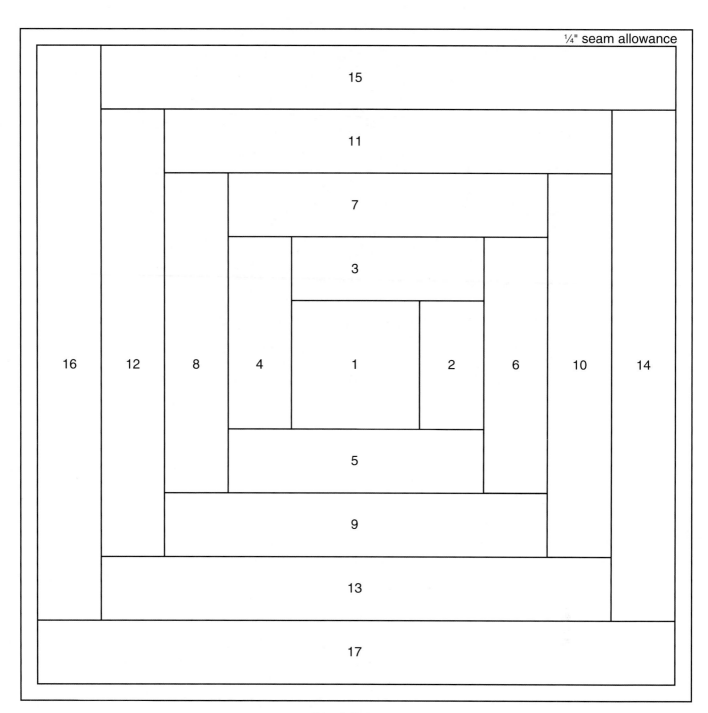

¼" seam allowance

15

11

7

3

16 12 8 4 1 2 6 10 14

5

9

13

17

Block Pattern

Pattern shown is the mirror image of the finished block.
Note: Pattern is reduced. Enlarge it 150 percent before tracing.

Bed Skirts Made Easy

A simple ruffled bed skirt is easy to make and gives you an opportunity to spotlight a favorite fabric from your quilt.

The yardage needed for the bed skirt will be determined in steps 2 and 3. In addition to the bed skirt fabric, you will need a fitted bedsheet to fit your bed size.

1. Remove the mattress from the box spring and cover the box spring with the fitted sheet. Using an air-soluble marker, draw a line on the fitted sheet where the box spring top and sides meet; see **Diagram 1**. Remove the sheet from the box spring.

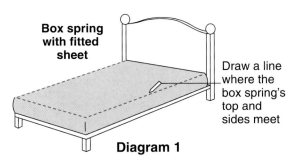

Box spring with fitted sheet

Draw a line where the box spring's top and sides meet

Diagram 1

2. To determine the length of the bed skirt strip, measure along the sides and end of the box spring and multiply by 2. Add 2 inches to the measurement for finishing the ends. To determine the depth of the bed skirt, measure from the top of the box spring to ½ inch from the floor. Add 1 inch for the hem and ½ inch for the seam allowance.

3. To determine the yardage needed, first determine the number of strips you can cut from the fabric. You should be able to cut either two or three strips across the width of your fabric. For example, if your fabric is 40 inches wide and the cut width of your bed skirt strips is 16 inches, you can cut two lengthwise strips from the width of the fabric. Then, take the total length needed (from Step 2) and divide that number by the number of strips you can cut

from the width of your fabric (from Step 3). Divide by 36 (inches per yard) and round up to the nearest ⅛ yard to get total yards needed. For example, if the length of the bed skirt strip is 408 inches of fabric, divide by 2 (strips you can cut across the width of fabric), and it equals 204 inches of fabric needed. Divide 204 by 36 to get a total yardage of 5.66 yards. Round to the nearest ⅛ yard for 5¾ yards needed for the bed skirt.

4. Cut the number of strips needed and sew the strips together end to end. Hem one long edge and both short ends by pressing under ½ inch twice and stitching in place. Gather the remaining long edge with at least two rows of gathering stitches.

5. With right sides together and the long, hemmed edges of the bed skirt toward the center of the fitted sheet, pin the gathered edge of the strip to the fitted sheet ½ inch inside the marked line; see **Diagram 2**. Sew on the marked line.

Wrong side of hemmed bedskirt

Right side of fitted sheet

½" between gathered bedskirt and marked line

Diagram 2

Marked line where box spring top and side meet

Gathered edge of bedskirt

6. Fit the sheet with the attached skirt onto the box spring. It's guaranteed not to slip!

Row Houses

Skill Level: Challenging

*J*udy Spahn has combined cool, shimmering colors and an out-of-the-ordinary setting to create a stunning wallhanging or lap quilt with a contemporary twist. The quilt seems to be in perpetual motion, and this whirling effect is intensified by the strong diagonal lines of Judy's original border treatment.

Before You Begin

If you study the photograph carefully, you'll notice that this quilt is made of two different House blocks. The blocks are identical, except that House 2 is the reverse of House 1. It is this mirror image, along with the unique arrangement of all 24 House blocks, that gives this quilt its vitality and character.

The instructions are written based on quick-cutting techniques. With the exception of a few simple shapes that require templates, all of the pieces are strips and squares that can be rotary cut. In addition, an easy strip-piecing technique is provided for parts of the House blocks and pieced borders. Strips of fabric are sewn together to form strip sets. These strip sets are then cut apart into individual units that are incorporated into the blocks and borders.

While most of the seams for this quilt require simple, straight-line sewing, a few set-in seams are required. Read through "Set-In Seams" on page 189 to familiarize yourself with the simple procedure for set-in pieces, as well as for more detailed instruc-

tion on the strip-piecing method described above.

Choosing Fabrics

This quiltmaker relied on a variety of solid fabrics in a cool color scheme of dusty blues, green, teals, lavenders, and grays to give her quilt its sleek, contemporary look. Most of the fabrics are matte finished, but a few are polished cottons, and one or two are not cotton at all but luxurious

Quilt Size

Finished Quilt Size	44" × 54½"
Finished Block Size	8"
Number of Blocks	
House 1	20
House 2	4

NOTE: *Because the specific block arrangement (including mirror images) is critical to the overall design of the quilt, no variations in size or layout are provided.*

Materials

Fabric	Amount
Muslin	1⅓ yards
Assorted dusty blue, green, teal, lavender, and gray solids	2 yards
Navy solid	1¾ yards
Backing	3 yards
Batting	50" × 61"
Binding	½ yard

NOTE: *Yardages are based on 44/45-inch-wide fabrics that are at least 42 inches wide after preshrinking.*

Cutting Chart

Fabric	Used For	Strip Width or Piece	Number to Cut	Second Cut Dimensions	Number to Cut
Muslin	Unit 1	4"	2		
	Unit 2	4"	1		
	Unit 2	3"	1		
	I	Template I	24		
	I reverse	Template I	24		
	J	1¾"	1	1¾" × 2¾"	4
	Unit 3	2½"	5		
Assorted dusty solids	Unit 3	3"	5		
Navy solid	Border	1"	5		
	Unit 1	1½"	4		
	Unit 2	1½"	2		
	B	1"	3	1" × 4½"	24
	C	1"	4	1" × 6"	24
	D	Template D	20		
	D reverse	Template D	4		
	F	1"	2	1" × 3"	24
	Unit 3	1¼"	10		

From the assorted dusty solids, cut the following pieces for each block. All of the pieces for a single block should be cut from the same fabric. Refer to the *Block Diagram* as needed.

Fabric	Used For	Dimensions	Number to Cut per House
Assorted dusty solids	A	4½" × 5½"	1
	E	Template E*	1
	G	3" × 3"	1
	H	Template H	1

Cut one E for 20 of the houses and one E reverse for 4 of the houses.

silk shantung. These latter fabrics add sheen that contributes to the quilt's glossy good looks.

For another contemporary look, try working in solids of black, white, and gray. In fact, any mix of neutrals—including beige, brown, taupe, tan, and cream—would make a striking quilt. Or replace the navy framework with black and the muted, dusty tints with rich purples, teals, greens, blues, and pinks for a quilt with a strong Amish flavor.

To help develop a unique color scheme for the quilt, photocopy the **Color Plan** on page 210, and use crayons or colored pencils to experiment with different color arrangements.

Cutting

All of the measurements include ¼-inch seam allowances. Refer to the Cutting Chart and cut the required number of strips in the sizes needed. Cut all strips across the fabric width (crosswise grain).

Make templates for pieces D, E, H, and I using the full-size pattern pieces on page 36. Refer to page 186 for complete details on making and using templates. The Cutting Chart indicates how many of each piece to cut with each template.

Refer to the **Block Diagram** as you work. For House 1, place the D, E, and I templates wrong

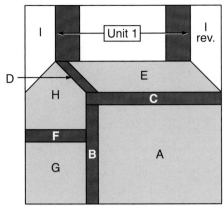

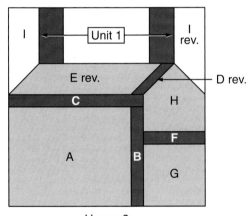

House 1

House 2

Block Diagram

Cut sizes

A = 1" × 4½"
B = 5½" × 4½"
C = 6" × 1"
F = 3" × 1"
G = 3" × 3"

the D reverse, E reverse, and I reverse pieces. Turn the I template over to cut the I pieces.

Note: Cut and piece one sample block before cutting all the fabric for the quilt.

Piecing the House Blocks

Refer to the **Block Diagram** as you assemble each block. For ease of construction, each pattern piece is identified by a letter. The strip-pieced chimney unit is labeled Unit 1. In each House block, the A, E, G, and H pieces should be cut from the same fabric. Note that in the House 2 blocks, the D and E pieces are replaced with D reverse and E reverse. You'll need a total of twenty House 1 blocks and four House 2 blocks for this quilt.

House 1 Blocks

Step 1. Pin, then sew a 1½-inch navy strip to either side of a 4-inch muslin strip, as shown in **Diagram 1**. Make another strip set in the same manner, and press all seams toward the navy strips. Using a rotary cutter and ruler, square up one end of each strip set. Cut twenty-four 2¾-inch segments from the strip sets, as shown. Label these segments Unit 1.

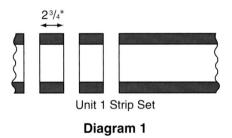

Unit 1 Strip Set

Diagram 1

side up on the wrong side of the fabric to cut those pieces. Turn the I template over to cut the I reverse pieces.

For House 2, place the D, E, and I templates right side up on the wrong side of the fabric to cut

Sew Easy

To prevent fabrics from turning shiny when the seam lines are pressed, press blocks from the reverse side or use a pressing cloth. Always test press a scrap when using unusual fabrics such as silk, wool, or polished cotton to determine the correct temperature setting for your iron.

Step 2. Sew a navy B strip to the right edge of a dusty solid A rectangle, as shown in **Diagram 2**. Press the seams toward B. Add a C segment along the top edge of the A/B unit, as shown, pressing the seams toward C. Set the unit aside.

Diagram 2

Step 3. Sew a D piece to the left edge of E, as shown in **Diagram 3**, to form the roof unit. Press the seams toward E. Join the roof unit to the top of the house, as shown. Press the seams toward C and set aside.

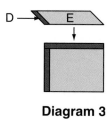

Diagram 3

Step 4. To make the house front, stitch an F strip along one edge of a G square, as shown in **Diagram 4**. Press the seam toward G. Add an H piece to the opposite side of F, pressing the seam toward H.

Diagram 4

Step 5. Sew the house front to the left of the house/roof unit, as shown in **Diagram 5**. Start stitching ¼ inch from the raw edge at the point where the H, D, and C pieces come together, and stitch from this pivot point first in one direction, then in the other, as indicated by the arrows. Refer to page 189 for additional information on pivoted, or set-in, seams.

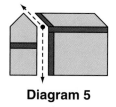

Diagram 5

Step 6. With right sides together, pin, then sew a Unit 1 to the top edge of the house, as shown in **Diagram 6A**.

Begin and end stitching ¼ inch from the raw edges, as shown in **6B**, and press the seams toward the house.

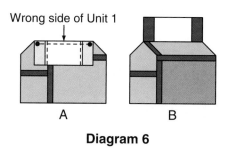

Wrong side of Unit 1

A   B

Diagram 6

Step 7. Set in the I and I reverse pieces, as shown in **Diagram 7**. For both of the pieces, begin stitching ¼ inch from the raw edge at the angle where the chimney meets the roof, and stitch to the other edge, as indicated by the arrows in the diagram. Press the seams away from the I pieces.

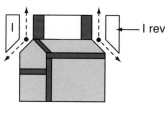

Diagram 7

Step 8. Repeat Steps 1 through 7 to make twenty House 1 blocks.

House 2 Blocks

The House 2 block is assembled in the same fashion as the House 1 block with the following exceptions:

• The A pieces are sewn to the *left* side of the B pieces, as shown in **Diagram 8A**.

• The D reverse pieces are sewn to the *right* edge of the E reverse pieces, as shown in **8B**.

• The house front (G/F/H unit) is stitched to the *right* edge of the house/roof unit.

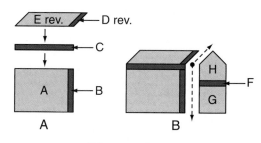

Diagram 8

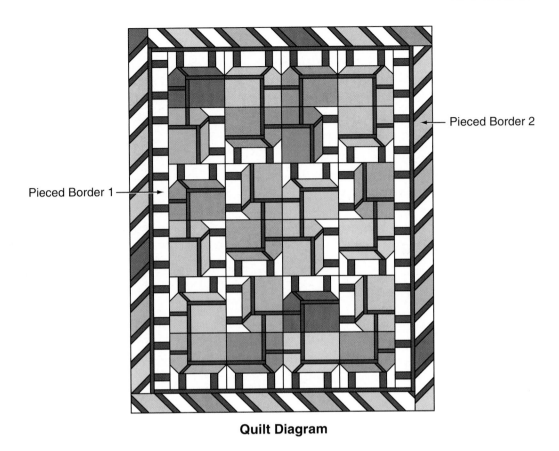

Quilt Diagram

Assembling the Quilt Top

Step 1. Use a design wall or other flat surface to lay out the House blocks exactly as shown in the **Assembly Diagram.** The diagram indicates where

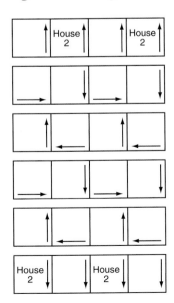

Assembly Diagram

to place the House 2 blocks. Unlabeled squares in the diagram indicate placement of House 1 blocks. For both types of blocks, the arrows show which direction the chimneys of each should be pointing. You may also find it helpful to refer to the photograph on page 28.

Step 2. Sew the blocks together in six horizontal rows, as shown. Each row has four blocks. Press the seams in opposite directions from row to row.

Step 3. Sew the rows together, carefully matching seams where the blocks meet. Press the quilt top.

Piecing the Borders

There are two separate pieced border units for this quilt. Pieced Border 1 (the inner border) is used only on the quilt sides. Pieced Border 2 (the outer, diagonally striped border) surrounds the quilt on all sides. These two pieced borders are separated by a narrow, unpieced navy border.

Pieced Border 1

Step 1. Pin, then sew a 1½-inch navy strip to either side of a 4-inch muslin strip. Add a 3-inch muslin strip to one of the navy strips to complete a strip set, as shown in **Diagram 9.** Press the seam allowances toward the navy strips. Square up one end of the strip set, and cut twelve 2¾-inch segments from the strip set, as shown. Label these segments Unit 2.

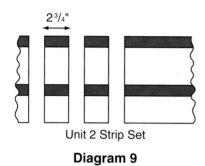

2¾"

Unit 2 Strip Set

Diagram 9

Step 2. Join six Unit 2 segments side by side, as shown in **Diagram 10.** Press the seams toward the navy strips. Make two of these border strips for the quilt sides.

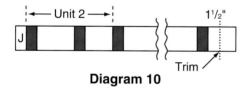

Unit 2   1½"   J   Trim

Diagram 10

Step 3. Trim the last muslin segment on the *right* end of each border strip so that it is 1½ inches wide. Sew a 1¾ × 2¾-inch muslin J piece to the left end of each border strip, as shown in the diagram. Press the seams toward the navy strips. Set the two Pieced Border 1 units aside.

Pieced Border 2

Step 1. Sew together a 2½-inch muslin strip, a 1¼-inch navy strip, a 3-inch dusty solid strip, and a 1¼-inch navy strip side by side, staggering their starting points by a distance equal to the strip width, as shown in **Diagram 11.** Make five such strip sets.

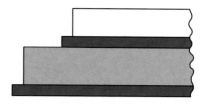

Diagram 11

Step 2. Align the 45 degree line of your rotary ruler with the seam line between the muslin and navy strips, as shown in **Diagram 12.** Use a rotary cutter to trim the end of the strip set, as shown. Realign your ruler so that the diagonal edge of the fabric is aligned with the 3½-inch line on the ruler and the 45 degree line is still in line with the seam of the strip set. Now cut a 3½-inch diagonal section from the strip set. Cut 26 segments in this manner and label them Unit 3.

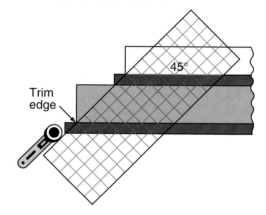

Trim edge   45°

Diagram 12

Sew Easy

Because the Pieced Border 2 strips have the bias edges on the outside of the strips, be careful not to stretch the edges as you sew them to the quilt top. You may find it helpful to stay stitch the edges by machine stitching a scant ¼ inch from all raw edges. This extra step will keep your borders nice and even and prevent fabric-stretching headaches down the road.

Step 3. Sew six Unit 3 segments together, varying the colors, to make a top border. Repeat, making a bottom border in the same manner. Make two side borders in the same manner using seven Unit 3 segments in each border.

Adding the Borders

Step 1. Fold a Pieced Border 1 in half crosswise and crease. Unfold it and position it right side down along one side of the quilt top, with the crease at the quilt's midpoint. Pin at the midpoint and ends first, then along the entire length of the edge, easing in fullness if necessary. Sew the border to the quilt top, using a ¼-inch seam allowance. Press the seams toward the border. Repeat this procedure to add the remaining Pieced Border 1 to the opposite side of the quilt.

Step 2. You will need to piece two of the navy border strips so that they are long enough to fit the sides of the quilt top. Cut one of the navy border strips in half, and sew one half to two of the remaining navy border strips. Press the seams open. The top and bottom borders do not need to be pieced.

Step 3. Measure the quilt from side to side, taking the measurement through the center of the quilt, including the pieced borders. Trim the two unpieced navy border strips to this length. Using the procedure described in Step 1, sew a border strip to the top and bottom of the quilt. Press the seam allowances toward the navy strip.

Step 4. Measure the length of the quilt, taking the measurement through the center of the quilt and including the navy borders. Trim the remaining two navy border strips to this length. Stitch the borders to the quilt sides in the same manner as you did for the top and bottom borders. Press the seams toward the navy borders.

Step 5. Position a Pieced Border 2 along the top edge of the quilt top, with right sides together and the navy pieces aligned with the navy chimneys in the blocks. Pin the border in place, with the ends of the border extending beyond the edge of the quilt top. Use a rotary cutter and ruler to square up the *left* edge of the strip. The strip should overhang the right edge of the quilt top by at least 3¼ inches, as shown. *Do not square up the right edge of the strip yet!* With the wrong side of the quilt top facing you, sew the border to the quilt top, using a ¼-inch seam. By having the border on the bottom as you sew, the bias edges of the border will be eased in to fit the quilt top by the feed dogs. Stop sewing approximately 3 inches from the edge of the quilt top and backstitch. Leave the end of the border strip free. Open out the border and press. See **Diagram 13**.

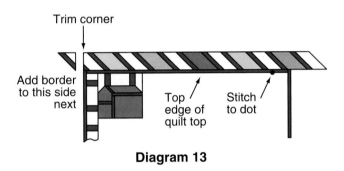

Diagram 13

Step 6. Attach the left border next, aligning the diagonal navy pieces in Pieced Border 2 with the navy strips in Pieced Border 1. The ends of the border will overhang the top and bottom edges of the quilt top slightly. Square up both ends of the border strip so they are even with the quilt top, and stitch the border in place.

Step 7. Attach the bottom border and then the right border in the same manner as you did for the top and left borders. To complete the quilt top, finish sewing the seam on the top border, and square up the right end of the border with the edge of the quilt top. Press the seams toward the border strips.

Quilting and Finishing

Step 1. Mark the quilt top for quilting. The quilt shown is outline quilted around each shape with the exception of the navy strips, which are left unquilted.

Step 2. Cut the backing fabric in half crosswise. Remove the selvages and cut a 32-inch-wide panel from each piece. Sew the pieces together along the long edges. Press the seam open. The seam will run parallel to the top and bottom of the quilt. Refer to page 205 for more information on pieced backings.

Step 3. Layer the backing, batting, and quilt top and baste the layers together. Trim the excess backing and batting so they are approximately 3 inches larger than the quilt top on all sides. Quilt all marked designs, adding any additional quilting as desired.

Step 4. Referring to the directions on page 206, make and attach double-fold binding from the navy fabric. You will need approximately 205 inches of binding.

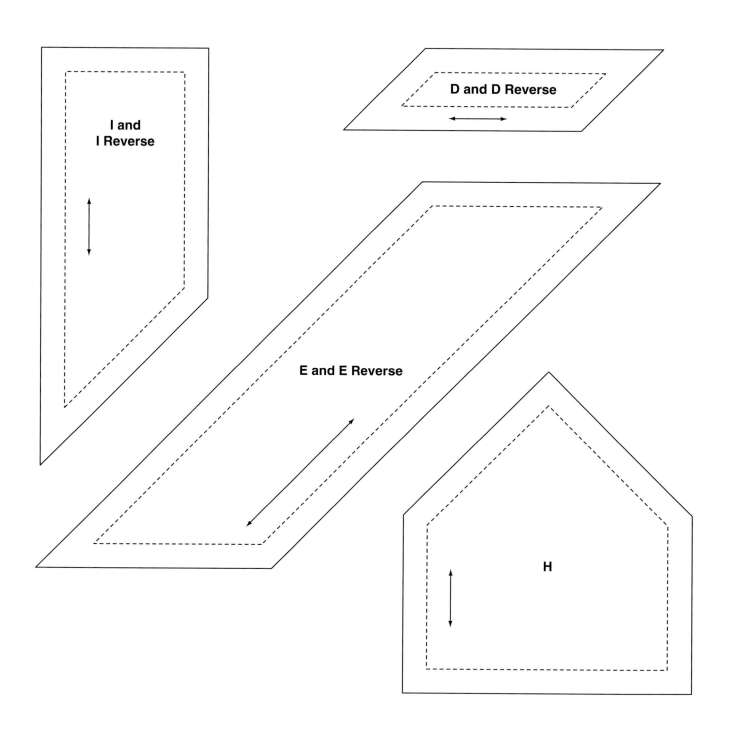

Tell the Story

As quilters, we understand the importance of including a label on our quilts so that future generations will know something about the quilt's history. However, keeping a journal of all the quilts you've made or all the quilts you own is equally important and another assurance that the stories of how the quilts came to be can live on.

Antique quilts are the most challenging to document, but often a little research can provide details. Start by documenting how and where you acquired the quilt. Did Grandma give it to you or did you purchase it at a flea market? Record every known detail, such as the block pattern, the quilt size, the condition of the quilt, and how much you paid for it. If the quilt was given to you by a family member who is still living, ask her about the story behind the quilt. If the quiltmaker is deceased, try and find out information about her from people she might have known. A quilt appraiser should be able to give you an approximate date of when the quilt was made; be sure to include it in your journal. Take pictures of the front and back of the quilt and record any visible dates or lettering.

Quilts that you have made are easier to document, but you should do it while the details are fresh in your mind. Include detailed photographs of the quilt, fabric swatches, receipts, and other interesting items related to the quilt whenever possible. Use a large envelope or zip-pered plastic bag to hold the items. If the quilt pattern is one of your original designs, consider having it copyrighted. Be sure to include as many of the following items as possible in your written documentation:

- Project name
- Pattern name and where it was obtained (book, magazine, friend)
- Occasion for which the quilt was made
- Quiltmaker
- Start and finish dates
- Quilt owner
- Quilt size
- Techniques used for piecing and quilting
- Any shows the quilt has been entered in and any awards won
- The story behind the quilt (why it was made, why those fabrics were selected, and anything funny or unusual that happened while the quilt was being made)

To further preserve the quilt's history, register it with a local or national registry project. In the event that your journal is lost or the quilt is stolen, this service can provide the information or help necessary for recovery of the quilt.

Trailing Starflower

Skill Level: Easy

A cheerful mix of stars, flowers, and heartwarming plaids lends this small quilt a charming folk art feel. Quiltmaker Bethany S. Reynolds of Ellsworth, Maine, works visual magic using simple appliqué, colorful embroidery floss, and the nostalgic touch of yo-yos to enhance her homespun garden.

Before You Begin

This project allows you to try a wide variety of quiltmaking techniques. You'll use both templates and your rotary cutter to cut the pieces. Construction methods include piecing, appliqué, making yo-yos, quilting, and tying. You can even try decorative hand or machine stitching for additional embellishment.

You might think such a variety of techniques would earn this quilt an intermediate or challenging rating. Not so! In fact, it offers the perfect opportunity for a confident beginner to sharpen skills in many areas. The piecing is easy, with stars and starflowers appliquéd to the background blocks, eliminating set-in seams. The appliqué pieces are few, and the shapes are simple. And the yo-yos and other embellishing techniques are just plain fun!

You may wish to read "Quiltmaking Basics," beginning on page 184, before you begin this quilt. In addition to specific instructions about making and using templates, and using rotary cutters, you'll find lots of hints and tips to help with your appliqué technique.

Quilt Sizes

	Wallhanging	Lap (shown)
Finished Quilt Size	40½" × 40½"	56½" × 72½"
Finished Star Block Size	12"	12"
Number of Large Star Blocks	4	12
Number of Small Starflowers	9	20

Materials

Fabric	Wallhanging	Lap
Light solid or subtle print	1⅝ yards	3¾ yards
Dark green plaid	¾ yard	1 yard
Dark red plaid	⅝ yard	1⅜ yards
Assorted light plaids (*total*)	⅓ yard	⅝ yard
Assorted dark plaids (*total*)	⅓ yard	⅝ yard
Medium blue plaid	⅛ yard	¼ yard
Embroidery floss (*six-strand*)	2 skeins	2 skeins
Backing	2¾ yards	3¾ yards
Batting	48" × 48"	64" × 80"
Binding	⅓ yard	½ yard

NOTE: *Yardages are based on 44/45-inch-wide fabrics that are at least 42 inches wide after preshrinking.*

Choosing Fabrics

This quiltmaker has chosen to work almost exclusively in homespun and madras plaids. For the background, sashing, and borders, she has selected a grayed-green, linen-weave cotton to enhance the folk art appearance of the quilt. As a substitute, you might select any light solid or subtle "reads-as-solid" cotton print in a neutral shade.

Light and dark value plaids alternate in the points of the large

39

Cutting Chart

Fabric	Used For	Strip Width or Pieces	Number to Cut Wallhanging	Number to Cut Lap	Second Cut Dimensions	Number to Cut Wallhanging	Number to Cut Lap
Light solid or subtle print	Borders	2½"	4	7			
	Block backgrounds	12½"	2	4	12½" squares	4	12
	Sashing strips	4½"	4	11	4½" × 12½"	12	31
	Corner squares	4½"	1	3	4½" squares	9	20
Dark green plaid	Vine	24" square	1	—			
		36" square	—	1			
	D*	Template D	24	62			
Dark red plaid	B	Template B	72	160			
Assorted light plaids	A	Template A	16	48			
Assorted dark plaids	A	Template A	16	48			
Medium blue plaid	C	Template C	9	20			

* After cutting vines from squares, cut leaves from leftovers before cutting additional fabric.

stars. For a scrappy look, select as many different plaids as possible. Neither lights nor darks need to be identical in value. Since the perceived value of a fabric is dependent on the value of its neighboring fabrics, some of your plaids may do "double duty" as both lights and darks.

For example, a medium blue fabric looks dark when positioned against a pastel, but it becomes a light or medium when positioned next to black. It might be helpful to review the values of the various fabrics you have selected to be sure you have a good mix of values to create lots of visual interest.

In the quilt shown, the vines and leaves are all sewn from the same dark green plaid. The small starflowers are a deep red-and-black plaid, with medium blue plaid yo-yo centers.

While the concentration of homespuns and plaids creates a cozy, country look, the design would be equally attractive in a colorful mix of plaids, stripes, and prints. Or you might prefer to focus solely on the wonderful reproduction prints currently available, including the soft pastels of the 1920s and 1930s.

To develop your own color scheme for this quilt, photocopy the **Color Plan** on page 210, and use crayons or colored pencils to experiment with different color arrangements.

Cutting

The pieces for this quilt are cut using a combination of templates and rotary-cutting techniques. Make templates for pieces A, B, C, and D from the full-size patterns on page 46. Refer to page 186 of "Quiltmaking Basics" for complete details on making and using templates.

With the exception of pattern pieces C and D, all of the full-size pattern pieces and the rotary-cutting measurements given include ¼-inch seam allowances. Refer to the Cutting Chart for the number of pieces or strips to cut from each fabric. Cut all strips across the width of the fabric (crosswise grain).

Note: We recommend that you cut and piece a sample block before cutting all of the fabric for your quilt.

Piecing the Large Stars

Step 1. Select four light A star points and four dark A star points. Position them as shown in the **Block Diagram**, alternating light and dark points.

Block Diagram

Step 2. Pin a light A piece to a dark A piece with right sides together. Sew the pieces together, beginning and ending with a backstitch exactly ¼ inch from each end, as indicated by the dots in **Diagram 1A**. Be careful not to sew into the ¼-inch seam allowance. Finger press the seam allowance toward the dark point. Your unit should look like **1B**.

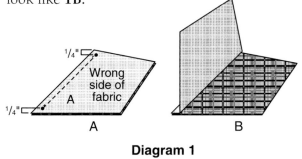

Diagram 1

Step 3. Repeat, sewing together the remaining three pairs of light and dark A star points.

Step 4. Sew two of the pairs together. Begin sewing ¼ inch from the edge, as shown by the dot in **Diagram 2A**, and backstitch. Continue sewing to the other dot (where the previously sewn seam ends). End with a backstitch. This unit should look like the one in **2B**. Finger press the seam allowance in the same direction as the others. Join the two remaining pairs to assemble the other half of the star.

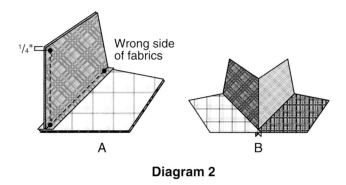

Diagram 2

Step 5. Pin the two star halves together with right sides facing. Rather than sewing completely across the star from one side to the other, begin stitching ¼ inch from one edge of the star and sew toward the center, stopping exactly at the point where all of the seams meet, as shown in **Diagram 3A**. Finger press the seam allowances out of the way. Sew the remaining seam, starting ¼ inch from the opposite side of the star, and sewing again only to the star center, as shown. Press the final seam in the same direction, fanning out the star center, as shown in **3B**.

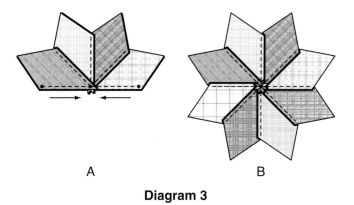

Diagram 3

Step 6. Repeat Steps 1 through 5 to assemble the number of large stars required for your quilt.

Appliquéing the Large Stars

In this quilt, the large stars are appliquéd onto, rather than pieced into, a background square. Refer to page 200 in "Quiltmaking Basics" for general information on appliqué.

Step 1. Use your preferred method to prepare all of the large stars for appliqué. If you use the needle-turn method, no additional preparation is necessary. If you prefer to turn the seam allowances in advance, turn under and baste the ¼-inch seam allowance you have left "free" around the outer edge of the star.

Step 2. Center a star on a 12½-inch background square. Appliqué the star to the square. Repeat to appliqué all the large Star blocks.

Sew Quick

If you are lucky enough to have a sewing machine with fancy decorative stitches, you may prefer to machine appliqué the Star blocks, starflowers, vines, and leaves. Try a blanket stitch and contrasting thread for a warm, homespun look.

Sew Easy

Here's an easy way to position an appliqué motif in the center of a background square. Fold the square in half and carefully finger crease to mark the vertical center. Open the square, then refold in the opposite direction, finger creasing to mark the horizontal center. In the same manner, fold and crease both diagonal lines. The two creases will intersect at the exact center of the block, plus serve as guides for aligning appliqué pieces. Certain appliqué pieces, however, look best when they are slightly lower than center.

Piecing the Small Starflowers

Each corner square in this quilt is adorned with a smaller version of the large star that appears in the basic quilt block. The little stars are called starflowers, and each is finished with a decorative yo-yo center. Follow Steps 2 through 5 in the instructions for "Piecing the Large Stars" to complete the required number of starflowers for your quilt. Use the dark red plaid B star points you have cut to make the starflowers. The starflowers will be appliquéd to the corner squares after the quilt top has been assembled.

Note: Before you begin piecing the starflowers, trim the inner point of template B to reduce bulk and allow for easier piecing.

Making the Yo-Yo Centers

Step 1. Thread a hand sewing needle with a length of thread that matches the yo-yo fabric. Double the thread and tie a knot at the end. Working with the right side of a blue C circle away from you, use the drawn line as a guide to turn over a ¼-inch seam allowance. Take a backstitch to secure the thread. Stitch a running stitch approximately ⅛ inch from the outer edge of the circle, turning and basting the ¼-inch seam as you work, as shown in **Diagram 4**. Stitch around the entire perimeter of the circle.

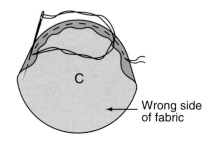

Wrong side of fabric

Diagram 4

Step 2. Draw up the thread to gather the edge tightly. Knot the thread and flatten the yo-yo at its center, as shown in **Diagram 5A**.

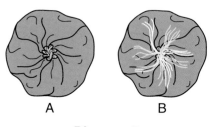

A   B

Diagram 5

Step 3. To make the stamens, thread a length of six-strand embroidery floss and take a stitch in the center hole of the yo-yo. Cut the floss, leaving approximately ¾ inch on both ends. Tie a double knot to secure. Repeat, making two more embroidery ties. Trim the threads so they are even, and untwist the strands, as shown in **5B**.

Step 4. Repeat Steps 1 through 3 to make the number of yo-yo centers required for the small starflowers in your quilt.

Step 5. Use a thread that matches the yo-yos to hand appliqué them to the centers of the starflowers, as shown in **Diagram 6.**

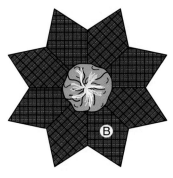

Diagram 6

Appliquéd Sashing

The sashing strips are appliquéd before they are sewn into the quilt top.

Making the Vines

We recommend that you use bias strips to make the gracefully curving vines for the sashing strips of your quilt. Refer to instructions on page 202 for information on preparing bias strips. For the wall-hanging, use the 24-inch square of dark green plaid to cut a total of twelve 24-inch-long bias strips. For the lap-size quilt, use the 36-inch square of dark green plaid to cut a total of thirty-one bias strips, each 24 inches long. Keep in mind that since the fabric is layered, each cut will yield two strips, and that some of these strips may be long enough to be divided into two 24-inch-long strips.

For either size quilt, cut the bias strips 1⅜ inches wide. Then fold, press, and sew the strips as instructed in "Appliquéing Leaves and Vines."

Preparing Leaves for Appliqué

Use your preferred method to prepare all leaves (D pieces) for appliqué. Refer to page 201 for information on freezer paper appliqué.

Appliquéing Leaves and Vines

Step 1. Gently shape a prepared vine to a 4½ × 12½-inch sashing strip, as shown in **Diagram 7**. Pin or baste in place.

Diagram 7

Step 2. Pin or baste a leaf on each side of the vine, as shown in the diagram.

Step 3. Use your preferred method to appliqué the vine and leaves to the sashing strip. Trim away any excess vine that extends beyond the ends of the sashing strip.

Step 4. Repeat to appliqué the required number of sashing strips for your quilt.

Assembling the Quilt

Step 1. Use a design wall or other flat surface to arrange the Star blocks, sashing strips, and corner squares, as shown in the **Assembly Diagram** on page 44. Take care to position the appliqué sashing as shown. The wallhanging has two horizontal rows of two Star blocks each. The lap-size quilt has four horizontal rows of three Star blocks each.

Step 2. Sew the blocks, sashing strips, and corner squares into horizontal rows, as shown. Press seam allowances toward the sashing strips.

Step 3. Sew the rows together, matching seams carefully. Press the quilt.

Assembly Diagram

Step 3. Fold a side border strip in half crosswise and crease. Unfold it and position it right side down along the side of the quilt, with its crease at the quilt's horizontal midpoint. Pin at the midpoint and ends first, then along the entire length of the quilt, easing in fullness if necessary. Sew the border to the quilt, and press the seam toward the border. Repeat on the opposite side of the quilt.

Step 4. Measure the width of the quilt, taking the measurement through its horizontal center rather than along the top or bottom edge, and including the side borders. Trim the top and bottom border strips to this measurement.

Step 5. Repeat the process described in Step 3 to attach the top and bottom borders to the quilt top.

Appliquéing the Starflowers

Step 1. Center, then pin or baste a starflower on each corner square, as shown in the **Quilt Diagram.** The starflowers will overlap the squares and cover the ends of the vines.

Step 2. Use your preferred method to appliqué the starflowers to the quilt.

Quilting and Finishing

Step 1. Mark the top for quilting. The quilt shown has been machine quilted. The large Star blocks have an offset star motif, as shown in **Diagram 8.** All other shapes are outlined, and the background is stipple quilted.

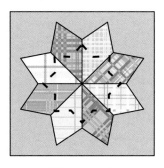

Diagram 8

Adding the Borders

Step 1. Although the pre-cut, 2½ × 42-inch border strips are sufficient in length for the wall-hanging, you will need to piece strips to achieve the required lengths for the side and the top and bottom borders of the lap-size quilt. Cut one of the strips in half. Sew one full-length strip and one half strip together for the top and the bottom borders. Piece two of the 2½-inch-wide border strips end to end for each of the side borders.

Step 2. To determine the exact length for the side borders, measure the length of the quilt top, taking the measurement through its vertical center rather than along its sides. Trim the side border strips to this measurement.

Step 2. Regardless of which quilt size you've chosen to make, the backing will need to be pieced. **Diagram 9** illustrates the layout for both quilt backs.

Wallhanging   Lap

Diagram 9

For the backing for the wallhanging, cut the backing fabric in half crosswise and trim the selvages. Cut a 24½-inch-wide panel from the entire length of each piece of backing fabric. Sew the two panels together lengthwise, and press the seam open. When you are layering the quilt top, batting, and backing for basting, turn the backing so that the seam is parallel to the top edge of the quilt, as shown in the diagram.

Wallhanging   Lap

Quilt Diagram

For the lap-size quilt, cut the backing fabric in half and trim the selvages. Trim each piece to 40 inches wide. Sew the two pieces together lengthwise, and press the seams open. When basting the quilt, the backing seam should be parallel to the top edge of the quilt, as shown in **Diagram 9** on page 45.

Step 3. Layer the backing, batting, and quilt top, and baste the layers together. Quilt by hand or machine, adding additional quilting designs of your choice as desired.

Step 4. Referring to the directions on page 206 in "Quiltmaking Basics," make and attach double-fold binding to finish at a width of ¼ inch. To calculate the amount of binding you will need for the quilt size you are making, add the length of the four sides of the quilt plus 9 inches.

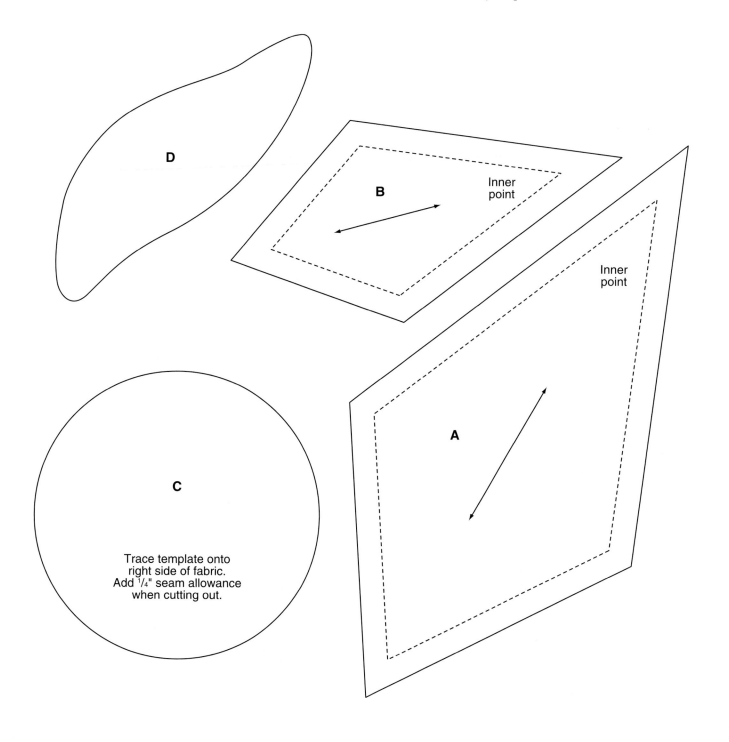

D

B

Inner point

Inner point

A

C

Trace template onto right side of fabric. Add ¹/₄" seam allowance when cutting out.

Quilting through the Seasons

Quilters don't need an excuse or a reason to make a quilt, but the seasons and the special occasions they bring with them offer loads of inspiration.

Spring

Open the windows and drink in the arrival of fresh air and the promise of warmer weather. Now is the time to put away the heavier quilts you've been using all winter and give your décor a face-lift with something new. With Easter on the horizon, your color palette can range from pastels to jelly bean brights. And don't forget Mother's Day. Your mother, grandmother, or aunt will treasure a handmade quilt long after she's finished her breakfast in bed. Celebrate the moment with a quilt that captures the beauty of a springtime bouquet. Dad's special day is just around the corner as well. Wouldn't he love a quilt made from his old ties or maybe a traditional bow tie quilt? June weddings signal yet another reason to show off your quilting skills. Grace the newly-weds with a quilt that spells romance, and they're sure to live happily ever after.

Summer

Begin the lazy days of summer sprawled out on a well-loved quilt under the shade of a big, old tree. Take along your favorite cold beverage and a stack of quilting books and magazines, and soak up loads of ideas for hot-weather projects. For Fourth of July gatherings, be sure to include a wallhanging or door banner that welcomes guests with patriotic colors. Heat up a summertime cookout with a fun table topper scattered with fish, sailboats, and beach items. Or how about making your friends a quilted flag or star pin? Be sure to include a few hand-stitched projects on your list. They're perfect for taking on vacation or toting to the kids' baseball games. Whatever you choose, keep it quick and simple so you can enjoy all the fun summer has to offer.

Fall

This season evokes memories of the first day of school, picking apples, leaves crunching under foot, and watching football games while wrapped up in a warm, comfy blanket and cheering for the home team. Now's the time to start stitching for the cooler days ahead, using some of those memories as inspiration. Pick an apple quilt for the teacher, a sports-themed quilt for the man in your life, or a colorful leaf quilt for yourself. Halloween conjures up a cauldron of opportunities to boo-tify any corner of your home, and Thanksgiving offers a cornucopia of warm, inviting motifs. Light some pumpkin- or apple-pie-scented candles and set the mood for autumn stitching.

Winter

Light the fireplace, pour a mug of hot chocolate, and wrap up in your favorite quilt. Can you think of anything cozier on a cold, blustery day? Of course, making a quilt is always a warm option, too. Pull out the flannels and wools and make some gifts for the upcoming holiday. Quilted ornaments make wonderful additions to the tree as well as great gifts for hostesses or unexpected guests. If you can't get outside to roll up a frosty snowman, quilt one! He'll last all winter and provide lots of cheer. When the holidays are over, toast the New Year with a resolution to make more time to quilt. You deserve it.

Spiderwebs and Dewdrops

Skill Level: Intermediate

_T_his spectacular wallhanging sparkles in the light, thanks to metallic spiderweb quilting and iridescent beading. Quiltmaker Susan Stein confesses to having made this quilt, which is quite lovely in its own right, several years prior to deciding to add the embellishments, which truly make the quilt a knockout.

Before You Begin

We recommend that you read through all of these directions, as well as "Quiltmaking Basics," beginning on page 184, before starting this project, especially if this is your first time making a Double Wedding Ring quilt. Even if you've made Wedding Ring quilts, you'll find tips and pointers throughout the book to make the process fun and rewarding.

Choosing Fabrics

The rings in this quilt are pieced from a gradation of solid hand-dyed fabrics, which move from warm to cool along the length of each arc. A midnight blue solid fabric is used for all other parts of the quilt. While hand-dyed fabrics add a richness to the quilt, you can achieve a similar effect with commercially dyed fabrics if hand-dyed fabrics are not available in your area. You can also order many hand-dyed fabrics online.

The vibrant pinks and teals contrast with the midnight blue to give this quilt a feel similar to that of an Amish color palette. Yet the iridescent black beads and a rainbow metallic quilting thread that highlights the colors in the rings make this quilt distinctively contemporary.

If you would like to experiment with blending shades of other colors for the arcs, such as blues into greens or pinks into purples, photocopy the **Color Plan** on page 209, and use crayons or colored pencils to try different color arrangements.

Quilt Sizes

	Wallhanging (shown)	Twin
Finished Quilt Size	40½" × 40½"	72" × 93"
Finished Ring Size	15"	15"
Number of Rings	9	48
Number of Pieced Arcs	48	220

Materials

Fabric	Wallhanging	Twin
Midnight blue	2 yards	7⅝ yards
Magenta	¼ yard	⅞ yard
Rose	⅓ yard	1 yard
Lavender	⅓ yard	⅞ yard
Orchid	⅓ yard	⅞ yard
Blue	⅓ yard	⅞ yard
Teal	⅓ yard	⅞ yard
Aqua	⅓ yard	1 yard
Green	¼ yard	⅞ yard
Backing	2¾ yards	5¾ yards
Batting	48" × 48"	79" × 100"
Binding	½ yard	⅞ yard

NOTE: _Yardages are based on 44/45-inch-wide fabrics that are at least 42 inches wide after preshrinking._

Cutting Chart

Fabric	Used For	Piece	Number of Pieces	
			Wallhanging	Twin
Midnight blue	Background	A	9	48
	Melons	B	24	110
Magenta	Connecting diamonds	C	24	110
Green	Connecting diamonds	C	24	110
Rose	Outer wedges of arcs	D	48	220
Lavender	Inner wedges of arcs	E	48	220
Orchid	Inner wedges of arcs	E	48	220
Blue	Inner wedges of arcs	E	48	220
Teal	Inner wedges of arcs	E	48	220
Aqua	Outer wedges of arcs	D reverse	48	220

Fabric	Used For	Strip Width	Number of Strips	
			Wallhanging	Twin
Midnight blue	Border	6"	4	8
All eight other fabrics	Binding	2½"	1 of each	1 of each

Cutting

All measurements for cutting strips include ¼-inch seam allowances. Make templates for pieces A, B, C, D, and E from the patterns on page 55, referring to page 186 in "Quiltmaking Basics" for information about making and using templates. Then, referring to the Cutting Chart, cut the required number of pieces for your quilt size. For the border and binding, cut strips in the stated width across the full width of the fabric.

Note: Cut and piece one sample ring before cutting all of the fabric for the quilt.

Piecing the Arcs

Step 1. Each arc is constructed from the D, D reverse, and E pieces, beginning with a rose D piece and continuing to the right along the arc in the following order: lavender E, orchid E, blue E, teal E, and aqua D reverse. As you sew, be sure pieces are oriented so that curves arch in the same direction. Gently press seams to one side, taking care not to stretch the unit. Repeat until you've assembled all of the arcs required for your quilt. Each pieced arc should look like the example shown in **Diagram 1.**

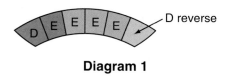

Diagram 1

Step 2. Center and sew one pieced arc to one side of each midnight blue melon, as shown in **Diagram 2.** To determine the center of the melon, fold it in half and lightly crease it. The seam between the two center E pieces marks the center of the arcs. For more specific information and tips on assembling curved pieces, refer to page 191. Press each seam toward the melon. You will use half of the pieced arcs for this step.

Diagram 2

Step 3. Sew a magenta C piece to each end of *half* of the remaining pieced arcs. Gently press all seams in the same direction. Sew a green C piece to each end of the remaining arcs and press. You now have two types of arcs, as shown in **Diagram 3.**

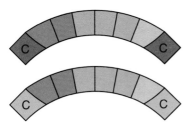

Diagram 3

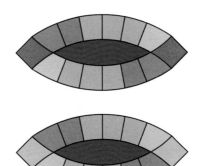

Diagram 4

Assembling the Quilt Top

Step 1. Sew the completed arc/melon units to the background A pieces, as shown in **Diagram 5,** leaving ¼ inch open at the beginning and end of each seam. For the wallhanging, you will have one A piece with an arc/melon unit sewn to all four sides, four A pieces with three units attached, and four A pieces with two units attached. For the twin-size quilt, you will have one A piece with arc/melon units attached to all four sides. Twelve A pieces will have units on three sides, and thirty-five A pieces will have two units attached. Be sure to alternate the colors of the tips from magenta to green, as shown.

Sew Quick

Since all of the arcs are identical, assembly line piecing can make arc construction quick and easy. For example, stack all rose D pieces alongside the lavender E pieces. Pair these pieces, with right sides together, then sew them together. Then go on to the next pair, the orchid E and blue E pieces. After assembling the pairs, sew them together to form the arcs, and you'll be sure to have your colors in the right sequence.

Step 4. Center and sew the arcs to the melon units, matching the seam of the C pieces with the seam on the tip of the partially completed melons. Press all seams toward the melons. Make two stacks for the new units, one with magenta ends and one with green ends, as shown in **Diagram 4.** Again, refer to page 191 for further explanation of sewing curved seams.

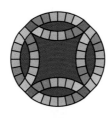

Make 1 for either size.

Make 4 for wallhanging.
Make 12 for twin.

Make 4 for wallhanging.
Make 35 for twin.

Diagram 5

Step 2. Use a design wall or other flat surface to lay out the units for the wallhanging, as shown in the **Wallhanging Assembly Diagram.** For the twin-size quilt, lay out eight horizontal rows of rings, with six rings in each row. Notice that arc units with the magenta tips are all placed horizontally in the rings, while those with green tips are positioned vertically.

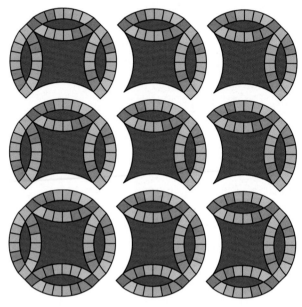

Wallhanging Assembly Diagram

Step 3. Sew units together in rows, starting and stopping seams ¼ inch from each end and backstitching. Then sew the rows together to complete the quilt top. For more assembly details, see page 193 in "Quiltmaking Basics."

Making and Attaching the Border

For either size quilt, the outside edge of the quilt center is appliquéd onto a preassembled border unit.

Step 1. For the wallhanging, trim two of the 6-inch-wide midnight blue border strips to 29½ inches long for the quilt sides, and trim two strips to 40½ inches long for the top and bottom borders. For the twin-size quilt, join four sets of two

6-inch-wide border strips. Cut two of the long strips to 81½ inches for the quilt sides, and trim the other two long strips to 72 inches for the top and bottom borders.

Step 2. For either size quilt, sew a side border to a top or bottom border, placing right sides together and aligning outer edges, as shown in **Diagram 6A.** Press the seams toward the side borders. See **6B.** Repeat for all corners to assemble the entire border unit, as shown in **6C.**

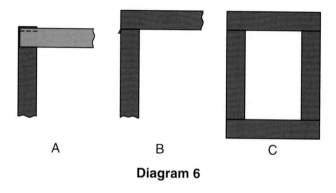

A   B   C

Diagram 6

Step 3. Prepare the outer rings for appliqué. Refer to page 201 for details about the freezer paper method of preparing the ring edges. Center the completed quilt top on the border unit. Pin or baste in place, then hand or machine appliqué the top to the border around the outer rings. The **Wallhanging Diagram** shows how the completed wallhanging will look. The twin-size quilt is finished the same way but has more rings to be appliquéd. Trim away excess fabric from the inner portion of the border as necessary. If you use the freezer paper method, remove the paper when the appliqué is complete.

Quilting and Finishing

Step 1. Mark the quilt top for quilting. The quilt shown has a glittery spiderweb, stitched with metallic thread, stretching across the midnight blue center of each ring. Midnight blue thread was used to machine quilt in the ditch around the rings and melons. The quiltmaker also used shimmering black seed beads, staggered at ½-inch in-

Wallhanging Diagram

tervals, in the borders and melon of her quilt. Each bead is stitched by hand, embellishing the surface of the quilt. The beading also acts as quilting since the beads are stitched through all layers of the quilt.

If you wish to add beads to your quilt, construct a prepunched see-through grid to simplify the task of marking bead positions.

Step 2. To make a see-through grid, first determine the spacing you will use for bead placement and whether the beads will be positioned in matching or staggered rows. Use a ruler to determine placement points, then mark the points on a sheet of template plastic. Final template size is up to you, but a large sheet of plastic will allow you to mark more bead positions before having to reposition it. Use an ice pick, awl, or similar tool to punch through each marked hole. One-eighth-

inch paper punches work well for narrow templates.

Position the template over an area that will be beaded. Use a light-color pencil to mark the fabric at each hole. Move the sheet around if necessary to mark positions, avoiding seam allowance areas in the borders. After the quilt has been quilted, sew a bead at each mark, then tie it off on the back and bury the thread ends in the batting layer.

Step 3. Regardless of which quilt size you've chosen to make, the backing will have to be pieced.

For the wallhanging, cut the backing fabric into two equal lengths, and trim the selvages. Cut a 32-inch-wide panel from one length and a 16-inch-wide panel from the other length. Sew the two panels together, as shown in **Diagram 7** on page 54. Press the seam open.

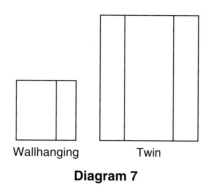

Wallhanging   Twin

Diagram 7

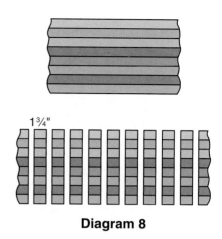

1¾"

Diagram 8

Step 4. For the twin-size quilt, cut the backing fabric into two equal lengths, and trim the selvages. Cut one of the pieces in half lengthwise, and sew one half to each side of the full-width piece, as shown. Press the seams open.

Step 5. Layer the backing, batting, and quilt top, and baste. Quilt as desired.

Adding the Binding

The binding is pieced from short segments of the fabrics used in the rings. Strip piecing is used to speed up the process. You will need four separate binding strips for your quilt.

Step 1. To determine the lengths of the pieced binding strips needed for each side, measure the quilt vertically and add approximately 5 inches, then measure the quilt horizontally and add approximately 5 inches.

Step 2. Sew the 2½-inch-wide strips together lengthwise in any order you find pleasing. Each time you add a strip, sew in the opposite direction from the previous strip to prevent warping. Set each seam by pressing it flat, just as it was sewn, then gently open the strip and press from the right side. Press all seams in the same direction.

Step 3. Using a rotary cutter, trim one end of the strip set, as shown in **Diagram 8**, then cut as many 1¾-inch segments from the strip set as possible.

Step 4. Sew the segments together end to end, as shown in **Diagram 9**, constructing two binding strips for each length calculated in Step 1. Make another strip set if necessary, adjusting its width to yield the number of strip units required to complete your binding.

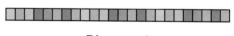

Diagram 9

Step 5. Placing right sides together, match the raw edge of a side binding strip to the raw edge of one side of your quilt, allowing the binding to extend beyond both ends. Sew the binding to the quilt with a ¼-inch seam allowance.

Step 6. Turn the binding to the back of the quilt and fold the raw edge under to meet the raw edge of the quilt top. Blindstitch the binding to the quilt backing. Trim excess binding flush with the top and bottom edges of the quilt. Stitch across each end of the binding to help prevent fraying. Repeat for the opposite side of the quilt.

Step 7. Apply the top and bottom binding strips in the same manner, but do not trim the binding flush with the quilt sides. Instead, trim the binding ends so they extend beyond the quilt edge by about ½ inch. Fold under the binding ends before stitching them in place.

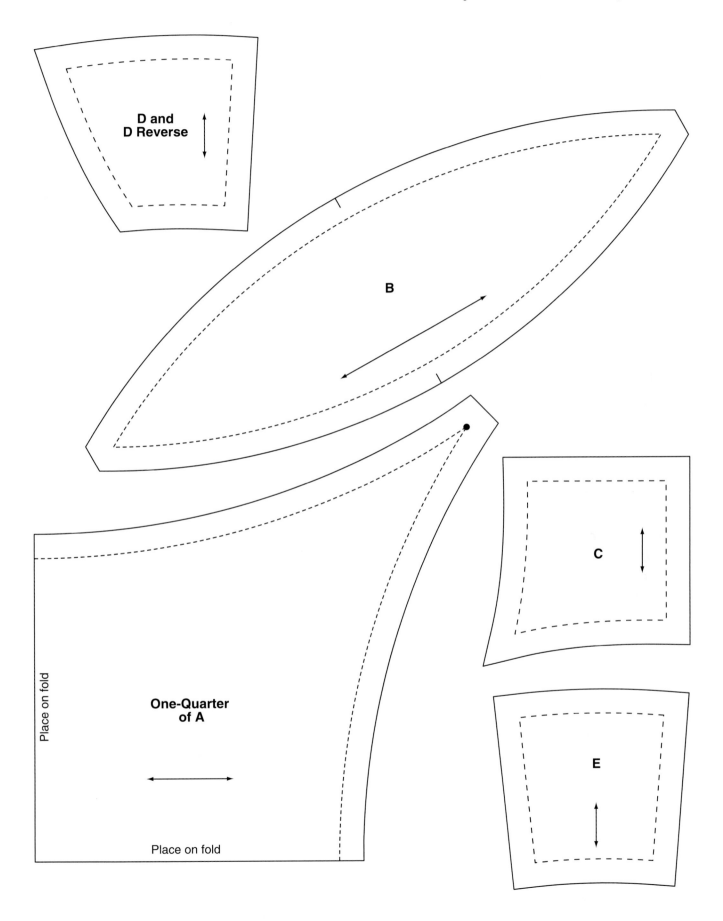

**D and
D Reverse**

B

C

Place on fold

**One-Quarter
of A**

Place on fold

E

The Eclectic Neighborhood

Skill Level: Challenging

*I*nspired by a workshop with Mary Golden, quiltmaker Margaret Harrison put a new spin on a familiar pattern. This up-to-the-minute wallhanging seems to have it all: rich colors, diminutive houses, bold strip piecing, and a dazzling set. Hand and machine quilting add touch-me texture in a comfortable blending of old and new.

Before You Begin

This quilt is rated challenging primarily because of its unusual setting, which involves set-in seams. In addition, each of the nine blocks has a different arrangement of setting triangles. But don't be intimidated! If you read through the directions and study the diagrams carefully, you'll discover familiar quick-cutting and strip-piecing methods for making the setting triangles and squares. Plus, the small-scale houses use paper foundation piecing, so you can achieve expert accuracy without having to cut tiny pieces from templates.

You will need to make nine copies of the Block Pattern on page 64. Trace the blocks or photocopy them on a high-quality photocopier that won't distort their shape. If you trace the blocks by hand, be sure to copy the numbers, as they indicate the piecing order for the block.

You may also want to refer to "Quiltmaking Basics," beginning on page 184, which contains more detailed instructions to help you with rotary cutting, strip piecing, and set-in seams.

Quilt Size

Finished Quilt Size	29" × 29"
Finished Block Size	
House Block	4"
Overall Block	7"
Number of Blocks	9

NOTE: *Due to the number of block variations and the specific block arrangement required for this quilt, no variations in size or layout are provided.*

Materials

Fabric	Amount
Fuchsia/blue/green plaid	½ yard
Dark blue-violet print	¼ yard
Medium blue-violet print	½ yard
Navy solid	⅔ yard
Tan stripe	⅛ yard
Medium blue-green print	⅛ yard
Purple-and-green plaid	⅛ yard
Teal solid	⅛ yard
Sky blue mottled print	¼ yard
Medium blue streaky print	⅛ yard
Light purple mottled print	⅛ yard
Dark blue swirly print	⅛ yard
Fuchsia solid	⅛ yard
Medium purple solid	⅛ yard
Dark purple solid	⅛ yard
Dark blue-violet solid	⅛ yard
Medium gray solid	⅛ yard
Dusty blue solid	⅛ yard
Light blue solid	⅛ yard
Backing	1 yard
Batting	33" × 33"
Binding	⅜ yard

NOTE: *Yardages are based on 44/45-inch-wide fabrics that are at least 42 inches wide after preshrinking.*

Cutting Chart

Fabric	Used For	Strip Width	Number to Cut
Fuchsia/blue/green plaid	Borders	3"	4
Dark blue-violet print	Borders	¾"	4
	Pieced squares and triangles	1"	2
Medium blue-violet solid	Row 1	1½"	2
	Row 2	2½"	1
	Setting triangles	Template A	8
	Setting triangles	Template B	4
Navy solid	Row 1	1½"	2
	Pieced squares and triangles	1"	2
Tan stripe	Row 1	1½"	1
Medium blue-green print	Row 1	1½"	1
Purple-and-green plaid	Row 2	3"	1
Teal solid	Row 3	1¾"	1
Sky blue mottled print	Row 2	2"	2
	Row 3	1¾"	2
Medium blue streaky print	Setting triangles	Template A	8
Light purple mottled print	Setting triangles	Template A	8
Dark blue swirly print	Setting triangles	Template A	4
Fuchsia, medium purple, dark purple, and dark blue-violet solids	Pieced triangles	1⅛"	2 each color
Medium gray, dusty blue, and light blue solids	Pieced triangles and squares	1"	2 each color

Choosing Fabrics

This quiltmaker chose her favorite purples, fuchsias, and teals to add richness and depth to her contemporary-looking design. You might enjoy duplicating this cool color palette or prefer an autumn look of reds, golds, browns, and rusts.

To develop your own color scheme for this quilt, photocopy the **Color Plan** on page 209, and experiment with different color arrangements.

Cutting

All of the measurements include ¼-inch seam allowances. Refer to the Cutting Chart and cut the required strips, cutting across the fabric width.

Make templates for patterns A and B on page 64. See page 186 for details on making and using templates. To trace the templates onto fabric, place them right side up on the wrong side of the fabric.

Note: Cut and piece one sample block before cutting all the fabric for the quilt.

Piecing the House Blocks

The blocks are pieced in three sections, which are joined to complete the block. Refer to the **Block Diagram** for color placement as you assemble each block. Notice that the strip widths give ample seam allowances. After stitching, simply trim the excess fabric with your scissors or rotary cutter, taking care not to cut through the paper.

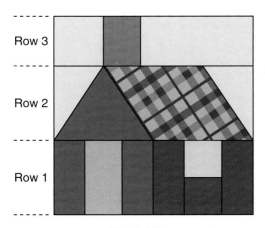

Block Diagram

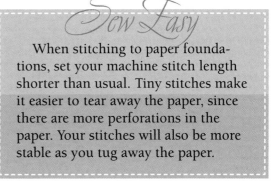

Step 1. To make Row 1, you will need the following strips: navy solid, blue-green print, medium blue-violet solid, and tan stripe. To form the window, begin with the navy and blue-green strips and place them right sides together with the navy strip on top. Hold the strips underneath your paper pattern so that they are underneath section 2 (the navy fabric will be against the paper). The edges of the strips should extend at least ¼ inch beyond the boundaries of section 2 on all sides, as shown in **Diagram 1**. Pin in place. Stitch along the line between sections 1 and 2, extending the stitching slightly beyond both ends of the line, as shown.

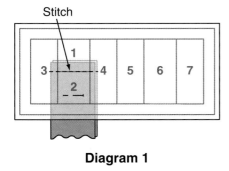

Diagram 1

Step 2. Turn the paper over, trim the seam to ¼ inch, and then open out the strips. Press. Trim the strips so that the navy extends at least ¼ inch beyond the bottom of section 2 and the blue-green extends ¼ inch beyond the top of section 1.

Step 3. With the fabric side of the block facing you, lay the remainder of the navy strip on top of

the section 1 and 2 pieces, *with right sides together* and raw edges even on the right edge, as shown in **Diagram 2A**. Holding the strip in place, flip the paper over, and stitch along the line between section 3 and sections 1 and 2. Again, start and stop stitching slightly beyond the ends of the line, as shown in **2B**. Turn the paper over, trim the seam to ¼ inch. Open out the strips and press. Trim the navy strip so that it extends ¼ inch beyond section 3 on all raw edges.

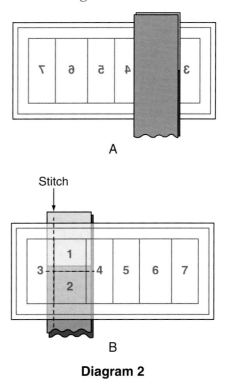

Diagram 2

Step 4. Continue adding fabric, following the numerical order on the pattern. Section 4 will be another navy piece, followed by a blue-violet piece, a tan stripe piece, and a blue-violet piece. Remember to trim the seams each time after you stitch to avoid bulk in the finished block. Also, be sure to leave enough fabric for a seam when you trim beyond the block boundaries.

Step 5. Row 2 is completed in exactly the same fashion as Row 1, except the seam lines are diagonal. Since you'll be sewing to a paper foundation, your fabric will be stabilized and will not stretch as you sew along the bias edge. Begin with the purple-and-green plaid strip for the roof and the sky blue mottled strip for the sky. Hold the strips with right sides together with the plaid strip on top. Then align the strips underneath the paper foundation, as shown in **Diagram 3**, so that you will have enough fabric to cover sections 1 and 2 when the strips are opened up.

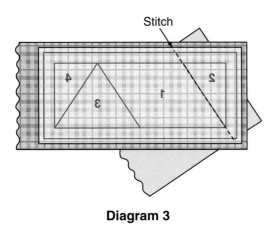

Diagram 3

Step 6. Continue piecing Row 2, adding the medium blue-violet strip for the roof peak (section 3) and finishing with the remainder of the sky blue mottled strip for section 4.

Step 7. Row 3 is pieced from sky blue mottled strips and teal solid strips. Hold the strips with right sides together and the blue strip on top. Place the Row 3 paper foundation over the strips, as shown in **Diagram 4**, so that at least ¼ inch extends beyond the top and bottom of the row for seams. Stitch along the line between sections 1 and 2. Turn the paper over, trim the seam, and open up the strips. Press. Trim excess fabric,

leaving enough to extend beyond the block boundaries for seams. Add the remaining section of Row 3 in the same manner.

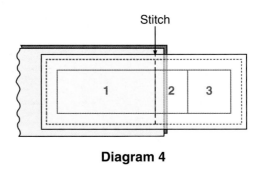

Diagram 4

Step 8. Turn all three rows so the paper side is face up. Using your rotary-cutting equipment, trim the excess fabric and paper from the three sections of the block. Be sure to trim on the dashed outer lines, not the inner solid seam lines. See **Diagram 5**.

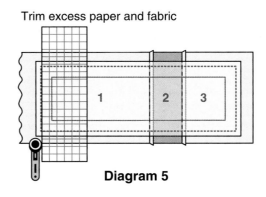

Diagram 5

Step 9. With the paper foundations still in place for stability, sew Row 1 to Row 2. Sew exactly on the dashed seam line. Sew Row 3 to the top of Row 2 in the same manner. When the block is complete, remove the papers, taking care not to stretch the seams. Use tweezers where seams intersect to get out the last bits of paper.

Step 10. Repeat Steps 1 through 9 to complete nine House blocks.

Piecing the Setting Triangles and Squares

Some of the setting triangles are strip pieced, while some are cut from a single fabric. For the strip-pieced triangles, sew together strip sets first, then use the triangle template to cut the triangle from the strip set. The same template is used to cut the single-fabric triangles.

Step 1. Sew together $1\frac{1}{8}$-inch-wide fuchsia, medium purple, dark purple, and dark blue-violet solid strips along their long edges to form strip sets. Press all seams in one direction. Make a total of twelve strip sets. See **Diagram 6**.

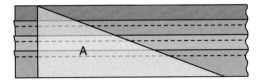

Diagram 6

Step 2. Lay template A *right* side up on the *wrong* side of the strip set, with the long straight edge of the template aligned with the raw edge of the fuchsia strip, as shown. Lay your rotary ruler along one edge of the template to cut one side of the triangle. Repeat along the other triangle side. Cut a total of twelve purple pieced A triangles.

Step 3. The blue pieced A triangles are made in the same manner. Sew together 1-inch-wide dark blue-violet print, navy, medium gray, dusty blue, and light blue strips along their long edges to form strip sets. Press all seams in one direction. See **Diagram 7**. Following the procedure described in Step 2, cut four blue pieced A triangles, with the *longest* edge of template A aligned with the raw edge of the light blue strip, as shown.

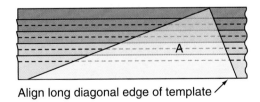

Align long diagonal edge of template ╱
Diagram 7

Step 4. From the leftover blue strip set, cut four 3-inch-wide squares and set them aside.

Devote your valuable time to stitching instead of searching! Keep an extra pack of needles, a spare lightbulb, a few bobbins filled with neutral-color thread, and the instruction manual close at hand when you begin any machine-sewing project.

Assembling the Blocks

There are nine blocks in this quilt. Each is composed of a House block surrounded by four A triangles. In addition to the purple and blue pieced A triangles, some of the A triangles are cut from a dark blue swirly print, a medium blue streaky print, and a light purple mottled print.

Although the blocks are pieced in exactly the same manner, each has a different color placement and arrangement of the triangles that surround the center block. Refer to the **Assembly Diagram** for color placement and to **Diagram 8** on page 62 for stitching assistance. Use a design wall or other flat surface to lay out the blocks before you begin piecing them. For each block variation, position

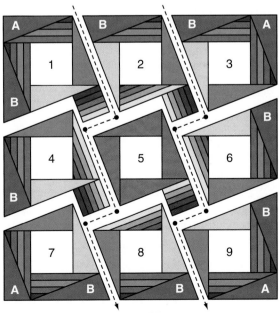

Assembly Diagram

the bottom triangle first and work clockwise as you stitch the triangles to the House block.

Step 1. Sew the appropriate A triangle to the bottom edge of the House block, as shown in **Diagram 8A.** With right sides together, align the short edge of the triangle with the left edge of the House block. The long pointy tail of the triangle will extend beyond the right edge of the House block. Stop sewing approximately 1 inch from the raw edge on the right of the House block, as indicated by the arrow. This seam will be finished after the last triangle has been added. Press the seam away from the House block.

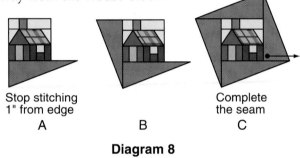

Stop stitching
1" from edge
A

B

Complete
the seam
C

Diagram 8

Step 2. Sew the appropriate A triangle to the left edge of the House block, as shown in **8B.** Align the short edge of the triangle with the top edge of the House block. This time sew the complete seam. Press the seam toward the triangle.

Step 3. Continue adding the remaining triangles to the block, sewing the top triangle next, then the right triangle, in the same manner as in Step 2. When the last triangle has been added, go back and complete the first unfinished seam, sewing in the direction of the arrow in **8C.** Press.

Step 4. Repeat Steps 1 through 3 to complete all nine blocks.

Assembling the Quilt Top

Step 1. Refer to the **Assembly Diagram** on page 61 and use a design wall or other flat surface to lay out the blocks, the strip-pieced squares, and the medium blue-violet A and B setting triangles. The diagram is number coded to indicate which block variation should appear in each position in the quilt top. Refer to the photograph on page 56 for additional assistance.

Step 2. Sew a pieced square to the lower right corner of Block 1, as shown in **Diagram 9.** Press the seam away from the square. Repeat for Blocks 2, 4, and 5.

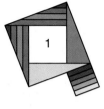

Diagram 9

Step 3. Referring again to the **Assembly Diagram** for positioning, sew the medium blue-violet setting triangles to the outer edges of the house blocks. Note that some blocks have both A and B triangles added, while others have only B triangles. The center block has no setting triangles. Press all seams toward the setting triangles.

Step 4. From this point on, all of the blocks are sewn together with set-in seams. Refer to page 189 for additional information on set-in seams. The blocks are sewn in vertical rows of three blocks each. Then the vertical rows are sewn together.

First, sew Block 1 to Block 4, as illustrated in **Diagram 10.** Begin stitching ¼ inch from the raw edge where the pieced square and Block 1 meet. Sew from the inner corner outward in each direction, as indicated by the arrows. Press the seams as desired. In a similar fashion, sew Block 4 to Block 7 to complete the first row.

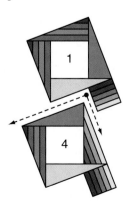

Diagram 10

Quilt Diagram

Step 5. Using the same procedure, complete the second vertical row by sewing Block 2 to Block 5, then Block 5 to Block 8. Complete the third row by sewing together Blocks 3, 6, and 9.

Step 6. Sew the rows together, stitching in the direction indicated by the arrows in the **Assembly Diagram.** Stop stitching and pivot ¼ inch from the raw edges at each corner marked with a dot. Press as desired.

Adding the Borders

Step 1. Sew the dark blue-violet print border strips to the fuchsia/blue/green plaid border strips in four pairs. Press the seams toward the plaid strips. Trim each to 31 inches long.

Step 2. Fold a border in half crosswise and crease. Unfold it and position it right side down along one side of the quilt top, with the crease at the quilt's horizontal midpoint. The narrow blue-

violet strip should be positioned so that, when sewn, it is closest to the center of the quilt. Pin and sew the border in place, using a ¼-inch seam. Begin and end sewing ¼ inch from the raw edge of the quilt top. Repeat this procedure to attach the remaining borders to the other three sides of the quilt top. Press seams away from the borders.

Step 3. Miter the corner seams, carefully matching the seams of the two border fabrics, as shown in the **Quilt Diagram.** Refer to page 204 for complete details on mitering corners.

Quilting and Finishing

Step 1. Mark the quilt top for quilting. In the quilt shown, the House blocks are hand quilted in the ditch. The triangles around the center house are hand quilted in a swirly motif that follows the pattern of the fabric. The strip-pieced triangles are machine quilted in the ditch, with straight lines echoed in the unpieced triangles. The outer border is machine quilted in parallel lines that extend from the setting triangles.

Step 2. Trim the selvages from the backing fabric. Layer the backing, batting, and quilt top, and baste the layers together.

Step 3. Quilt all marked designs, adding any additional quilting as desired.

Step 4. Referring to the directions on page 206, make and attach navy double-fold binding. You will need approximately 126 inches of binding.

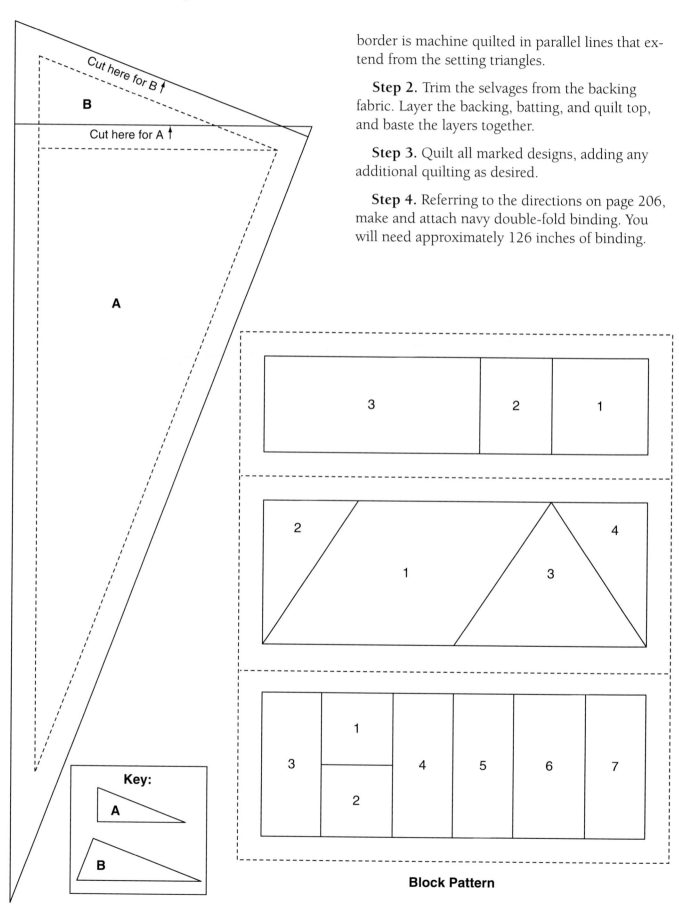

Block Pattern

Gifts for Quilting Friends

No one understands a quilter like another quilter, so when a gift-giving occasion rolls around, you probably are thinking about purchasing your quiltmaking friend a quilt-related item. She'd love anything you gave her, but here are some suggestions that are always appropriate and appreciated. After you've picked one out, wrap it up in quilt-themed gift wrap or a brown paper gift bag you've embellished with quilting motifs. Look for all of these items wherever quilting supplies are sold.

• Give quilt-themed stationary to help a quilting friend keep track of her design ideas and thoughts in style. Get her a notepad to keep next to her machine to jot down items she needs from the quilt shop. Add a stack of self-adhesive notes so she can stick tidbits of information anywhere. Don't forget a box of decorative business-size cards with her name and address. They're useful as luggage tags, name tags, calling cards, gift tags, and so much more.

• Satisfy her love of specialty fabrics with a bundle of hand-painted or hand-dyed fabric. Each piece is unique, just like her.

• Protect her rulers and help her keep them organized with a ruler rack.

• If she never seems to be able to find the right color thread, buy her a thread holder. Add a few spools of neutral color threads that will go with any color fabric.

• Is she constantly toting her sewing supplies to a class in a plastic bag or trying to get it all together so she can quilt while she's on the road? A travel case could be the answer. They come in a variety of sizes to accommodate everything from the basic necessities to a large-size cutting mat to a sewing machine. Take your pick!

• If there's an item she's been longing for, but you find it's out of your price range, give her a gift certificate to the shop that carries the item. If enough friends have the same idea, her waiting days are over.

• Make sure she keeps all your quilting dates with a quilt-themed calendar. Pencil in a few dates throughout the year so she has a surprise when she flips to a new month.

• Stickers and rubber stamps are perfect when you need that little something extra to stick in with her birthday card or into her Christmas stocking.

• Leave no doubt as to her favorite hobby with a sweatshirt or T-shirt printed with quilting motifs.

• Pay for a quilting class at her favorite quilt shop.

• Texturize her quilting palette with an assortment of decorative threads.

• Buy her a subscription to her favorite magazine. If she's already a subscriber, have the company extend her subscription so she can enjoy it longer.

• Indulge her with chocolate, chocolate, and more chocolate. Most quilters won't care what kind or type it is as long as it's chocolate. And the sugar-free chocolates are yummier than ever!

Skill Level: Intermediate

$\mathcal{J}$ohanna Wilson's expert piecing and Bonnie Erickson's spectacular feathered machine quilting make this wallhanging a real knockout. Johanna chose just two fabrics, but unlike many quilts made from a pair of fabrics, this one packs a colorful punch. The paisley print used is rich with burgundies, greens, teals, golds, and browns, providing a range of strong colors. Solitude is just one of more than two dozen quilts Johanna has designed using the traditional Fox and Geese block in original settings.

Before You Begin

This quilt is constructed using rotary cutting techniques and your choice of quick-piecing methods.

Each 12-inch star block is actually made up of four 6-inch Fox and Geese blocks. To form the intricate-looking diagonal setting, the 12-inch blocks are separated by plain setting squares, and pairs of 6-inch blocks are placed near the outer edges of the quilt corners.

Choosing Fabrics

The original quilt contains only two fabrics. A medium tan print is used for setting squares and rectangles and all background areas of the blocks. For a blended, consistent background, choose a very small print or one that "reads" as a solid. For example, the print you choose may appear to be solid at first glance, but when examined more closely, you find it is actually an overall print or pattern. A print of this type will add more texture to your quilt than a true solid.

For the star points, choose a medium-scale print. The print can be multicolor, as in the quilt shown, but be sure that all colors in the print contrast with the background fabric that you have chosen so the star points are clearly distinguishable from the background fabric.

To develop your own color scheme, photocopy the **Color Plan** on page 215, and use colored pencils or crayons to experiment with different color arrangements.

Quilt Sizes

	Wallhanging (shown)	King
Finished Quilt Size	54½" × 54½"	102½" × 102½"
Finished Block Size	6"	6"
Number of Blocks	32	128
Number of 3" Triangle Squares	72	280
Number of 1½" Triangle Squares	128	512

Materials

Fabric	Wallhanging	King
Tan print	4 yards	11⅞ yards
Teal print*	2 yards	5 yards
Backing	3½ yards	9⅓ yards
Batting	62" × 62"	110" × 110"

NOTE: *Yardages are based on 44/45-inch-wide fabrics that are at least 42 inches wide after preshrinking.*

* *Yardages include binding.*

Cutting Chart

Fabric	Used For	Strip Width	Number to Cut Wall	King	Second Cut Dimensions	Number to Cut Wall	King
Tan	Setting squares	12½"	2	8	12½" squares	4	24
	Setting rectangles	6½"	3	6	12½" × 6½"	8	16
	Border rectangles	21½"	1	1	21½" × 3½"*	8	8
	Border rectangles	18½"	—	1	18½" × 3½"	—	8
	Large triangle squares	25"	1	4	25" squares	1	4
	Small triangle squares	20"	1	2	20" squares	1	4
	Pieced blocks	2"	7	26	2" squares	128	512
Teal	Large triangle squares	25"	1	4	25" squares	1	4
	Small triangle squares	20"	1	2	20" squares	1	4
	Border corners	3½"	1	1	3½" squares	4	4

* Cut these pieces on the lengthwise grain.

Cutting

Refer to the Cutting Chart for the number of pieces to cut from each fabric for your quilt size. All measurements include ¼-inch seam allowances.

Note: Cut and piece one sample block before cutting all of the fabric for the quilt.

Making the Triangle Squares

Two sizes of triangle squares are used in this quilt. Each Fox and Geese block contains four 1½-inch triangle squares and two 3-inch triangle squares (finished sizes). The 3-inch triangle squares are also used in the border.

Triangle squares can be made quickly and accurately using the grid method, which is described on page 187.

Step 1. For the 1½-inch triangle squares, use a 2⅜-inch grid with eight squares across and eight squares down. Make one grid for the wallhanging or four grids for the king-size quilt.

Step 2. Use a 3⅞-inch grid with six squares across and six squares down for the 3-inch triangle squares. Make one grid for the wallhanging or four grids for the king-size quilt.

Making the Fox and Geese Blocks

Step 1. Sew a 2-inch square to a small triangle square, as shown in **Diagram 1A**. Press toward the dark triangle. Repeat to make four units. Sew the units together in pairs, as shown in **1B**. Press.

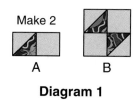

Make 2

A   B

Diagram 1

Step 2. Sew a large triangle square to one end of each bow-tie unit, positioning the units as shown in **Diagram 2A**. Press toward the large dark triangles. Sew together, as shown in **2B**. Press.

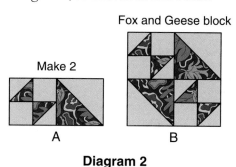

Fox and Geese block

Make 2

A   B

Diagram 2

Step 3. Repeat Steps 1 and 2 to complete the number of Fox and Geese blocks needed for your quilt size. The remaining large triangle squares will be used in the border.

Assembling the Star Blocks

Step 1. Position and sew two Fox and Geese blocks together, as shown in **Diagram 3**. Repeat, sewing all but four Fox and Geese blocks into pairs. Set the remaining four blocks aside to be used in the quilt corners.

Diagram 3

Step 2. Sew two units from Step 1 together to create a Star block, orienting them as shown in **Diagram 4**. Match the seams carefully, and press the adjoining seams in opposite directions where possible.

Star Block

Diagram 4

Step 3. Repeat, assembling five Star blocks for the wallhanging and twenty-five for the king-size quilt. The remaining Fox and Geese block pairs will be used in the border.

Step 4. Sew the leftover large triangle squares together in pairs, as shown in **Diagram 5**. These will be used in the border.

Diagram 5

Assembling the Quilt Top

Step 1. Refer to the photograph of the wallhanging or the **King-Size Assembly Diagram** on page 70, and use a design wall or other flat surface to lay out the Star blocks, setting pieces, and Fox and Geese blocks in horizontal rows.

Step 2. Sew the blocks and the setting squares and rectangles together in rows, pressing the seams toward the setting pieces. Sew the rows together, matching seam intersections carefully. Press the entire quilt top.

Step 3. Lay out the border rectangles, the remaining 3-inch triangle squares, and the border corners around the perimeter of the quilt. For the king-size quilt, use the larger rectangles at the corners and the smaller rectangles for the middle area of the border.

Step 4. Sew the top and bottom borders together in horizontal rows. Sew these borders to the quilt top, carefully matching seams and being sure the dark portion of the triangle squares is adjacent to the quilt top.

Step 5. Sew the side borders together in the same manner as the top and bottom borders, and sew one to each side of the quilt top.

Quilting and Finishing

Step 1. Mark the top for quilting. In the quilt shown on page 66, feathered wreaths were used in the center of each setting square, feathered curves in each setting triangle, and feathered ropes in each border rectangle. To highlight the feathered quilting, the remaining background areas were stipple quilted. The dark star points were quilted in the ditch.

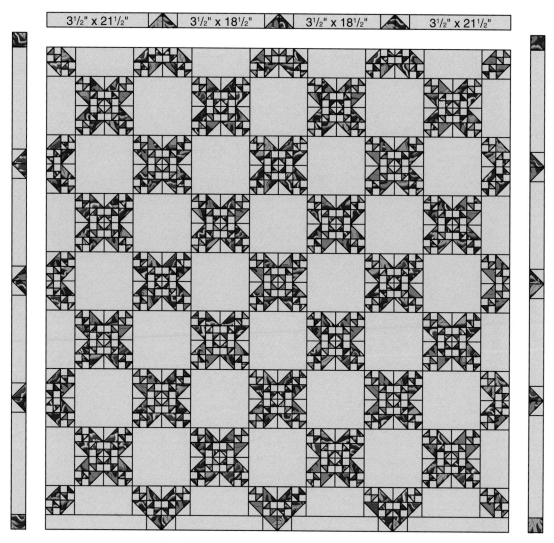

| 3¹/₂" x 21¹/₂" | 3¹/₂" x 18¹/₂" | 3¹/₂" x 18¹/₂" | 3¹/₂" x 21¹/₂" |

King-Size Assembly Diagram

Step 2. Regardless of which quilt size you're making, the backing will have to be pieced. For the wallhanging, cut the backing fabric in half crosswise and trim the selvages. Cut two 11-inch-wide pieces from the entire length of one segment. Sew one narrow piece to each side of the full-width piece, as shown in **Diagram 6.** Press the seams open.

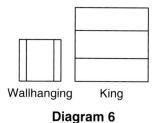

Wallhanging   King

Diagram 6

For the king-size quilt, cut the backing fabric into three equal lengths and trim the selvages. Cut a 35-inch-wide panel from the entire length of two of the segments and sew one to each side of the full-width piece, as shown. Press the seams open.

Step 3. Layer the backing, batting, and quilt top. Baste the layers together, then hand or machine quilt as desired.

Step 4. Referring to the directions on page 206, make and attach double-fold binding from the teal fabric. To calculate the amount of binding you will need, add up the length of the four sides of the quilt plus 9 inches.

A Quilting We Will Go

Where would you go if you were planning a vacation? Visualize it in your mind and then imagine yourself quilting. Now, that's an ideal vacation! Look for quilt tour ads in quilting magazines, check the Internet for vacation packages geared toward quilting, or make up your own destination. Here are a few ideas to get you started.

Beach: Find a nice seaside cottage, leave the windows open, and listen to the waves hitting the sand as your sewing machine hums happily along. When the beach beckons, grab your handwork and head for the lounge chair where you can soak up the sun and stitch to your heart's content.

Mountains: A high-altitude vacation can provide beautiful scenery any time of year. Enjoy the peace and tranquility of freshly fallen snow during the winter, lushness of mountain greenery during the spring and summer, and masses of blazing colors throughout the fall season. Book your accommodations at or near a ski resort that offers year-round activities for added fun.

Cruise ship: Head for an adventure on the high seas with a cruise geared toward quilting! Visit exotic ports of call between classes and enjoy the local cuisine. Shop at local quilt shops for souvenirs to add to your stash and a chance to meet quilters from another region.

Shop hop: Pick an area rich with quilt shops and go visit. Stay at a cozy bed-and-breakfast where you can be pampered after a long day of shopping. Be sure to take advantage of any nonquilting sites along the way. Get a carload of quilting friends together and take a weekend road trip, visiting as many shops as you can (and enjoy the local sights and flavors while you're at it).

National quilt shows: Big or small, quilt shows ooze with inspiration and creativity, but one trip to a national quilt show will leave you in absolute awe. Row after row of stunning quilts made by quilters from all over the world line the aisles, followed by multitudes of vendors selling the latest and greatest fabrics and quilting supplies. Take advantage of the opportunity to learn techniques from nationally known instructors and meet quilters from near and far. Count on being tired but happy after this quilting vacation.

Home: Send everyone else away and enjoy the pleasure of your own sewing space! Everything you need is at your fingertips, and there's no one to sidetrack you with other demands. Watch your favorite quilting videos and shows, browse through your favorite magazines, or just sew. Go to bed when you want, eat when and what you want, and never get out of your pajamas. Just because you're home doesn't mean it can't be a vacation.

All-American Schoolhouses

Skill Level: Easy

*T*winkling stars, bright corner squares, and bold striped sashing add patriotic flair to the time-honored Schoolhouse motif in this quilt pieced by Sharyn Craig. With its ample helping of red, white, and blue, this wallhanging is the perfect accent for Independence Day or any day! Most of the strips for this all-American beauty are the same width, so rotary cutting is a breeze.

Before You Begin

With the exception of a few simple shapes that require templates, all of the pieces are strips and squares that can be rotary cut. In addition, an easy strip-piecing technique is provided for making the pieced sashing and parts of the Schoolhouse block. Strips of fabric are sewn together into sets, which are cut into smaller units that are used as sashing or incorporated into the Schoolhouse blocks.

General information about making Schoolhouse blocks and details on strip-piecing techniques begin on page 189.

Choosing Fabrics

This quiltmaker stretched the traditional red, white, and blue color scheme to encompass burgundy and dusty blue, giving this quilt a popular country look. You might prefer the more traditional bright red and deep navy for your all-American tribute. A subtle white-on-white print adds visual texture.

To develop your own color scheme for the quilt, photocopy the **Color Plan** on page 211, and use crayons or colored pencils to experiment with different color arrangements.

Quilt Sizes

	Wallhanging (shown)	Crib
Finished Quilt Size	33½" × 33½"	44½" × 55½"
Finished Block Size		
Schoolhouse	8"	8"
Star	3"	3"
Number of Blocks		
Schoolhouse	4	12
Star	9	20

Materials

Fabric	Wallhanging	Crib
White-on-white print	⅞ yard	1½ yards
Dark blue star print	⅝ yard	⅞ yard
Dark dusty blue print	⅝ yard	1 yard
Medium dusty blue stripe	⅝ yard	⅔ yard
Medium dusty blue print	¼ yard	⅜ yard
Burgundy print	¼ yard	¼ yard
Red-and-black print	¼ yard	⅜ yard
Backing	1⅛ yards	2¾ yards
Batting	38" × 38"	51" × 62"
Binding	⅜ yards	⅝ yard

NOTE: *Yardages are based on 44/45-inch-wide fabrics that are at least 42 inches wide after preshrinking.*

Cutting

All of the measurements include ¼-inch seam allowances. Referring to the Cutting Chart,

Cutting Chart

Fabric	Used For	Strip Width or Piece	Number to Cut Wallhanging	Crib	Second Cut Dimensions	Number to Cut Wallhanging	Crib
White-on-white print	Sashing	1½"	6	16			
	Unit 2	1½"	1	2			
	Unit 3	1½"	2	2			
	Unit 1	2"	2	2			
	Unit 1	3½"	1	1			
	C	Template C	4	12			
	C reverse	Template C	4	12			
	G	Template G	36	80			
	I	1½"	2	3	1½" square	36	80
Dark blue star print	Border	4½"	4	5			
Dark dusty blue print	Sashing	1½"	3	8			
	Unit 3	1½"	3	3			
	E	1½"	2	4	1½" × 5½"	8	24
	A	Template A	4	12			
Medium dusty blue stripe	B	Template B	4	12			
Medium dusty blue print	Unit 2	1½"	2	4			
	D	1½"	2	3	1½" × 3½"	4	12
Burgundy print	Unit 1	1½"	2	2			
	Border corners	4¼"	1	1	4¼" squares	4	4
Red-and-black print	F	Template F	36	80			
	F reverse	Template F	36	80			
	H	1½"	1	1	1½" squares	9	20

cut the required number of strips in the widths needed. Cut all strips across the fabric width. Some of the strips will be subcut into shorter lengths, as listed under "Second Cut Dimensions."

Make templates for pieces A, B, and C for the Schoolhouse blocks and F and G for the Star blocks using the full-size patterns on page 78. See page 186 for complete details on making and using templates. The Cutting Chart indicates how many pieces to cut with each template. Place the B, C, and F templates wrong side up on the wrong side of the fabric to trace and cut pieces. For the reverse pieces, turn the C and F templates right side up to cut C reverse and F reverse.

Note: Cut and piece one sample block before cutting all the fabric for the quilt.

Piecing the Schoolhouse Blocks

Refer to the **Schoolhouse Block Diagram** as you assemble this block. For ease of construction, strip-pieced units are numbered as Unit 1, Unit 2, and Unit 3. All other pieces have letter labels. Refer to the Quilt Sizes chart on page 73 to determine how many blocks you will need for your quilt size.

Step 1. Row 3, the sky and chimneys, is made entirely from a Unit 1 strip set. Sew 1½-inch-wide burgundy print strips to either side of a 3-inch-wide white strip. Then sew a 2-inch white strip to each burgundy strip. See **Diagram 1**. Press the seams toward the burgundy strips.

Step 2. Square up one end of the strip set and cut 1½-inch-wide segments from it, as shown,

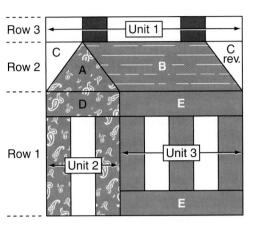

Row 3

Unit 1

C   C rev.

Row 2

A   B

D   E

Row 1

Unit 2   Unit 3

E

Schoolhouse Block Diagram

Cut sizes

D = 1½" × 3½"
E = 1½" × 5½"

4½"

Diagram 3

Step 5. Sew a medium dusty blue D piece along the top edge of each Unit 2, as shown in **Diagram 4**. Press the seams toward D.

D

Diagram 4

until you have one Row 3 for each Schoolhouse block.

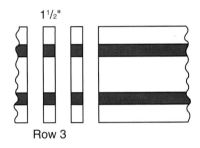

1½"

Row 3

Diagram 1

Step 3. To make Row 2, sew an A, B, C, and C reverse piece together in the sequence shown in **Diagram 2**. Press all seams toward B. Repeat, making a Row 2 for each Schoolhouse block.

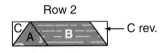

Row 2

C   A   B   — C rev.

Diagram 2

Step 4. Row 1 is made from Unit 2 and Unit 3 strips sets as well as from the D and E segments. To make the Unit 2 strip set, sew a 1½-inch-wide medium dusty blue print strip to either side of a 1½-inch-wide white strip, as shown in **Diagram 3**. Press the seams toward the blue strips. Square up one end of the strip set, and cut one 4½-inch Unit 2 segment for each Schoolhouse block.

Step 6. To make a Unit 3 strip set, sew together three 1½-inch-wide dark dusty blue print strips and two 1½-inch-wide white strips, alternating colors, as shown in **Diagram 5**. Press seams toward the blue strips. Square up one end of the strip set, and cut a 3½-inch-wide Unit 3 segment for each Schoolhouse block, as shown.

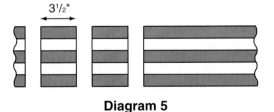

3½"

Diagram 5

Step 7. Sew a dark dusty blue E piece along the top and bottom edges of each Unit 3, as shown in **Diagram 6A**. Press the seams toward E. Sew each of these units to a Unit 2, as shown in **6B**, to complete Row 1. Press the seams toward Unit 2.

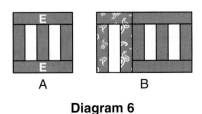

E

E

A   B

Diagram 6

Step 8. Join Rows 1, 2, and 3 of each School-house block, as shown in the **Schoolhouse Block Diagram** on page 75. Press the seams as desired.

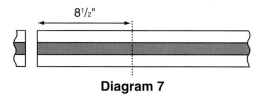

Sew Easy

An empty fabric bolt makes a great portable ironing board. Wrap it in a thick towel, pin securely, and position it at your sewing station so you can press as you go. You'll save precious time—and you'll be recycling, too!

Making the Sashing Strips

Step 1. Sew a 1½-inch-wide white strip to each side of a 1½-inch-wide dark dusty blue strip. See **Diagram 7.** Press the seams toward the blue strip.

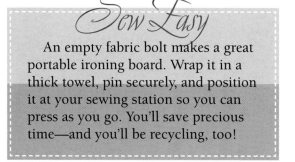

Diagram 7

Step 2. Square up one end of a set, and cut as many 8½-inch segments as possible from the long strip set. Continue making strip sets and cutting segments until you have assembled twelve sashing strips for the wallhanging or thirty-one for the crib quilt.

Piecing the Star Blocks

Step 1. Sew red F and F reverse triangles to either side of a G triangle, as shown in **Diagram 8.** Press the seams toward the red triangles. Make four of these units for each block.

Step 2. Lay out the pieced triangle units and the H and I squares in three rows of three, forming a star, as shown in the **Star Block Diagram.** Sew the squares together into horizontal rows, pressing the seams in opposite directions from row to row. Sew the rows together. Press.

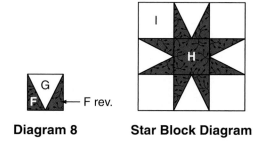

Diagram 8   **Star Block Diagram**

Assembling the Quilt Top

Step 1. Referring to the **Assembly Diagram**, use a design wall or other flat surface to lay out the Schoolhouse blocks, Star blocks, and sashing strips. The quilt in the photograph is a wallhanging with two rows of two Schoolhouse blocks each. The layout for the crib quilt is the same except it contains four horizontal rows of three Schoolhouse blocks each. In each quilt, the blocks are separated by sashing strips and Star blocks.

Step 2. Sew the Star blocks and sashing strips together into rows, then sew the Schoolhouse blocks and sashing strips into horizontal rows, as

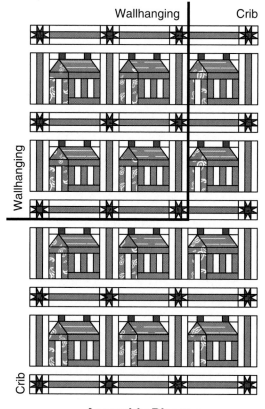

Assembly Diagram

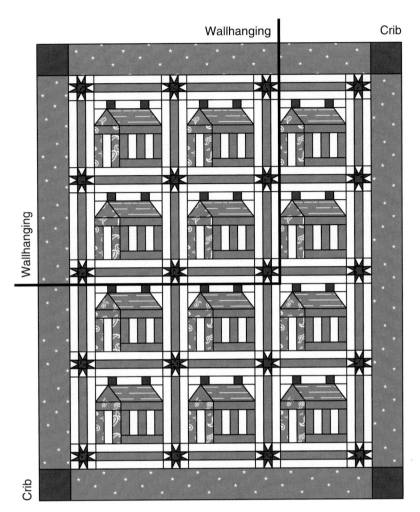

Wallhanging   Crib

Wallhanging

Crib

Quilt Diagram

shown in the diagram. Press the seams in opposite directions from row to row. Sew the rows together, carefully matching seams. Press.

Adding the Borders

Step 1. If you are making the crib quilt, you'll need to piece two long border strips for the side borders. Cut one of the 4½-inch dark blue star print border strips in half, and sew one half each to two of the remaining border strips. See page 206 for details on the diagonal seaming method of connecting fabric strips. Press the seams open.

Step 2. For either size quilt, measure the length of the quilt, taking the measurement through the vertical center of the quilt, not the sides. Trim two

borders to this length for the *side* borders. Measure the width of the quilt, taking the measurement through the horizontal center of the quilt. Trim the remaining two border strips to this length for the top and bottom borders.

Step 3. Fold one side border strip in half crosswise and crease. Unfold it and position it right side down along one side of the quilt top, with the crease at the horizontal midpoint. Pin at the midpoint and ends first, then along the length of the entire side, easing in fullness if necessary. Sew the border to the quilt top, using a ¼-inch seam allowance. Press the seams toward the border. Repeat on the opposite side.

Step 4. Sew a 4¼-inch burgundy corner square to each end of the top and the bottom border strips, as shown in **Diagram 9**. Press the seams away from the corner squares.

Diagram 9

Step 5. In the same manner as for the side borders, pin a border strip to one end of the quilt, matching seams and easing in fullness. Stitch, using a ¼-inch seam allowance. Press the seams toward the border. Repeat on the opposite end. See the **Quilt Diagram** on page 77.

Quilting and Finishing

Step 1. Mark the quilt top for quilting. The quilt shown is quilted in the ditch around each schoolhouse, star, and sashing strip. The border is quilted in a continuous cable motif.

Step 2. For the crib quilt, you will need to piece the backing. Cut the backing fabric in half crosswise, and trim the selvages. Join the two pieces along the long edges and press the seam open. The seam will run parallel to the top and bottom of the quilt. Refer to page 205 for more information on pieced backings. For the wallhanging, simply trim the backing selvages.

Step 3. Layer the backing, batting, and quilt top; baste. Quilt as desired.

Step 4. Use the dusty blue striped fabric to make and attach double-fold bias binding, referring to page 206. For the wallhanging, you will need 140 inches of binding; for the crib quilt, you will need 206 inches of binding.

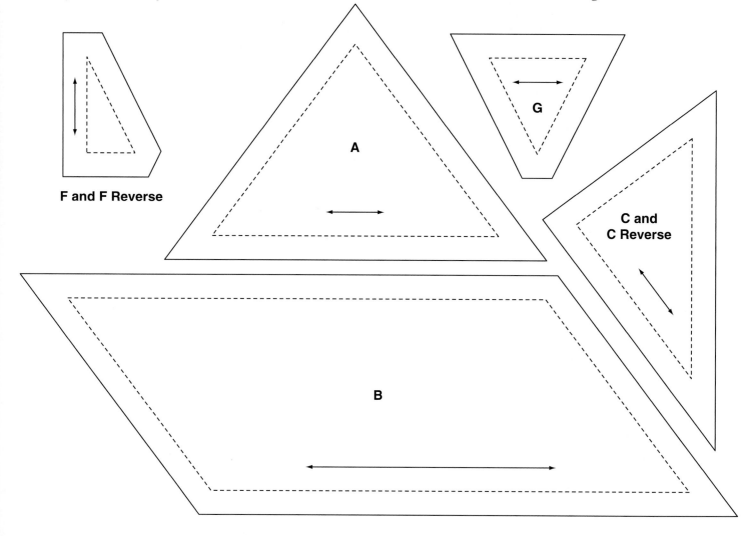

Classroom Etiquette

Taking a class at a quilt shop or through a guild is a great way to expand your knowledge of quilting and get to know other quilters better. Whether the class is taught by a well-known expert or someone local who is knowledgeable about the technique, these tips will go a long way in making the event fun for everyone involved.

• Get as much information as possible about the class before you sign up so you're not disappointed or overwhelmed when you get there. If you are required to know certain techniques, be sure you know them well. It takes time away from other students if you're not up to speed on basic techniques.

• Sign up as early as possible and pay on time. Many teachers require a minimum amount of students to make the class cost-effective, and they will cancel the class if that minimum is not met within a certain amount of time. Don't disappoint yourself and others by waiting until the last minute.

• Be sure you know the cancellation policy and abide by it. Do not demand your money back after the specified time or request a cash refund when the policy is to give in-store credit or credit for another class. The teacher has time and money invested in preparing for the number of students signed up.

• Get to class on time. If the class is a workshop, make sure you have your machine set up and ready to sew before class starts. If being late is unavoidable, try to catch up quietly without causing others to fall behind.

• Be prepared. Have all of the fabrics and tools required on the materials list, in addition to basic sewing supplies. If you do not receive a materials list when you sign up for the class, ask for one or make sure you know what items are required. You may not be able to borrow from someone else when you get to class.

• Know how to operate your machine. Take your sewing machine manual with you in case troubleshooting advice is needed. Many teachers have become pros at figuring out different machines, but every minute they spend threading your machine or adjusting your tension is time away from the class technique.

• Be courteous of others around you. Give them enough space to work and don't talk while the teacher is giving instructions.

• Turn off the sound on your cell phone. If you receive a call or need to make one, excuse yourself from the room *before* you answer or dial the phone.

• Offer advice when you can but don't usurp the teacher's lecture or presentation. Share your thoughts as long as others are interested and have time to listen to what you can offer.

• Ask permission from the instructor before taking photographs of her or his work, reproducing handouts from the class, or teaching techniques to others.

• Clean up your work area before you leave, and be sure to ask other students if they need assistance getting their supplies or machines to their cars. Quilters are a friendly lot, so lend a hand when you can.

• Be sure to fill out class evaluation forms. Teachers and the facilities managers use those comments to refine class goals, make the classrooms more comfortable, and make improvements for upcoming classes.

• A quick thank-you on your way out will let the teacher know that you appreciate her hard work. It's tough standing on your feet all day, dealing with many quilting personalities, and talking until you're hoarse, and quilting teachers do it with grace class after class. An appreciative word is a great reward for a long day's work.

Robbing Peter to Pay Paul

Skill Level: Challenging

*L*ively and vibrant, this quilt features a border formed by a skillful arrangement of color. Quiltmaker Becky Herdle of North Branford, Connecticut, made this quilt over a two-year period while searching for an appropriate purple solid for the outer blocks. The quilt pattern is named Robbing Peter to Pay Paul because each assembled block "borrows" a portion from an adjacent block. The construction, however, isn't as difficult as it may seem since the blocks are actually square.

Before You Begin

At first glance, this quilt appears to be pieced almost entirely with curved seams. While there are four curved seams within each block, the arcs are split lengthwise down the middle, allowing the blocks to be sewn together side by side with straight seams.

You will need to make templates from pattern pieces A and B on page 86. For information about making and using templates, see page 186.

This quilt has a unique border treatment. The blocks are assembled to form the quilt top, then the top is appliquéd onto the pre-assembled black borders. Read through the directions before beginning this project to become familiar with the various block types used.

Choosing Fabrics

The quiltmaker created the appearance of a border by using a consistent color scheme two blocks deep around the perimeter of the quilt. The inner portion of the quilt is sewn with a variety of solids in lighter values than those used around the edges.

To re-create the quilt shown, choose a black solid first, then select many clear, light solids in both warm and cool tones for the interior of the quilt. In this case, the quiltmaker used twelve different solids for the center area of the quilt top.

To help develop your own unique color scheme for the quilt, photocopy the **Color Plan** on page 213, and use crayons or colored pencils to experiment with different color arrangements.

Cutting

All measurements include a ¼-inch seam allowance. Referring to the Cutting Chart, cut the

Quilt Sizes

	Twin	Double (shown)
Finished Quilt Size	69" × 89"	79" × 89"
Finished Block Size	5"	5"
Number of Blocks	221	255

Materials

Fabric	Twin	Double
Black	6¾ yards	7¾ yards
Assorted light solids	4¼ yards	5¼ yards
Purple	2¾ yards	3 yards
Pink	1⅔ yards	1⅞ yards
Turquoise	1⅛ yards	1¼ yards
Backing	5¾ yards	7½ yards
Batting	75" × 95"	85" × 95"
Binding	¾ yard	¾ yard

NOTE: *Yardages are based on 44/45-inch-wide fabrics that are at least 42 inches wide after preshrinking.*

Cutting Chart

Fabric	Used For	Piece or Strip Width	Number to Cut Twin	Number to Cut Double
Black	Background	A	162	183
	Arcs	B	156	200
	Borders	4"	8	9
Assorted light solids	Background	A	59	72
	Arcs	B	268	324
Purple	Arcs	B	260	280
Pink	Arcs	B	156	168
Turquoise	Arcs	B	104	112

required number of pieces for your quilt size. Pattern pieces A and B, on page 86, are used to cut all of the pieces for this quilt.

Note: Cut and piece one sample block before cutting all of the fabric for the quilt.

Assembling the Blocks

Although all of the blocks are sewn in exactly the same manner, several color combinations were used to assemble the quilt shown on page 80. The **Block Diagram** illustrates the basic block types used in the quilt and gives you the total number of each block type required for your quilt size.

Types 1 and 2 are used two-deep along the top, bottom, and sides of the quilt. Types 3 and 4 are used in the outermost corners of the quilt. Type 5 is used to define the inside corners of the pieced "border." Types 6 and 7 are alternated in the center portion of the quilt. Type 8 is used to define the outer corner of the center portion of the quilt. Types 9 and 10 are used in the perimeter of the center portion of the quilt.

Step 1. Referring to **Diagram 1**, use a fine-point marker to mark the center of each curved side of a piece. Stack pieces by color.

Type 1
Make 48 for twin
Make 52 for double

Type 2
Make 48 for twin
Make 52 for double

Type 3
Make 2 for each quilt size

Type 4
Make 2 for each quilt size

Type 5
Make 4 for each quilt size

Type 6
Make 39 for twin
Make 50 for double

Type 7
Make 38 for twin
Make 49 for double

Type 8
Make 4 for each quilt size

Type 9
Make 16 for twin
Make 18 for double

Type 10
Make 20 for twin
Make 22 for double

Block Diagram

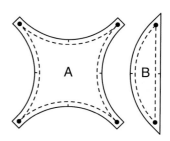

Diagram 1

Step 2. To make Type 1 blocks, gather one black A background, one turquoise B arc, two pink B arcs, and one purple B arc. With right sides together and the black A piece on top, match the center of the curved side of the turquoise arc with the center of one side of the black A piece, then pin at this point, as shown in **Diagram 2A**. Match the dots at the seam allowances and pin along the entire arc, as shown in **2B**. Sew the pinned pieces together. Press the seam toward the A piece.

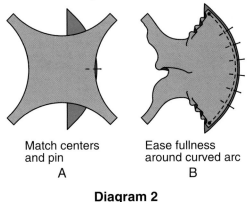

Match centers
and pin
A

Ease fullness
around curved arc
B

Diagram 2

Sew Easy

To reduce bulk in the seams before sewing the blocks together, trim a scant 1/8 inch from the seam allowance near the block corners.

Step 3. Add the three remaining arcs in the same manner. Sew a purple arc directly across from the turquoise arc, and sew the two pink arcs in the remaining slots across from each other, as shown in the **Block Diagram**. Press seams toward the A piece. Assemble the total number of Type 1 blocks required for your quilt size. Stack the blocks together and label them.

Step 4. To make blocks 2 through 10, use one A background and four B arcs, referring to the **Block Diagram** for color placement. Press seams toward the A piece.

Assembling the Quilt

Step 1. Lay out the completed blocks and remaining purple arcs around the outer edge, as shown in the **Assembly Diagrams** below and the Quilt Diagram on page 85.

```
4  1  2  1  2  1  2  1  2  1  2  1  2  1  3
2  5  1  2  1  2  1  2  1  2  1  2  1  5  2
1  2  8 10  9 10  9 10  9 10  9 10  8  2  1
2  1 10  6  7  6  7  6  7  6  7  6 10  1  2
1  2  9  7  6  7  6  7  6  7  6  7  9  2  1
2  1 10  6  7  6  7  6  7  6  7  6 10  1  2
1  2  9  7  6  7  6  7  6  7  6  7  9  2  1
2  1 10  6  7  6  7  6  7  6  7  6 10  1  2
1  2  9  7  6  7  6  7  6  7  6  7  9  2  1
2  1 10  6  7  6  7  6  7  6  7  6 10  1  2
1  2  9  7  6  7  6  7  6  7  6  7  9  2  1
2  1 10  6  7  6  7  6  7  6  7  6 10  1  2
1  2  9  7  6  7  6  7  6  7  6  7  9  2  1
2  1 10  6  7  6  7  6  7  6  7  6 10  1  2
1  2  8 10  9 10  9 10  9 10  9 10  8  2  1
2  5  1  2  1  2  1  2  1  2  1  2  1  5  2
3  1  2  1  2  1  2  1  2  1  2  1  2  1  4
```

Twin

```
4  1  2  1  2  1  2  1  2  1  2  1  2  1  3
2  5  1  2  1  2  1  2  1  2  1  2  1  5  2
1  2  8 10  9 10  9 10  9 10  9 10  8  2  1
2  1 10  6  7  6  7  6  7  6  7  6 10  1  2
1  2  9  7  6  7  6  7  6  7  6  7  9  2  1
2  1 10  6  7  6  7  6  7  6  7  6 10  1  2
1  2  9  7  6  7  6  7  6  7  6  7  9  2  1
2  1 10  6  7  6  7  6  7  6  7  6 10  1  2
1  2  9  7  6  7  6  7  6  7  6  7  9  2  1
2  1 10  6  7  6  7  6  7  6  7  6 10  1  2
1  2  9  7  6  7  6  7  6  7  6  7  9  2  1
2  1 10  6  7  6  7  6  7  6  7  6 10  1  2
1  2  9  7  6  7  6  7  6  7  6  7  9  2  1
2  1 10  6  7  6  7  6  7  6  7  6 10  1  2
1  2  8 10  9 10  9 10  9 10  9 10  8  2  1
2  5  1  2  1  2  1  2  1  2  1  2  1  5  2
3  1  2  1  2  1  2  1  2  1  2  1  2  1  4
```

Double

Assembly Diagrams

Step 2. Sew the straight side of a purple arc to the straight side of each turquoise arc in the outermost blocks around the entire perimeter of the quilt, as shown in **Diagram 3.** Leave the seams unpressed until the rows are sewn together.

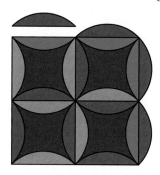

Diagram 3

Step 3. Sew the blocks in each horizontal row together. Press the seams in adjacent rows in opposite directions. Match the seams carefully, and sew the rows together. Press the quilt.

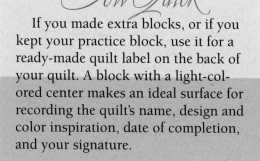

Sew Quick

If you made extra blocks, or if you kept your practice block, use it for a ready-made quilt label on the back of your quilt. A block with a light-colored center makes an ideal surface for recording the quilt's name, design and color inspiration, date of completion, and your signature.

Making the Outer Border

The outside edge of the quilt is centered and appliquéd to a preassembled border unit.

Step 1. To make the border unit for the twin-size quilt, piece together 4-inch-wide black strips, then cut two 67½-inch pieces for the top and bottom borders and two 91½-inch pieces for the side borders. For the double-size quilt, piece together 4-inch-wide black strips, then cut two 77½-inch pieces for the top and bottom borders and two 91½-inch pieces for the side borders.

Step 2. Beginning at any corner, sew a side border to a top or bottom border, as shown in **Diagram 4A,** placing the right sides together. Press the seam open, as shown in **4B.** Repeat for all corners to assemble the border, as shown in **4C.**

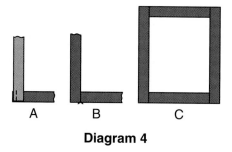

Diagram 4

Appliquéing the Top to the Border

Step 1. Make a plastic template the size of a finished arc, represented by the dashed lines on template B. Trace the shape onto the nonwaxy side of freezer paper, and cut it out. Make a freezer paper template for each of the arcs around the outer edge of the quilt.

Step 2. Align a freezer paper arc, waxy side up, with the wrong side of an outer purple arc. The freezer paper should fit snugly against the inner seam allowance where the purple arc connects to the blue arc. Use a medium-hot iron to press the outer seam allowance of the arc onto the freezer paper, as shown in **Diagram 5.** Repeat, pressing a new freezer paper template onto each outer arc.

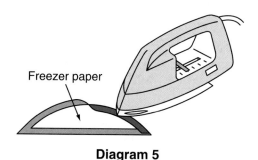

Freezer paper

Diagram 5

Step 3. Center and pin the quilt on the border. Two inches of black fabric should extend past the outer rings on all sides. Appliqué the quilt edges to the border and remove all freezer paper templates.

Step 4. Mark around a plate or other circular object to make a curve at each corner. Be sure the plate is in the same position for each corner so the curves will be the same size, as shown in **Diagram 6**. Trim the fabric outside the marked lines.

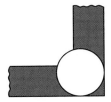

Diagram 6

Quilting and Finishing

Step 1. Mark the quilt top for quilting. The quilt shown has cross-hatching in the centers of all of the background A pieces. All A and B pieces were outline quilted ¼ inch away from seam allowances. The black border area was not quilted.

Step 2. To make the backing for the twin-size quilt, cut the backing fabric in half crosswise, and trim the selvages. Cut two 18-inch-wide panels from one of the pieces, and sew a narrow panel to each side of the full-size piece, as shown in **Diagram 7** on page 86. Press the seams open.

Quilt Diagram

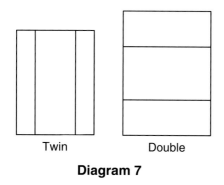

Twin   Double

Diagram 7

Step 3. For the double-size quilt, cut the backing fabric crosswise into three equal lengths, and trim the selvages. Cut a 28-inch-wide panel from two of the segments, then sew one of those to each side of the full-width piece, as shown. Press the seams open.

Step 4. Layer the quilt top, batting, and backing, and baste the layers together. Quilt as desired.

Step 5. Use the remaining black fabric to make and attach double-fold bias binding, referring to page 206. To calculate the amount of binding needed for the quilt size you are making, add the length of the four sides of the quilt, plus 9 inches.

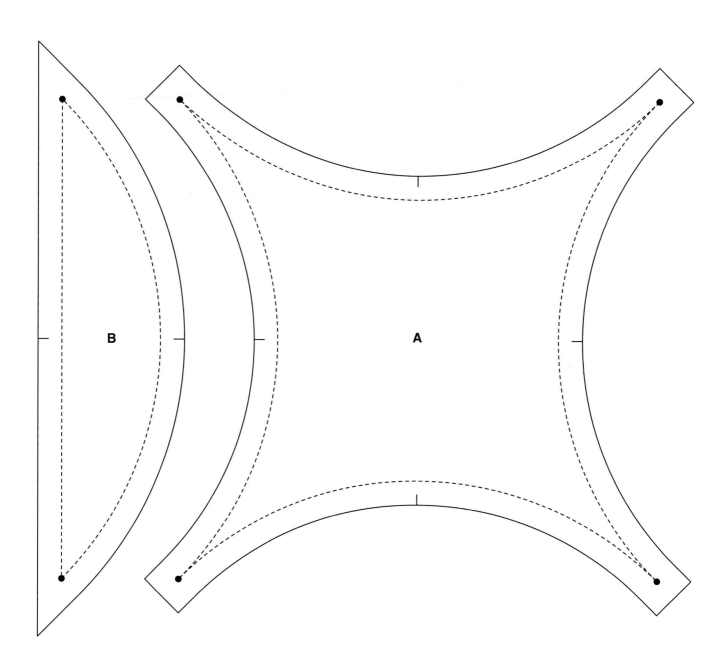

Organizing a Raffle Quilt

Quilts have long been used as a means to raise money for groups and charitable causes. While many only see the end result, the work leading to its success begins long before the first stitch is ever taken. Here are some guidelines to keep things running smoothly.

1. Begin planning as soon as possible.

2. Encourage all the members of the group to volunteer for some aspect of the raffle. Everyone can help in some way, even if they're not stitchers.

3. Obtain a raffle ticket license and find out the rules governing your area.

4. Establish a time line. Include everything from how much time it will take to select a design to how far ahead the quilt needs to be finished for photography. Decide now whether the quilt will be hand quilted or machine quilted because this can greatly affect the amount of time needed. Stick to your deadlines. Once the date of the raffle is set, the ticket chairperson can design the tickets and have them printed.

5. Select the pattern and fabrics. Selection should be based on wide general appeal. Traditional patterns and classic color schemes usually draw a better response than art-style quilts, but judge this by the area in which you live. Also consider the stitching abilities of the group members and the amount of time you've allotted for making the quilt.

6. Have one person cut out the required pieces so you won't have a variation in patch size.

7. Construct the quilt top. Decide whether you want just a few members to do the piecing or everyone in the group to make a block. Because everyone sews slightly differently, the more people you have stitching, the greater the chance of variation in the size of the blocks. If only a few members will do the piecing, find a day that works for everyone and work assembly style. If you go with the group approach, package all the pieces for one block in a zip-top sandwich bag and keep a record of the members who take a bag. Require that all of the blocks are the correct size before they are turned in and that they are turned in on time. Have a separate group assemble the top.

8. Select someone to mark the quilting pattern on the quilt top, if necessary.

9. Layer and baste the quilt sandwich together. This is a task that probably everyone in the group can do together. Provide needles and thread and make a party out of it.

10. Quilt the quilt.

11. Bind the quilt edges.

12. Take a photograph of the completed quilt and have enough copies made so that each member can have one.

13. Sell tickets. Seeing the actual quilt can be a great incentive for potential ticket buyers. Make arrangements with various business owners to display the quilt and sell tickets. Or make ticket packets for each member to sell to their families, friends, and coworkers. Include a photograph of the finished quilt in each packet so potential ticket buyers can see the quilt.

14. Raffle the quilt and notify the winner.

15. Have a party to show your appreciation for everyone who helped.

Amish Easter Baskets

Skill Level: Intermediate

*T*he rich dark colors of traditional Cake Stand blocks stitched together in an unusual Bear's Paw-type setting make a dramatic statement in this queen-size quilt. The quilt design was patterned after a similar but smaller antique quilt. In addition to expert piecing and quilting, this quilt also shows off Elsie Vredenburg's appliqué talents with the final touch of a hand-appliquéd sawtooth edging on the outer border. Elsie was inspired to add "Amish" to the name of this quilt because of all the dark solids she used.

Before You Begin

The directions for this quilt are written for rotary cutting and quick piecing. Yardage requirements include enough fabric to cut borders lengthwise before other pieces are cut from the fabric. This method takes advantage of the stability that the lengthwise grain adds to the borders. It also avoids seams in the borders, which are more likely to show on solid fabrics than on prints.

Choosing Fabrics

This quilt is made entirely of solid fabrics, including unbleached muslin. When selecting the dark solids, choose high-quality fabrics. These have a tight weave or high thread count and do not feel as though the dyes will rub off between your fingers. For an authentic Amish feel, consider using black in place of the muslin and traditional Amish brights in place of the navy, red, and green.

To help develop your own unique color scheme for the quilt, photocopy the **Color Plan** on page 211, and use crayons or colored pencils to experiment with different color arrangements.

Quilt Sizes

	Lap	Queen (shown)
Finished Quilt Size	60^1/$_2$" × 87"	87" × 113^1/$_2$"
Finished Block Size		
Single Basket	7^1/$_2$"	7^1/$_2$"
Four Basket	19"	19"
Number of Blocks		
Single Basket	24	48
Four Basket	6	12

Materials

Fabric	Lap	Queen
Unbleached muslin	4 yards	5^3/$_4$ yards
Navy blue	2^1/$_2$ yards	3^1/$_4$ yards
Dark red	2^1/$_2$ yards	3^1/$_4$ yards
Dark green	1 yard	1^3/$_8$ yards
Backing	5^1/$_8$ yards	7^2/$_3$ yards
Batting	67" × 93"	93" × 120"
Binding	^{3}/$_4$ yard	1 yard

NOTE: *Yardages are based on 44/45-inch-wide fabrics that are at least 42 inches wide after preshrinking.*

Cutting

All measurements include ^{1}/$_4$-inch seam allowances. Cut all borders, binding, and piping

89

Cutting Chart

Fabric	Used For	*Lengthwise* Strip Width	Number to Cut Lap	Queen
Muslin	Border	8"	4	4
Navy	Piping	$^3/_4$"	4	4
Red	Sawtooth border	2"	4	4
	Binding	$1^1/_2$"	4	4

Fabric	Used For	*Crosswise* Strip Width	Number to Cut* Lap	Queen
Muslin	Sashing strips	8"	4	9
	Block background	2"	8	14
	Basket handles	$2^3/_8$"	5	9
	Bottom triangles	$3^7/_8$"	2	3
Navy	Sashing/border squares	8"	2	3
	Sashing strips	8"	3	6
Red	Baskets	$5^3/_8$"	4	7
	Basket handles	$2^3/_8$"	7	14
	Center squares	$4^1/_2$"	1	2
Green	Basket bottoms	$5^3/_8$"	4	7
	Basket feet	$2^3/_8$"	2	3

Calculations are based on the fabric widths remaining after cutting the lengthwise pieces. Muslin strips are based on 42-inch-wide strips.

first, cutting on the lengthwise grain to minimize seams. Cut a 100-inch-long piece from the muslin for the queen-size quilt and a 75-inch-long piece for the lap-size quilt; you'll cut border strips from these lengths. Next, referring to the Cutting Chart, cut the required number of lengthwise strips in the width needed from the previously cut muslin lengths as well as from the navy and red fabrics. After you have finished the lengthwise cutting, refer to the second part of the Cutting Chart and cut the crosswise strips. When you have cut all of those strips, refer to the instructions that follow to cut the *crosswise* strips into individual pieces.

• For the sashing strips, cut the 8-inch-wide muslin strips into $19^1/_2$-inch-long pieces. Cut seventeen for the queen-size quilt and seven for the lap size.

• For the block background, cut the 2-inch-wide muslin strips into 2 × 5-inch rectangles. Cut ninety-six rectangles for the queen-size quilt and forty-eight for the lap size. From the remaining strips, cut 2-inch squares: forty-eight for the queen size and twenty-four for the lap size.

• For the bottom triangles of the basket blocks, cut the $3^7/_8$-inch-wide muslin strips into $3^7/_8$-inch squares. Cut the squares in half diagonally; see **Diagram 1.** Make forty-eight triangles for the queen-size quilt and twenty-four for the lap size.

• For the basket handles, cut the $2^3/_8$-inch-wide muslin strips into $2^3/_8$-inch squares. Cut the squares in half diagonally to make 288 triangles for the queen size and 144 triangles for the lap size.

• For the sashing and border squares, cut the 8-inch-wide navy strips into 8-inch squares. Cut ten for the queen size and six for the lap size.

• For the sashing strips in the basket blocks, cut the 8-inch-wide navy strips into $4^1/_2 \times 8$-inch rectangles. You need forty-eight for the queen size and twenty-four for the lap size.

• For the top half of the baskets, cut the $5^3/_8$-inch-wide red strips into $5^3/_8$-inch squares. Cut the squares in half diagonally.

• For the basket handles, cut the $2^3/_8$-inch-wide red strips into $2^3/_8$-inch squares. Cut the squares in half diagonally to make 288 triangles for the queen-size quilt and 144 for the lap size.

• For the center squares of the four-basket blocks, cut the $4^1/_2$-inch-wide red strips into $4^1/_2$-inch squares. You need twelve squares for the queen-size quilt and six for the lap size.

• For the basket bottoms, cut the $5^3/_8$-inch-wide green strips into $5^3/_8$-inch squares. Cut the squares in half diagonally, as shown.

• For the basket feet, cut the $2^3/_8$-inch-wide green strips into $2^3/_8$-inch squares. Cut the squares in half diagonally, as shown.

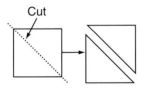

Diagram 1

Piecing the Basket Blocks

Step 1. Sew $5^3/_8$-inch red and green triangles together to form a triangle square for the center of the basket block, as shown in **Diagram 2**.

Diagram 2

Step 2. Sew the $2^3/_8$-inch muslin and red triangles together to form triangle squares. You will need six red-and-muslin triangle squares per basket. Press the seams toward the red fabric.

Step 3. Sew the triangle squares together in strips of three, referring to **Diagram 3** for color placement. Add a muslin square to the end of one strip, as shown in the diagram.

Diagram 3

Step 4. Attach the shorter triangle-square strip to the large red-and-green triangle square, as shown in **Diagram 4**. Sew the other triangle-square strip to the block, as shown.

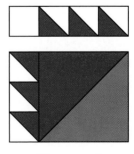

Diagram 4

Step 5. Sew a $2^3/_8$-inch green triangle to the end of a muslin rectangle. Make two such units for each basket, referring to **Diagram 5** for placement of the triangles.

Diagram 5

Step 6. Sew the rectangle units to the green sides of the partial block. Press the seams toward the rectangles. To complete the single-basket block, add a muslin triangle to the corner, as shown in the **Block Diagram.** Press the seam away from the muslin.

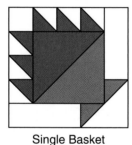

Single Basket   Four Basket

Block Diagram

Step 7. Repeat Steps 1 through 6 to make forty-eight basket blocks for the queen-size quilt and twenty-four blocks for the lap-size quilt.

Assembling the Quilt Top

The individual basket blocks are assembled into larger blocks containing four basket blocks separated by navy sashing strips, as shown in the **Block Diagram.** The four-basket blocks are then pieced together with muslin sashing strips and navy sashing squares.

Step 1. To make a four-basket block, lay out four baskets, four navy sashing strips, and one red center square in three horizontal rows. Make sure each basket handle points toward a corner.

Step 2. Stitch the units together into rows. Press the seams toward the navy sashing strips. Sew the rows together. Press the seams toward the navy strips. The finished block should measure $19\frac{1}{2}$ inches square, including seam allowances. Repeat to make twelve four-basket blocks for the queen-size quilt and six blocks for the lap quilt.

Step 3. Referring to the **Assembly Diagram,** lay out the blocks, muslin sashing strips, and navy sashing squares in rows. The quilt shown is the queen size. For the lap size, you'll have only three horizontal rows of two blocks each, with two muslin/navy sashing strip units between them.

Step 4. Sew the blocks and sashing pieces together into rows. Press the seams toward the sashing. Sew the rows together, matching seam intersections. Press all seams in one direction.

Adding the Borders

The muslin borders and navy corner squares are stitched to the quilt, then a red sawtooth

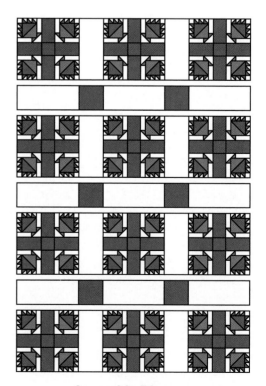

Assembly Diagram

border is appliquéd to the edge. The navy piping is added during the binding stage.

Step 1. Measure the width of the quilt top through the center of the quilt rather than along the top or bottom edge. Cut two border strips to this exact length. Measure the length of the quilt top, again through the center of the quilt. Cut the remaining strips to this exact length.

Step 2. Fold one short border strip in half crosswise and crease. Unfold it and position it right side down along the top edge of the quilt, with the crease at the midpoint. Pin at the midpoint and ends first, then along the length of the entire end, easing in fullness if necessary. Sew the border to the quilt top using a ¼-inch seam allowance. Press the seam toward the border. Repeat to add the border to the bottom of the quilt.

Step 3. Sew a navy border corner square to each end of the two side borders. Stitch the borders to the quilt sides as you did for the top and bottom borders, matching seam lines, pinning at the midpoints, and easing in fullness if necessary.

Step 4. To make the sawtooth border, make a mark every 2 inches along the length of one side of the 2-inch-wide red strip, beginning at one end, as shown in **Diagram 6**. On the opposite side of the strip, make a mark 1 inch from the end. Continue making marks every 2 inches so they are halfway between those on the other side. Mark the remaining strips in this manner.

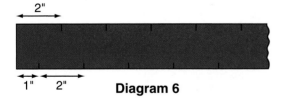

Diagram 6

Step 5. Pin a red strip to the outside edge of the quilt border, and baste it in place with a ¼-inch seam allowance. On the unbasted edge of the strip, cut diagonally from one mark to the next mark on the opposite edge. Cut up to the ¼-inch seam, as shown in **Diagram 7**. Use the line of basting as a handy guide to know when to stop cutting.

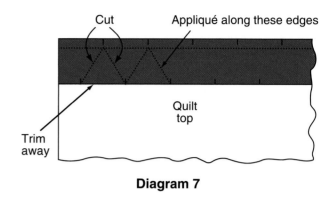

Diagram 7

Step 6. Turn under the fabric in a diagonal line from one mark to the opposite mark to make a sawtooth point. Trim away excess fabric if necessary. Appliqué the point in place, using the needle-turn appliqué method described on page 200 in "Quiltmaking Basics." Repeat for all borders.

Sew Easy

You will find it much easier to appliqué your sawtooth border if you snip only one or two sawtooth points at a time. You will reduce the chance of stretching your border fabric out of shape and increase the chance of a flat, nicely fitted border.

Quilting and Finishing

Step 1. Mark the top for quilting. The quilt shown was quilted with a double pumpkin seed pattern in the red squares, a feathered square in the navy sashing squares, and a serpentine feather in the sashing strips. Diagonal lines about ¼ inch apart fill in the background of the muslin. Each basket was quilted in diagonal lines from the top corner above the basket point to the corner below the base. The lines continue through the navy sashing squares, where they form a crosshatch design.

Step 2. Regardless of which quilt size you've chosen to make, the backing will have to be pieced. For the lap quilt, divide the 5⅛ yards of backing fabric into two equal length pieces, and trim the selvages. Cut one of the pieces in half lengthwise, and sew one half to each side of the full piece (see **Diagram 8**). Press the seams open.

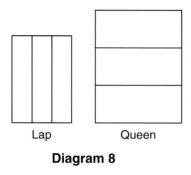

Lap   Queen

Diagram 8

Step 3. For the queen-size quilt, divide the 7²/₃ yards of fabric crosswise into three equal pieces, and trim the selvages. Sew the three pieces together along the long sides, as shown in **Diagram 8**, and press the seams open.

Step 4. Layer the quilt top, batting, and backing; baste the layers together. Quilt as desired.

Step 5. To add the navy piping, fold the ³/₄-inch strips in half lengthwise, right sides together, and press. Lay one strip along one edge of the quilt top, with raw edges even. Hand baste in place. Add a piping strip to each side of the quilt in the same manner, making sure the strip extends to the edge of the quilt on each end. Then, referring to the directions on page 206 in "Quilt-making Basics," make and attach double-fold binding. Add the lengths of the four sides of the quilt plus 9 inches to calculate the number of inches of binding you will need. After the binding is attached, about ¹/₈ inch of navy piping will be visible, as evident in the **Quilt Diagram.**

Quilt Diagram

Tools and Supplies

Nearly every hobby requires tools and supplies to do the job right and make the process more enjoyable. Quilting is no exception. Invest in the best quality goods you can afford, and then keep them in tip-top shape so you can enjoy many years of quilting pleasure. Purchase quality products from a reputable source, and don't be afraid to consult them when you need help selecting the right one for your needs.

Sewing machine: Keeping your machine in good working order is essential to the life of the machine as well as to the proper formation of stitches. Consult your machine manual to routinely perform basic cleaning and oiling procedures, and have your machine cleaned by a certified technician at least once a year. If your machine needs repairs, take samples with you to show the technician the problem whenever possible. Cover the machine when it is not in use.

Pins and needles: Don't wait until your sewing machine needle breaks to change it. Some sewers change the needle after a specific number of hours of use, while others change it after every project. Don't expect the same needle to work with every fabric and thread. Keep an assortment of sewing machine needles, hand sewing needles, and pins on hand to use with different threads, fabric, and techniques. Throw away any rusty, bent, broken, or dull pins and needles.

Scissors: Have scissors sharpened on a regular basis. Dull scissors can mangle fabrics and make cutting tasks a chore. Make sure you have one pair of scissors specifically for cutting fabrics and another pair for cutting paper and template plastic.

Thread: Whether you are hand or machine piecing or quilting, use good-quality thread. Bargain threads tend to shed, shred, and break often, making sewing more of a chore than a pleasure. The buildup of lint created by these threads can cause serious problems with your machine as well.

Rotary cutters, mats, and rulers: Always use your rotary cutter with a mat and ruler designed specifically for rotary cutting. Using other equipment can damage the rotary cutter blade, the surface being cut on, and the person doing the cutting. Change your rotary cutter blade frequently. A dull blade requires more pressure to cut through fabric, which can scar the mat and reduce its life. Close the safety shield when the cutter is not in use and keep it away from children. Store your mat flat and keep it away from heat and direct sunlight to avoid warping. Clean your mat with lukewarm water and mild detergent when necessary. Extend the life of your mat by varying where you cut it.

Broken Star

Skill Level: Intermediate

*T*he Broken Star quilt pattern, a variation of the beloved Lone Star, was introduced by *McCall's* in 1920, and its dramatic beauty has stood the test of time. This particular version, pieced by Kathryn England, contains more than 1,000 shimmering diamonds in cool blues, greens, and violets. But don't let the numbers fool you. The strip-piecing directions make cutting and assembly quicker than you'd think!

Before You Begin

This quilt is assembled using quick-cutting and quick-piecing techniques. Six different strip sets are sewn, then angled segments are cut from each and sewn together to create the large diamonds that form the star points. Setting squares and triangles fill in the gaps around the star points, so if you are unfamiliar with sewing set-in seams, you may want to refer to page 189 before beginning this project.

Choosing Fabrics

The quiltmaker used light, medium, and dark values of green, blue, and orchid in the quilt shown on the opposite page. The points on each end of the large diamonds are dark fabrics, and as they move inward to wider rows, patches shade from dark to light, and then back to dark again at the center of each of the diamonds.

This placement of color value links the diamonds and creates a radiating, circular-shaped star pattern from the center of the quilt outward. To develop a color scheme for the quilt that you are going to make, photocopy the **Color Plan** on page 209, and use colored pencils or crayons to experiment with different color arrangements.

Quilt Sizes

	Queen (shown)	King
Finished Quilt Size	95" × 95"	102" × 102"
Number of Large Diamonds	32	32
Finished Setting Square Size	12¾"	12¾"

Materials

Fabric	Queen	King
White-and-blue print	4¾ yards	5⅜ yards
Black-and-gray print	1¼ yards	1¼ yards
Medium blue print	1 yard	1 yard
Dark blue print	1 yard	1 yard
Light blue print	⅞ yard	⅞ yard
Light blue-and-gray print	⅞ yard	⅞ yard
Light green print	¾ yard	¾ yard
Light orchid print	¾ yard	¾ yard
Dark orchid print	¾ yard	¾ yard
Medium green print	½ yard	½ yard
Medium orchid print	½ yard	½ yard
Dark green print	¼ yard	¼ yard
Backing	8¾ yards	9¼ yards
Batting	102" × 102"	109" × 109"
Binding	⅝ yard	¾ yard

NOTE: *Yardages are based on 44/45-inch-wide fabrics that are at least 42 inches wide after preshrinking.*

Cutting Chart

Fabric	Used For	Strip Width	Strips Needed
White/blue print	Setting squares	13¼"	7
	Setting triangles	19¼"	1
	Outer border*	3¼"	9
■ Black/gray print	Strip sets	2"	18
■ Medium blue print	Strip sets	2"	15
■ Dark blue print	Strip sets	2"	15
■ Light blue print	Strip sets	2"	12
■ Light blue/gray print	Strip sets	2"	12
■ Light green print	Strip sets	2"	9
■ Light orchid print	Strip sets	2"	9
■ Dark orchid print	Strip sets	2"	3
	Inner border	1½"	9
■ Medium green print	Strip sets	2"	6
■ Medium orchid print	Strip sets	2"	6
■ Dark green print	Strip sets	2"	3

The border strip widths are for the queen-size quilt. For the king-size quilt, cut ten 6¾-inch-wide strips from the white-and-blue print fabric for the outer border. Cut the same number and width strips for the inner border as for the queen-size quilt.

Cutting

All measurements include ¼-inch seam allowances. Refer to the Cutting Chart for the number and dimensions of each piece or strip required for this quilt.

Note: We recommend that you piece one sample strip set and cut the star segments from it before cutting and stitching all strip sets.

• For the setting squares that surround the center star and fill in the corners of the quilt, cut the 13¼-inch white-and-blue print strips into twenty 13¼-inch squares.

• For the setting triangles that fill in the sides of the quilt, cut the 19¼-inch white-and-blue print strip into two 19¼-inch squares. Cut the squares in half diagonally in both directions. (This puts the more stable straight of grain at the edge of the quilt and helps eliminate stretching.)

Making the Strip Sets

To quick-piece the large diamonds that make up the center star and the broken star that surrounds it, you will make strip sets that will be cut into segments of joined small diamonds. These rows of small diamonds will be stitched together to form the large diamonds.

Step 1. To make Strip Set A, sew together strips in the order shown in **Diagram 1.** Stagger the strips by approximately 1½ inches, as shown. Press all the seams toward the dark green strip, as indicated by the arrow. Make three of Strip Set A.

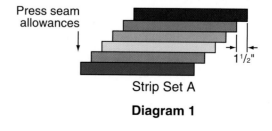

Press seam allowances

Strip Set A

Diagram 1

Step 2. Use a rotary cutter and a ruler with a 45 degree angle marking to cut 2-inch-wide segments from the strip set. First, position the ruler so that the 45 degree angle line is parallel to one of the seam lines in your strip set, then trim off the staggered edges of one end, as shown in **Diagram 2A**.

Then, slide the ruler over so that the 2-inch marking is aligned with the edge you just cut and the 45 degree line is still parallel to the seam line, as shown in **2B**. Cut a 2-inch segment from the strip set. Continue cutting 2-inch-wide segments from the three strip sets until you have thirty-two Strip Set A segments.

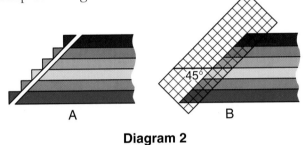

Diagram 2

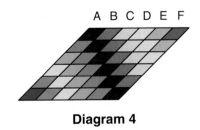

Sew Easy

To make sure all of your diamonds are truly diamond-shaped, be sure to align the 45 degree line with the strip set seams. If you notice it's not quite lining up as you measure and cut your segments, realign it perfectly and trim off some of the diagonal edge of the strip set before measuring your next segment. Don't worry about wasting $1/4$ inch or so of fabric after every few cuts to straighten your strip sets. The little bit of waste you trim off will ensure that each strip segment is accurate.

Step 3. Make Strip Sets B, C, D, E, and F in the same manner, referring to **Diagram 3** for the color orders of those sets. Cut a total of thirty-two segments from each type of strip set, keeping like segments together. Be sure to press the seam allowances of each strip set in the

direction of the arrow so assembling the large diamonds will be easier.

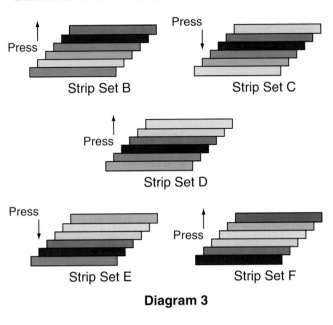

Diagram 3

Assembling the Diamonds

Step 1. To make a large diamond, sew one segment from each type of strip set together, as shown in **Diagram 4**. Match the seams carefully by pinning through the seam allowances $1/4$ inch from the raw edges. Notice that because the seams are angled at 45 degrees, the seam allowances will not butt together. Pin each seam allowance in place before stitching. Wait to press seam allowances.

A B C D E F

Diagram 4

Step 2. Repeat, assembling a total of thirty-two identical large diamonds. Press the seams on half of the large diamonds toward the green small diamonds and press the seams on the other half of the large diamonds toward the orchid diamonds. This allows the diamonds to fit together more easily as you assemble the quilt top.

Assembling the Quilt Top

As you sew the components of this quilt together, do not sew into the seam allowances at the beginnings and ends of seams. These free seam allowances let you set in diamonds, squares, and triangles at angled intersections. For more information about set-in seams, see pages 189–191.

Sew Easy

To make sure you leave exactly ¼ inch open at each end of a diamond seam, mark the ¼ inch on your sewing machine throat plate with masking tape. Or, measure the seam allowances on each diamond end and mark them with a pencil dot. These guides tell you exactly where to start and stop sewing.

The Center Star

Step 1. Matching seams carefully, sew two large diamonds together, as shown in **Diagram 5A,** with the dark green patches aligned along the lower edge. Be sure to start sewing ¼ inch from the raw edges and backstitch. Likewise, stop sewing ¼ inch from the end of the seam and backstitch. Sew together another pair of large diamonds in the same manner, then join the pairs to create a half star, as shown in **5B.**

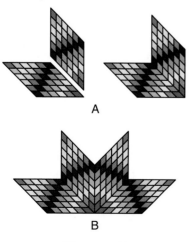

A

B

Diagram 5

Step 2. Repeat Step 1 to make another half star. Sew the two halves together, as shown in **Diagram 6.** Press all seams to one side so they fan out around the star.

Diagram 6

Step 3. Set a white-and-blue 13¼-inch square into each opening around the star, as shown.

Sew Easy

When setting in squares around the center star, align the edges of the star points precisely with the side of each square. Avoid problems with stretchy bias by matching and pinning the ends first, then pinning at each seam to ease in any fullness. To match the ends, poke a pin through the ¼-inch seam allowance of both the square and the diamond. The tip of the end diamond will extend beyond the edge of the square, as shown.

The Broken Star

Step 1. Sew together three large diamonds, matching seams carefully and aligning the dark orchid small diamonds to meet at the unit's center, as shown in **Diagram 7**. Leave the seam allowance open ¼ inch at the outer edges (the black diamonds) to accommodate the final setting squares. Repeat, making a total of eight sets of three diamonds.

Diagram 7

Step 2. Set a group of three diamonds into each opening between setting squares on the center star, as shown in the **Assembly Diagram** on page 102.

Step 3. To complete a quilt corner, sew a setting square to the outer diamond edges, as shown in the upper right corner of the **Assembly Diagram.** Sew two more setting squares together, and set them in next to the previous setting square, again referring to the upper right corner of the diagram. Press seam allowances toward the squares. Repeat for the remaining three corners.

Step 4. Sew setting triangles into the remaining openings, aligning raw edges and stitching from the outer edges toward the quilt center. Stop ¼ inch from the end of the seam and backstitch. Repeat for the other seam of each triangle. Press the seam allowances toward the triangles.

Adding the Borders

This quilt has a narrow, dark orchid inner border and a wider, white-and-blue print outer border.

Step 1. Measure the width of the quilt through the horizontal center, rather than along an edge. Sew the 1½-inch dark orchid border strips together end to end to achieve two borders this exact length to make top and bottom borders.

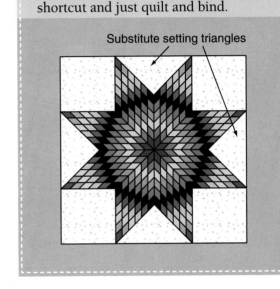

Sew Quick

If you love the Lone Star at the heart of this quilt design and don't have time to piece a bed-size quilt, make just the center! Replace the top, bottom, and side setting squares with setting triangles for a square wallhanging, as shown below. Cut the setting triangles as described in the Cutting Chart for the outer section of the Broken Star. You'll need four setting triangles and four setting squares for this size quilt. Add borders to your liking or take a shortcut and just quilt and bind.

Substitute setting triangles

Step 2. Fold one border strip in half crosswise and crease. Unfold it and position it right side down along the top of the quilt, with the crease at the vertical midpoint. Pin at the midpoint and ends first, then across the width of the entire quilt, easing in fullness if necessary. Sew the border to the quilt. Repeat on the bottom of the quilt. Press seam allowances toward the borders.

Step 3. Measure the length of the quilt through the vertical center, including the top and bottom borders. Sew the remaining 1½-inch dark orchid border strips together end to end to make two side borders this exact length. Attach the side borders in the same manner as you did for the top and bottom borders.

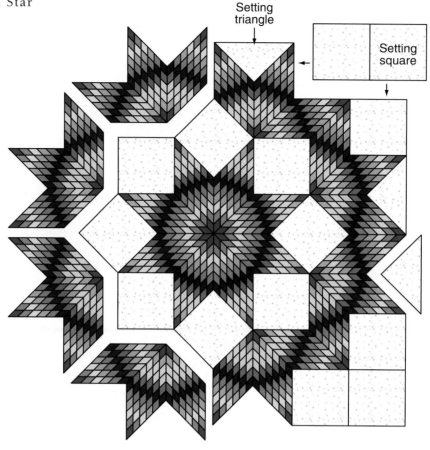

Setting
triangle

Setting
square

Assembly Diagram

Step 4. Following the directions in Steps 1 through 3, calculate lengths for the outer border strips. Piece together the white-and-blue strips as necessary, and sew them to the quilt as directed above. Press the seams toward the dark orchid border to prevent show-through.

Quilting and Finishing

Step 1. Mark the top for quilting. In the quilt shown, the large diamonds are outline quilted. The background areas are quilted with a variety of feather and heart motifs.

Step 2. To make the quilt backing for either size quilt, cut the backing fabric into three equal segments and trim the selvages. For the queen-size quilt, cut a 31-inch-wide panel from the entire length of two of the pieces, then sew them to either side of the full-width piece, as shown in **Diagram 8.** For the king-size quilt, cut a 35-inch-

wide panel from the entire length of two of the pieces, then sew them to the full-width piece. Press the seams open.

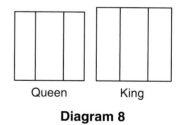

Queen   King

Diagram 8

Step 3. Layer the backing, batting, and quilt top. Baste the layers together. Quilt by hand or machine, adding additional quilting as desired.

Step 4. Referring to the directions on page 206, make and attach double-fold binding. To make the ½-inch binding shown in the photo, cut your binding strips 2½ inches wide. To calculate the amount of binding you will need, add up the length of the four sides of the quilt plus 9 inches.

Safety First

Your hobby is meant to be fun and enjoyable, but it quickly can turn into a risky business if the rules of safety are not carefully observed. Here are some things to think about the next time you and your tools are together.

• Feet have a strange way of finding lost needles and pins, and they are the first to feel the effects of a dropped pair of scissors or an open rotary cutter. Unless your reflexes are ultra-quick, keep your piggies covered and safe (or you might end up showing off your doctor's stitching prowess instead of your own).

• Keep pins in a spill-proof container or a pincushion. Relegate needles to their packages (or else stab stitching will take on a whole new meaning). Beware the needle or pin that slips through your fingers to perform a vanishing act. Find it before it finds you. Use a magnetic device to retrieve sharp objects that seem to disappear into the abyss of a carpeted room.

• A pair of dropped scissors can mean not only a trip to the emergency room for you but also a trip back to the factory for the scissors. Scissors that land on hard surfaces can easily be knocked out of alignment, rendering them virtually useless until repaired. And, all kidding aside, don't forget what your mother told you about running with scissors either.

• Seam rippers are meant to do exactly what their name indicates—cut seams. Many quilters have found the hard way that seam rippers also can do a handy job of poking into unsuspecting fingers if they're left uncapped in a sewing basket. And how many of you have inadvertently swept your seam ripper off the table and into your leg as you moved your quilt around? Keep your seam ripper capped when it's not in use. And *do not* use your seam ripper to rip out the stitches you acquired at the emergency room!

• A spool of thread may not seem like a dangerous object, but if you leave it on the floor, you'll find out how wrong you are. When stepped on, cylindrical objects tend to turn a person into a waving mass of arms and legs. Thread and pets present an even bigger problem.

Cats in particular enjoy batting spools around and around chair and table legs until the thread has wound itself into a tangled web that's just waiting for its next victim. Unfortunately, the victim may be the cat. If the cat winds a part of himself into the web, the thread can cut off circulation. Threads are also appealing for animals to ingest. Once inside the animal, they can end up wrapped around organs, resulting in the need for surgery. This can even kill an animal. Store spools safely and dispose of long thread tails in a garbage can that cannot be reached by animals.

• Be bright and don't fall victim to the wrong end of a lightbulb. Unplug the electrical source before changing the bulb and don't force the bulb in or out of the socket. Some task lighting can become extremely hot, so be sure that nothing, especially fabric and paper, is left close to the source.

• Close your rotary cutter when it's not in use, and store it safely away from children. Dispose of used blades in a safety disposal case.

An ounce of prevention is worth at least two fat quarters!

Colorful Scrap Baskets

Skill Level: Intermediate

*T*his Cake Stand Basket is filled with colorful fruit or flowers, whichever your imagination prefers. Made entirely of deep, rich, solid fabrics in the Amish tradition, this modern twin-size quilt was inspired by an antique. Even the quilting patterns are typical of the intricate wreaths and vines quilted so exquisitely by the Amish. Traditional cross-hatching provides a backdrop for the splendid feathered quilting and vibrant colors of the baskets.

Before You Begin

The quilt shown in the photograph was stitched from a variety of solid fabrics in the Amish style. While the overall effect is that of a scrap quilt, each basket uses five colors. One color is used for the basket, one color is for the background, and three contrasting colors are for the basket's contents. To simplify the yardage and cutting charts, directions are given as though all baskets are cut from the same five fabrics. However, if you plan to make a scrap quilt, you may substitute small pieces of different fabrics as long as your total yardage equals that given. An assortment of fat eighths and fat quarters would work well in providing variety for your quilt.

Quilt Sizes

	Twin (shown)	Queen
Finished Quilt Size	66" × 78½"	91" × 103½"
Finished Block Size	8¾"	8¾"
Number of Blocks	20	42

Materials

Fabric	Twin	Queen
Basket fabric	1 yard	1¾ yards
Basket background fabric	1¼ yards	2 yards
Three contrasting fabrics	⅜ yard *each*	¾ yard *each*
Light gray	3⅛ yards	5¼ yards
Burgundy	⅜ yard	⅝ yard
Backing	5 yards	8⅜ yards
Batting	72" × 85"	97" × 110"
Binding	⅝ yard	⅞ yard

NOTE: *Yardages are based on 44/45-inch-wide fabrics that are at least 42 inches wide after preshrinking.*

Choosing Fabrics

This quilt combines many of the dark solid hues associated with Amish quilts: purple, burgundy, green, dark blue, and gray. Surprisingly, it contains no black, a color often found in Amish quilts. The color choices for blocks in this quilt appear to be almost randomly selected, yet several color combinations repeat, creating a subtle visual harmony. Whether the basket is dark or medium and the background bright or pale, the contrasting values of light, medium, and dark shades help your eyes dance over this delightful quilt.

To achieve a pleasing scrap look with some underlying unity, pick a basic color scheme as this

Cutting Chart

Fabric	Used For	Strip Width	Number of Strips	
			Twin	Queen
Basket fabric	Baskets	6⅛"	2	4
	Basket feet	2⅝"	2	3
	Basket handles	2⅝"	4	8
Background fabric	Bottom triangles	4⅜"	2	3
	Basket background	2¼"	7	14
	Basket handles	2⅝"	4	8
Contrast 1	Basket contents	2⅝"	3	6
Contrast 2	Basket contents	2⅝"	3	6
Contrast 3	Basket contents	2⅝"	3	6
Light gray	Setting squares	9¼"	3	8
	Side setting triangles	13⅝"	2	2
	Corner setting triangles	5¼"	1	1
	Outer border	7"	7	11
Burgundy	Inner border	2"	6	9

quiltmaker has done. Her shades of gray, burgundy, and deep purples and pinks blend appealingly. A touch of green adds an unexpected bit of brightness. This quilt design would work equally well with a uniform color scheme, in which the same colors are used for all the blocks. You should also feel free to use print fabrics, although it would no longer be considered an Amish-style quilt. Make several copies of the **Color Plan** on page 211, and use crayons or colored pencils to experiment with different color arrangements.

Cutting

All measurements include ¼-inch seam allowances. Referring to the Cutting Chart, cut the required number of strips in the width needed. Cut all strips across the fabric width (crosswise grain).

The basket pieces, setting squares, and setting triangles are all cut from strips. When you have cut the number of strips in the Cutting Chart, refer to the instructions here to cut the individual pieces. Many of the squares will be cut diagonally into halves or quarters. Refer to **Diagram 1** for this step.

Sew Quick

If you choose to make all of the blocks in your quilt identical, refer to page 187 before cutting and constructing the triangle squares required for the top half of the basket. The grid method discussed there will be a faster way to make the large number of identical blocks needed for the quilt.

• For the baskets, cut the 6⅛-inch-wide strips of basket fabric into 6⅛-inch squares. You need ten squares for the twin-size quilt and twenty-one squares for the queen size. Cut each square in half diagonally.

• For the basket handles, cut the 2⅝-inch-wide strips into 2⅝-inch squares.

• For the basket feet, cut the 2⅝-inch-wide strips into 2⅝-inch squares. Cut each square in half diagonally.

• For the basket background pieces, cut the 2¼-inch-wide basket background fabric strips into 2¼-inch squares. You need one for each basket block. Also cut two 2¼ × 5¾-inch rectangles for each block.

• For the bottom triangles, cut the 4⅜-inch-wide strips into 4⅜-inch squares. Cut each square in half diagonally.

• For the basket contents, cut the 2⅝-inch-wide strips of contrasting fabrics into 2⅝-inch squares.

• For the setting squares, cut the 9¼-inch-wide gray strips into 9¼-inch squares.

• For the side setting triangles, cut the 13⅝-inch-wide gray strips into 13⅝-inch squares. Cut each square diagonally in both directions.

• For the corner setting triangles, cut two 5¼-inch squares from the 5¼-inch gray strip. Cut each square in half diagonally.

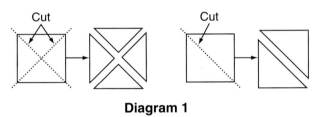

Diagram 1

Piecing the Blocks

Step 1. The basket handle is assembled from six identical triangle squares using three 2⅝-inch squares from your basket fabric and three from your background fabric. Draw a line from one corner to another on the wrong side of the lightest squares, as shown in **Diagram 2**.

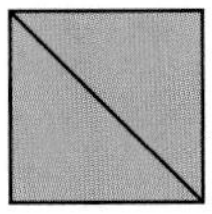

Diagram 2

Step 2. Place the basket and background squares together in pairs, right sides together, matching edges carefully. Sew a seam ¼ inch

away from each side of the diagonal line on each pair, as shown in **Diagram 3**.

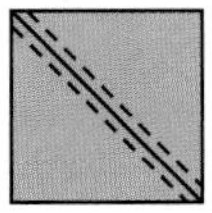

Diagram 3

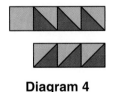

Sow Easy

Before stitching the squares together on each side of the diagonal line, lightly press each pair together. The heat will help hold them in place and prevent shifting while you stitch. The result is perfect triangle squares.

Step 3. Cut each pair apart on the drawn line to produce two triangle squares. Press seams toward the darker fabric.

Step 4. Sew the triangle squares together in sets of three, referring to **Diagram 4** for placement. Sew a 2¼-inch square of background fabric to the end of one row, as shown in the diagram.

Diagram 4

Step 5. Make three more triangle squares in exactly the same manner, this time using two 2⅝-inch squares of fabrics you've chosen for the basket contents. Note that the baskets in the quilt use three fabrics for this section. To simplify the diagrams and directions, we've paired a blue square with a light pink square and a blue square with a dark pink square.

Step 6. Cut two of the 2⅝-inch squares of contrasting fabric in half diagonally to make four triangles. Arrange and sew the three triangle squares from Step 5 with three of these triangles into rows, referring to **Diagram 5** for color placement. Save your extra triangle for your next block. Press the seams in adjoining rows in opposite directions, then sew rows together to form the basket contents.

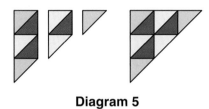

Diagram 5

Step 7. Sew the shorter handle unit to the side of the basket contents, as shown in **Diagram 6**.

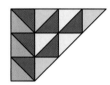

Diagram 6

Step 8. Now sew the remaining handle unit to the other side of the basket contents, as shown in **Diagram 7**.

Diagram 7

Step 9. Sew a large basket fabric triangle to the bottom of the partially assembled basket, as shown in **Diagram 8**.

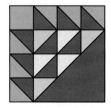

Diagram 8

Step 10. Sew a small basket fabric triangle to one end of two $2\frac{1}{4} \times 5\frac{3}{4}$-inch rectangles, referring to **Diagram 9** for placement. Press seams toward the darker fabric.

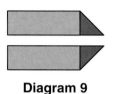

Diagram 9

Step 11. Sew the rectangle units to the partially completed basket block, as shown in **Diagram 10**. Press the seams toward the darker fabric.

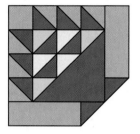

Diagram 10

Step 12. Sew a $4\frac{3}{8}$-inch bottom triangle to the bottom of the basket, as shown in the **Block Diagram**, completing the block. Press the seam toward the triangle.

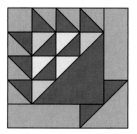

Block Diagram

Step 13. Repeat Steps 1 through 12 until you have assembled the number of blocks required for your quilt.

Assembling the Quilt Top

Step 1. Use a design wall or other flat surface to lay out the basket blocks, setting squares, side setting triangles, and corner setting triangles into diagonal rows, referring to the **Assembly Diagram.** For the queen-size quilt, your layout will be six baskets across by seven baskets down. Note that for either quilt, the baskets all point toward the vertical center of the quilt.

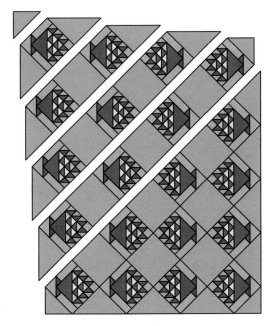

Assembly Diagram

Step 2. Once you are pleased with your block arrangement, sew the blocks and setting pieces together into rows. Press the seam allowances toward the setting squares and triangles. Sew the rows together, matching seams carefully. Press.

Adding the Borders

Step 1. For either size quilt, sew the 2-inch-wide inner border strips together end to end.

Step 2. Measure the width of the quilt top, taking the measurement through the horizontal center of the quilt rather than along the top or bottom. Cut two border strips to this exact length.

Step 3. Fold one border strip in half crosswise and crease. Unfold it and position it right side down along the top edge of the quilt, with the crease at the vertical midpoint. Pin at the midpoint and ends first, then along the length of the entire edge, easing in fullness if necessary. Sew the border to the quilt top using a ¼-inch seam allowance. Press the seam allowance toward the border. Repeat on the other end of the quilt.

Step 4. Measure the length of the quilt, taking the measurement through the vertical center of the quilt and including the top and bottom borders. Cut the remaining long border strip to obtain two borders this exact length.

Step 5. Stitch the side borders to the quilt top as you did for the top and bottom borders, pinning at the midpoints and easing in fullness if necessary.

Step 6. In the same manner as for the inner border, piece together the 7-inch-wide outer border strips. Measure and sew the borders to the quilt top, adding the top and bottom borders first, followed by the side borders. The completed twin-size quilt top should look like the one in the **Quilt Diagram** on page 110. If you are making the queen-size quilt, you will have more basket blocks, but the borders will be the same as for the twin-size quilt.

Quilting and Finishing

Step 1. Mark the top for quilting. The quilt shown was quilted with vertical lines about ½ inch apart through each basket block. The setting squares were quilted with feathered wreaths and background cross-hatching. The setting triangles have half wreaths and cross-hatching. The borders were quilted with a feathered vine motif.

Step 2. Regardless of which quilt size you've chosen to make, the backing will have to be pieced. For the twin-size quilt, divide the 5 yards of backing fabric crosswise into two 2½-yard pieces, and trim the selvages.

Step 3. Cut one of the pieces in half lengthwise, and sew one half to each side of the full-

Quilt Diagram

width piece, as shown in **Diagram 11.** Press the seams open.

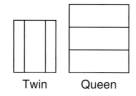

Twin   Queen

Diagram 11

Step 4. For the queen-size quilt, divide the $8^3/8$-yard length of fabric crosswise into three equal pieces, and trim the selvages.

Step 5. Sew the three pieces together along the long sides, as shown in **Diagram 11,** and press the seams open.

Step 6. Layer the quilt top, batting, and backing, and baste the layers together. Quilt as desired.

Step 7. Referring to the directions on page 206 in "Quiltmaking Basics," make and attach double-fold binding. To calculate the amount of binding needed for the quilt size you are making, add the lengths of the four sides of the quilt plus 9 inches. The total is the approximate number of inches of binding you will need.

Quick Suppers

You're merrily sewing along when someone says that nasty four-letter word . . . cook. Your family needs to eat, and you need to keep up your strength, too, so you can stretch that sewing session even farther. Eating is a requirement of life, but you don't have to be stranded in the kitchen when you'd rather be stitchin'. Try some of these ideas to make dinner appear on the table a little faster.

Quick Tip #1: Dig out the slow cooker that's been collecting dust in the attic and see how quickly you'll be inspired to make it part of your meal planning. Most dishes can be put together with little preparation, and there's not much to talk about in the way of cleanup. Invest in a cookbook devoted to this timesaving device, and you can enjoy a variety of meals throughout the year. The tantalizing smells wafting through the house are an added bonus.

Quick Tip #2: Use that little square box called a microwave for more than just defrosting food. When you've waited until the last minute to think about what's for dinner, microwaves can deal out entire meals in a fraction of the time those meals would take to make using traditional methods.

Quick Tip #3: Pick up the phone and dial up some take-out food. Sit and sew for a few more minutes while someone else goes to pick it up. Serve it all up on paper plates, and you'll be back at the sewing machine in no time.

Quick Tip #4: You've probably heard this tip before, but it really can save you time. First, pair up with a friendly neighbor who likes to cook. Each of you can double a recipe, and on alternating weeks you can deliver a piping-hot meal to the other family.

Quick Tip #5: Invite your spouse and kids to be chefs for a day. Have them plan and make the meal, and tell them that you'll stay out of the kitchen so you can be surprised with the menu! Naturally, you can head straight for your sewing space and sew up a storm while they cook.

Quick Tip #6: Set aside one day to cook and freeze several meals for the month. It may seem a lot to sacrifice initially, but you'll save time in the long run. Here's a recipe to get you started.

Mustardy Baked Turkey Drumsticks

2   pounds turkey drumsticks, skinned
¼   cup Dijon mustard
2   tablespoons packed brown sugar
2   cloves garlic, minced
1   teaspoon mustard powder
1   teaspoon hot-pepper sauce
¼   cup dried bread crumbs

Preheat the oven to 400°F. Line a 13" × 9" baking dish with foil. Place the drumsticks in the dish. In a small bowl, combine the Dijon mustard, brown sugar, garlic, mustard, and hot-pepper sauce. Brush over the drumsticks. Sprinkle with the bread crumbs. Bake for 45 minutes, or until no longer pink in the center. Check by inserting the tip of a sharp knife into the thickest part of 1 drumstick. Cut the meat off of the bones.

To freeze, pack the cooled cooked turkey in freezer-quality plastic bags. To use, thaw overnight in the refrigerator. Transfer the turkey to a 13" × 9" baking dish. Cover and bake at 400°F for 20 minutes or until hot.

On the Road Again...
Paducah Bound

Skill Level: Intermediate

*C*lever color placement makes this crib-size quilt, with its easy-to-construct blocks, seem more complicated than it actually is. The triangles in the pieced border complete the strong diagonals in the inner quilt. The quilt's unusual title refers to a challenge among a group of the quiltmaker's friends. Each year, these friends take their completed challenge projects to the American Quilter's Society show in Paducah, Kentucky, to "show" to each other. The quilt is based on a design by quiltmaker and author Trudie Hughes.

Before You Begin

Each block in this quilt is composed of a small Nine-Patch block, four corner squares, and four pieced rectangles. In half of the blocks, the small Nine-Patch blocks and corner squares are made with black print fabric, and in the other half they are made with medium gray print fabric. The pieced rectangles, made with magenta print and light gray print, are identical for all the blocks.

The directions are written based on using a quick-and-easy method for making the small Nine-Patch blocks. Strips of fabric are sewn together into strip sets. The strip sets are then cut apart and resewn into blocks. Read through the construction directions, beginning on page 115, for further details on this strip-piecing technique.

Choosing Fabrics

The quiltmaker chose a limited color palette with a high degree

Quilt Sizes

	Crib (shown)	Lap
Finished Quilt Size	36½" × 50½"	50½" × 64½"
Finished Block Size	7"	7"
Number of Blocks		
Black and magenta	12	24
Gray and magenta	12	24

Materials

Fabric	Crib	Lap
Magenta print	1¼ yards	2 yards
Black print	1 yard	1½ yards
Light gray print	1⅜ yards	2 yards
Medium gray print	⅝ yard	⅞ yard
Backing	1⅝ yards	4¼ yards
Batting	42" × 56"	56" × 70"
Binding	⅜ yard	½ yard

NOTE: *Yardages are based on 44/45-inch-wide fabrics that are at least 42 inches wide after preshrinking.*

of contrast, creating a bold, graphic image. To add movement and energy, she used fabrics with interesting visual textures. For example, the magenta fabric used in the original quilt is a print, but it "reads" as a solid. In other words, it gives the overall appearance of a solid color but has a texture of dark lines, which break

Cutting Chart

Fabric	Used For	Strip Width	Number of Strips	
			Crib	Lap
Magenta print	Inner border triangles	5⅜"	1	1
	Template B	2⅞"	7	14
	Strip sets	1½"	6	8
Black print	Outer border	2¾"	5	7
	Block corners	2½"	3	6
	Strip sets	1½"	3	5
Light gray print	Template A/ A reverse	2½"	9	18
	Inner border triangles	2⅞"	1	1
	Inner border segments	2½"	6	7
Medium gray print	Block corners	2½"	3	6
	Strip sets	1½"	3	5

the monotony and help your eyes move across the quilt top. The texture is more apparent in the medium gray print and light gray print fabrics, where it adds depth and dimension to the design.

You may choose to work with more or fewer fabrics to create a different-looking quilt. For best results, make sure there is strong contrast between at least two of the fabrics—the background (light gray in the quilt shown) and the fabric used to create the diagonal pattern (magenta in the quilt shown).

To help develop your own unique color scheme for the quilt, photocopy the **Color Plan** on page 215, and use crayons or colored pencils to experiment with different color arrangements.

Cutting

All measurements include ¼-inch seam allowances. Referring to the Cutting Chart, cut the required number of strips in the width needed. Cut all strips across the fabric width (crosswise grain).

Make templates for pieces A and A reverse and

B, using the full-size patterns on page 120. Refer to page 186 in "Quiltmaking Basics" for complete details on making and using templates. For the A and A reverse pieces, cut 2½-inch-wide strips from the light gray fabric. Use the template right side up to cut the A pieces from the strips. Turn the template over and cut the A reverse pieces from the strips. You will need two A and two A reverse pieces for each block in your quilt. In the same manner, cut the magenta fabric into 2⅞-inch-wide strips. Use template B to cut four B pieces for each block in your quilt.

The block corners are cut from 2½-inch-wide strips. Cut the black and medium gray 2½-inch strips into 2½-inch squares. You will need four squares for each block.

You will need two sizes of triangles to make the pieced inner border. For the magenta triangles, cut the 5⅜-inch magenta strip into 5⅜-inch squares. You will need three squares for the crib quilt and four squares for the lap-size quilt. Cut each square in half diagonally both ways, as shown in **Diagram 1A**, producing four triangles from each square. For the light gray triangles, cut the 2⅞-inch strip into 2⅞-inch squares. Cut each square in half diagonally, as shown in **1B**.

Note: Cut and piece one sample block before cutting all the fabric for the quilt.

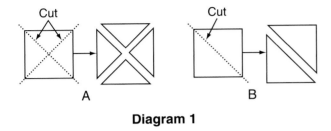

Diagram 1

Piecing the Blocks

Each block in the quilt contains a small Nine-Patch block, four corner squares, and four pieced rectangles. The blocks are made in two different color schemes—black and magenta, and medium gray and magenta—as shown in the **Block Diagram.** Except for the color, the blocks are identical.

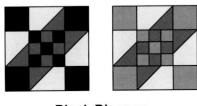

Block Diagram

Making the Small Nine-Patch Blocks

You will need small Nine-Patch blocks in two different color variations, as shown in **Diagram 2.** For illustration purposes, only the black-and-magenta blocks are shown in the diagrams that follow. Repeat all steps to make the required number of medium gray-and-magenta small Nine-Patch blocks.

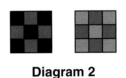

Diagram 2

The blocks are assembled using a strip-piecing technique. Each small Nine-Patch block requires two different segment variations, as shown in **Diagram 3.**

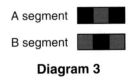

A segment

B segment

Diagram 3

Step 1. Refer to the Cutting Chart to determine the total number of 1½-inch strips you need to cut from each fabric. Cut all strips across the width of your fabric, from selvage to selvage. The strips should be approximately 42 inches long.

Step 2. To make the A segments for the black-and-magenta blocks, use a ¼-inch seam to sew a black strip to each side of a magenta strip, as shown in **Diagram 4A.** Press the seam allowances toward the black strips.

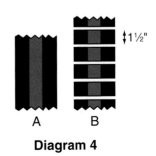

A   B

Diagram 4

Step 3. Using a rotary cutter and ruler, square up one end of the strip set. Cut 1½-inch-wide segments from the strip set, as shown in **4B** on page 115. You should be able to cut at least twenty-seven segments. Continue making strip sets and cutting them into segments until you have assembled the required number of black-and-magenta A segments for your quilt. You need two A segments for each small Nine-Patch block in your quilt. Repeat to make the medium gray-and-magenta A segments.

Step 4. To make the B segments for the black-and-magenta blocks, sew a magenta strip to each side of a black strip, as shown in **Diagram 5A.** Press the seams toward the black strip.

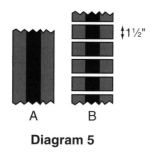

Diagram 5

Step 5. Using a rotary cutter and ruler, square up one end of the strip set. Cut 1½-inch-wide segments from the strip set, as shown in **5B.** You should be able to cut at least twenty-seven segments. Continue making strip sets and cutting them into segments until you have assembled the required number of B segments for your quilt. You need one B segment for each small Nine-Patch block in your quilt. Repeat to make the medium gray-and-magenta B segments.

Step 6. Sew two A segments and one B segment together, as shown in **Diagram 6**, matching seams carefully. Since the seam allowances on the segments are pressed in opposite directions, the intersections should fit together tightly. Stitch, using a ¼-inch seam allowance. Press. Complete all the black-and-magenta blocks, then repeat for the medium gray-and-magenta blocks.

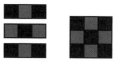

Diagram 6

Making the Pieced Rectangles

Step 1. Each block has four pieced rectangles: two made from a light gray A piece and a magenta B piece and two made from a light gray A reverse piece and a magenta B piece. Place a light gray A piece right sides together with a magenta B piece and align the edges. Using a ¼-inch seam allowance, stitch the pieces together, as shown in **Diagram 7A.** Open up the pieces and carefully press the seam allowance toward the magenta piece. See **7B.** Repeat, pairing each remaining light gray A piece with a magenta B piece.

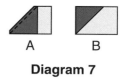

Diagram 7

Step 2. In the same manner, stitch each light gray A reverse piece to a magenta B piece. Open up the pieces and carefully press the seam allowances toward the magenta fabric. The resulting segments will be a mirror image of the Step 1 segments.

Assembling the Blocks

Step 1. To complete the black-and-magenta blocks, begin by sewing a 2½-inch black block corner to each side of an AB unit, as shown in **Diagram 8.** Press the seams toward the AB unit. Repeat, making a second identical unit.

Diagram 8

Step 2. Sew a reverse AB unit to each side of a black-and-magenta small Nine-Patch block, as shown in **Diagram 9**. Press the seams away from the Nine-Patch block.

Diagram 9

Step 3. As shown in **Diagram 10**, sew a Step 1 section to the top and bottom of the Step 2 section, making sure they are positioned correctly. Repeat, making the total number of black-and-magenta blocks required for your quilt size.

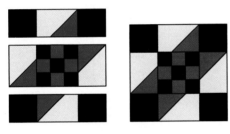

Diagram 10

Step 4. In the same manner, assemble the gray-and-magenta blocks, using the medium gray-and-magenta small Nine-Patch blocks and the medium gray corner squares.

Assembling the Quilt Top

Step 1. Use a design wall or other flat surface to lay out the blocks. Alternate the black-and-magenta blocks with the medium gray-and-magenta blocks, referring to the appropriate quilt diagram for correct layout for your quilt.

Step 2. Sew the blocks together in rows, pressing the seams in opposite directions from row to row. Sew the rows together, pressing seams carefully.

Crib-Size Quilt Diagram

Making the Pieced Inner Border

The pieced border is made from light gray fabric combined with magenta triangles to complete the strong diagonal lines of the quilt design. You will piece the inner border first, then join the inner border to the outer border, and then add them to the quilt top as a unit.

Step 1. Sew a light gray triangle to the two shorter sides of each magenta triangle, as shown in **Diagram 11**. These units will be combined with segments of 2½-inch-wide light gray fabric to complete the border.

Diagram 11

Lap-Size Quilt Diagram

Step 2. Refer to the appropriate quilt diagram to understand how the border relates to the quilt top. There are 10-inch-long (finished length) segments of light gray fabric between each of the triangle units made in Step 1. For the crib quilt, cut two 10½-inch-long segments for each side border and one segment each for the top and bottom borders. For the lap-size quilt, cut three 10½-inch-long segments for each side border and two each for the top and bottom borders.

The border corners are mitered. To complete the border strip and allow enough extra to miter the corners for either quilt, cut eight 18-inch-long segments—one for each end of each border strip.

Step 3. Join the Step 1 triangle units with the 10½-inch light gray segments, as shown in **Diagram 12**. Make sure the tips of the triangles are all pointing in the same direction. For the crib quilt, you will have three triangle units and two segments for each side border and two triangle units and one segment each for the top and bottom borders. For the lap-size quilt, you will have four triangle units and three segments for

Diagram 12

each side border and three triangle units and two segments each for the top and bottom borders. Add the 18-inch-long segments to each end of each border strip.

Step 4. Compare each completed border strip to the assembled quilt top. The magenta triangle points in the border should line up with the corresponding magenta B pieces in the blocks, ensuring a smooth line of color from the inner quilt out into the border. Some fullness can be eased in when the border is sewn, but if there is too much excess to ease in, it may be necessary to make slight adjustments in one or more seams joining the border units.

Adding the Borders

Step 1. The pieced inner border will be joined to the outer border, then the two will be sewn to the quilt top as a unit. You will need four outer border strips that are the same length as the corresponding pieced inner border strips. Sew the 2¾-inch-wide black border strips together end to end to make long borders, then trim them to the exact length needed. For the crib quilt, you'll need one and a half strips each for the side borders. The top and bottom borders will need just a few extra inches, not a full half-strip. Measure against the pieced border to determine how much you need, but don't cut a full strip for this little bit of extra; you should be able to piece it from scraps. For the lap-size quilt, you'll need two strips each for the side borders and one and a half strips each for the top and bottom borders.

Step 2. Sew the pieced inner borders and the outer borders together, making four border sets. Make sure you sew the outer border to the correct edge of the inner border so that the triangle points will be facing in the right direction when the borders are added to the quilt.

Step 3. Pin and sew the four borders to the quilt top, referring to page 204 in "Quiltmaking Basics" for complete instructions on adding mitered borders to your quilt.

Quilting and Finishing

Step 1. Mark the quilt top for quilting, if desired. The quilt shown is free-motion machine quilted.

Step 2. If you are making the crib quilt, the backing does not have to be pieced. **Note:** This assumes that your backing fabric is at least 42 inches wide, as specified in the Materials table on page 113. If your fabric is less than 42 inches wide, it may be necessary to add a narrow piece to one edge of the backing. The backing fabric should be at least 3 inches larger than the quilt top on all four sides.

Step 3. The backing for the lap-size quilt will have to be pieced. To make the most efficient use of the yardage, piece the back so that the seams run horizontally across the quilt, as illustrated in **Diagram 13**. To begin, cut the backing fabric crosswise into two equal pieces, and trim the selvages.

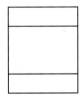

Diagram 13

Step 4. Cut one of the pieces in half lengthwise, and sew one half to each side of the full-width piece. Press the seams open.

Step 5. Layer the quilt top, batting, and backing, and baste the layers together. Quilt as desired.

Step 6. Referring to the directions on page 206 in "Quiltmaking Basics," make and attach double-fold binding. To calculate the amount of binding needed for the quilt size you are making, add up the length of the four sides of the quilt and add 9 inches. The total is the approximate number of inches of binding you will need.

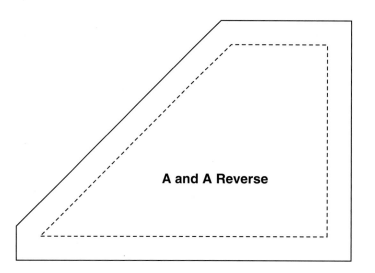

A and A Reverse

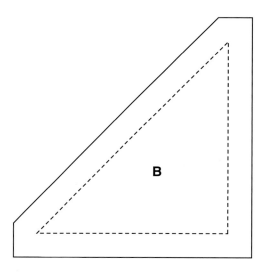

B

Quilt Shop Lock Up

Imagine that you've gone to your local quilt shop to pick up a few items you need for your latest project. It's close to closing time, and after the shop owner greets you she goes about her last-minute chores. You gather the things you need, and because there's still a little time before you have to go, you wander into the pattern room to take a peek at the new arrivals. Suddenly, the lights go out and you hear the familiar click of a door being closed. You're in familiar territory, but you can't see through the darkness to get to the door in time. You're locked in!

Now some people might begin to panic after figuring out what had just happened, but for a quilter, this situation is a dream come true. What quilter hasn't imagined being locked in a quilt shop with nothing to do but play with her favorite "toys"? You're surrounded by everything you could possibly need or want (including a phone, which you could use to call someone to get you out but choose to ignore). Where do you begin?

Start with the fabrics. No, start with finding the lights and turning them on so you can enjoy the fantasy. Once that's done, playtime can begin. Stroke every bolt of fabric, and drink in the pleasures brought by those fabulous fibers. Wouldn't they all look great with the rest of your stash? Take down a few you'd like to get to know better and set them aside.

Head for the books and patterns next. Take your time oohing and ahhing over the possibilities that await you. You probably won't get an uninterrupted expanse of time like this again. While you're dreaming of all those future projects you'd like to make, why not match up those fabrics you set aside with some of the designs you like best. Go find more fabrics if needed.

Look at that great cutting table! It's so much better for cutting than the dining room table, so you'd better go ahead and cut the pieces you need for those new projects. Don't forget to write down your yardage so you can settle up with the shop owner whenever she comes back. (You're really dreaming if you think this fantasy happened on a Saturday night and the shop isn't open again until Monday.)

Listen carefully. Do you hear sewing machines in the classroom just begging for attention? It just wouldn't be right not to show them the same consideration you did the other items in the store. The features of the latest models are at your fingertips. There are threads that need to be explored. And you've got pieces cut out that need to be sewn. How convenient!

In what seems like no time, you have a complete quilt top finished. Hunger strikes as daylight streams through the window. You reach for the candy bar in your purse just as the rattle of keys in the door brings you back to reality. The shop owner has returned.

"Oh my goodness. I got a few blocks down the road and remembered that I hadn't seen you leave. I am so sorry for locking you in here in the dark. I hope you were all right. Let me give you a fat quarter, on the house."

Dream on, quilters. It's good for the soul.

Paths to the Diamonds

Skill Level: Easy

Unlike the more common scrap Log Cabins, this contemporary interpretation of the traditional Barn Raising setting relies on a particular color scheme for its effect. Subtle tones of gray work well with the white and black prints to create a bold overall design. This large wallhanging was inspired by a lecture given by author and quiltmaker Mary Ellen Hopkins.

Before You Begin

The directions for this quilt are written based on using the chain piecing technique, although the foundation method would work equally well. Read through the general construction directions, beginning on page 194, to become familiar with the technique. All of the logs are cut to length, then the blocks are pieced in assembly line fashion. If you prefer to use the foundation method, prepare a foundation for each block using the pattern on page 128.

Choosing Fabrics

The blocks in this quilt are divided into two color schemes. While the red centers and the three light prints are the same in all sixty-four blocks, in half the blocks they are combined with gray prints and in the other half with black prints. For best results, select prints that vary in scale and texture. In the quilt shown, the same large-scale black-and-red floral was used in

Quilt Size

Finished Size	73½" × 73½"
Finished Block Size	8"
Number of Blocks	64

NOTE: Because specific color and value placement is critical to the overall design of this quilt, no variations in size or layout are provided.

Materials

Fabric	Amount
Red	1 yard
Light print 1	¾ yard
Light print 2	1 yard
Light print 3	1¼ yards
Black print 1	2 yards
Black print 2	¾ yard
Medium gray print 1	⅝ yard
Medium gray print 2	⅝ yard
Dark gray print	⅞ yard
Backing	4¾ yards
Batting	80" × 80"
Binding	⅝ yard

NOTE: Yardages are based on 44/45-inch-wide fabrics that are at least 42 inches wide after preshrinking.

two places in the blocks, as well as in the border.

If you wish to develop your own unique color scheme, pho-tocopy the **Color Plan** on page 214, and use crayons or colored pencils to experiment with different color arrangements.

123

Cutting Chart

Fabric	Strip Width	Number of Strips	Piece	Log Length	Number Needed
Red	1½"	8	Border		
	2½"	4	Log 1	2½"	64
Light print 1	1½"	10	Log 2	2½"	64
			Log 3	3½"	64
Light print 2	1½"	18	Log 6	4½"	64
			Log 7	5½"	64
Light print 3	1½"	24	Log 10	6½"	64
			Log 11	7½"	64
Black print 1	4"	8	Border		
	1½"	21	Log 4	3½"	32
			Log 5	4½"	32
			Log 12	7½"	32
			Log 13	8½"	32
Black print 2	1½"	11	Log 8	5½"	32
			Log 9	6½"	32
Medium gray print 1	1½"	7	Log 4	3½"	32
			Log 5	4½"	32
Medium gray print 2	1½"	11	Log 8	5½"	32
			Log 9	6½"	32
Dark gray print	1½"	14	Log 12	7½"	32
			Log 13	8½"	32

Cutting

All measurements include ¼-inch seam allowances. Referring to the Cutting Chart, cut strips in the width needed, then cut the strips into logs. Cut all strips across the fabric width (crosswise grain). You may find it helpful to pin a number label to each group of logs as you cut them. **Note:** Cut and piece one sample block before cutting all the pieces for the quilt.

Piecing the First Block

Refer to page 197 in "Quiltmaking Basics," and read through the directions for the technique you have chosen. Piece a sample block first; it will allow you to become acquainted with

the technique and to double-check the accuracy of your seam allowances. Cut enough light print and either gray print or black print logs for one block, and use the **Block Diagram** as a color sample and a guide for piecing order. The completed block should measure 8½ inches square.

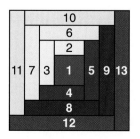
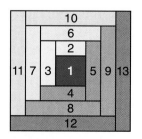

Block Diagram

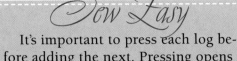

It's important to press each log before adding the next. Pressing opens up the seam, "stretching" a log to its full width. Always press the seam allowance toward the log you have just added.

Step 1. Place a light print log 2 right sides together with a red log 1, aligning the edges. Stitch the pieces together using a ¼-inch seam. Open out the pieces, as shown in **Diagram 1A,** and press the seam allowance toward log 2.

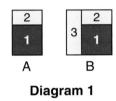

Diagram 1

Step 2. Referring to **Diagram 1B,** position log 3 right sides together with the pieced segment, and stitch. Press the seam allowance toward log 3.

Step 3. Add log 4 to the bottom of the pieced segment, as shown in **Diagram 2A.** Press the seam toward log 4.

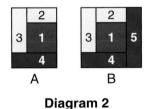

Diagram 2

Step 4. In the same manner, sew log 5 to the side of the pieced segment, as shown in **2B.** Press the seam allowance toward log 5.

Step 5. Continue to add logs in numerical order in a counterclockwise direction until all 13 logs have been added. Measure your completed block to make sure it is an accurate 8½ inches square. If it isn't, check your seam allowances and make any necessary adjustments.

Piecing the Remaining Blocks

Chain piecing can help speed up the block assembly process. Instead of making an individual block from start to finish, perform one step at a time on all blocks of the same color scheme.

Step 1. Stack the light print logs and the gray print logs near your sewing machine. Keep your sample block handy to use as a color guide. Stitch a log 2 to a red log 1 as described previously. Without removing the stitched pair from the sewing machine and without lifting the presser foot, insert and sew a second pair. Continue sewing until all remaining center sections are pieced. See **Diagram 3.**

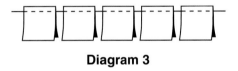

Diagram 3

Step 2. Cut the stitched segments apart. Press each seam allowance toward log 2. In the same manner, add the remaining logs to the blocks until you have completed all thirty-two gray print blocks.

Step 3. Repeat the process for the thirty-two black print blocks.

Assembling the Quilt Top

Step 1. The blocks are arranged in eight rows, with eight blocks in each row. Use a design wall or flat surface to arrange your blocks, as shown in **Diagram 4** on page 126.

Diagram 4 on page 126.

Sew Quick

It may not be necessary to pin short logs to the block as you sew, especially if you are using 100 percent cottons, which "stick" to each other nicely. As you begin adding longer logs, secure their edges with a few straight pins to help keep your piecing accurate.

Row 1

Row 2

Row 3

Row 4

Row 5

Row 6

Row 7

Row 8

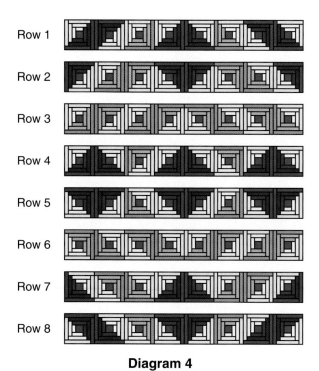

Diagram 4

Step 2. Sew the blocks into rows, pressing the seam allowances in opposite directions from row to row.

Step 3. Sew the rows together, carefully matching seams where blocks meet. If you've pressed the seam allowances in opposite directions, the seams should fit tightly against each other, helping you achieve a perfect match. Press seam allowances where rows were joined.

Adding the Borders

Step 1. Sew the 1½-inch-wide red border strips together in pairs, making four long borders.

Step 2. Measure the length of the quilt top, taking the measurement through the vertical center of the quilt rather than along the sides. Cut two of the long red border strips to this length.

Step 3. Fold one strip in half crosswise and crease. Unfold it and position it right side down along one side of the quilt top, with the crease at the horizontal midpoint. Pin at the midpoint and ends first, then along the length of the entire side, easing in fullness if necessary. Sew the border to the quilt top using a ¼-inch seam allowance. Repeat on the opposite side of the quilt.

Step 4. Measure the width of the quilt, taking the measurement through the horizontal center of the quilt and including the side borders. Cut the remaining two red border strips to this length.

Step 5. Fold one strip in half crosswise and crease. Unfold it and position it right side down along one end of the quilt top, matching the crease to the vertical midpoint. Pin at the midpoint and ends first, then across the entire width of the quilt top, easing in fullness if necessary. Stitch, using a ¼-inch seam allowance. Repeat on the opposite end of the quilt top.

Step 6. Sew the 4-inch-wide black print border strips together in pairs, making four long border strips.

Step 7. In the same manner as for the red border, measure, cut, and sew the 4-inch-wide border strips to the quilt sides.

Step 8. Measure, cut, and sew the 4-inch-wide border strips to the quilt ends. The completed quilt top should look like the one shown in the **Quilt Diagram.**

Quilting and Finishing

Step 1. Mark the quilt top for quilting. The angular lines of this quilt were softened by a quilting design of flowing fanlike curves that follow the contours of the dark diamond shapes. Segments of the motif are repeated in light areas, radiating outward from the center of the quilt.

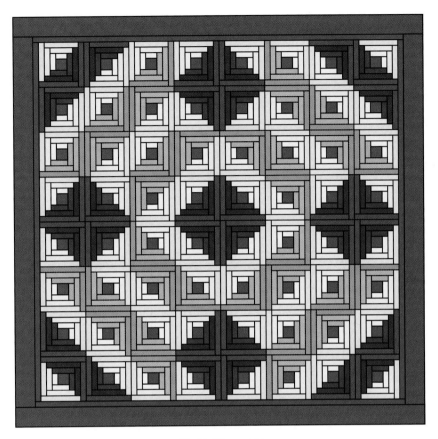

Quilt Diagram

Step 2. To piece the quilt back, first trim the selvages from the backing fabric. Cut the 4¾-yard piece of backing fabric into two equal segments, each 2⅜ yards long.

Step 3. Cut one of the segments in half vertically, producing two narrow segments that are each approximately 22 inches wide and 2⅜ yards long. Sew a narrow segment to each side of the uncut 2⅜-yard piece, as shown in **Diagram 5.** Press the seams open.

Step 4. Layer the quilt top, batting, and backing. Baste the layers together. Quilt as desired.

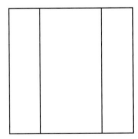

Diagram 5

Step 5. Make approximately 325 inches of double-fold binding. Refer to page 206 in "Quilt-making Basics" for complete directions on making and attaching binding.

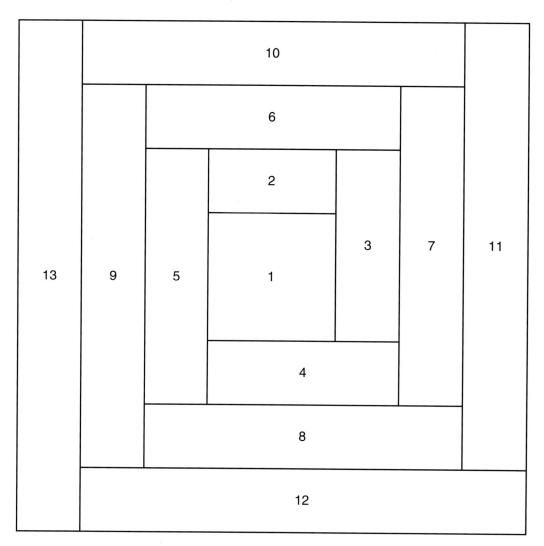

Block Pattern

Pattern shown is the mirror image of the finished block.
Note: Pattern is reduced. Enlarge it 150 percent before tracing.

Mail-Order Shopping

You can get all your quilting needs without ever leaving your house! Whether you mail your order, phone it in, or send it over the Internet, mail-order buying is becoming a popular alternative to traditional shopping methods. It's a great way to expand your choices, especially if you live in an area with a limited selection, plus you can shop almost any time of day or night. For a successful shopping experience, keep these basic rules in mind.

• Make purchases from a reputable source. If you're unfamiliar with the company, check them out before ordering. Make sure the company is authorized to sell large-ticket items, such as sewing machines, before ordering and be sure to familiarize yourself with their return policy.

• Avoid surprises by knowing exactly what you're ordering. If you're ordering fabric, ask for a sample first so you know it is exactly the right color. Make sure you know what items are included in kits (sometimes it's just fabric, other times the pattern is included).

• Check on shipping and handling charges, delivery time, method of delivery, minimum quantities, and substitutions.

• Double-check your order before submitting it. If you've phoned in your order, have the representative verify it. Make sure written orders are legible.

• Use your credit card to pay for your order, if possible. The credit card company can help you get a refund if you are unable to resolve a problem with the merchant.

• Keep a record of your order, along with the company's information (name, address, phone number, and Web site). Many companies will provide you with a confirmation number or order number. If you are ordering over the Internet, print out your order form. Write down the name of the person who took your order if you phoned it in. Make a copy of the order form before you mail it.

• Save your money and opt for ground shipping unless you need the items by a certain date.

• Contact the customer service department if you don't receive your items when expected or if the order is wrong.

• Inspect the package when it arrives for dents, dings, or other damage. Take photographs of any damage to the package in case the contents have also been damaged. Check the contents against your order form and report any missing items immediately.

• Whether you're dealing with a small or large company, take a moment to e-mail or call and let them know that you appreciate their quick service, friendliness, or their assistance. Companies love to hear compliments from customers!

Little Red Schoolhouses

Skill Level: Easy

The endearing image of the country schoolhouse springs to life in Mary Stori's nostalgic interpretation of a bona fide classic. The crisp color scheme rings so true, you can almost hear the recess bell! You'll whip up this lap quilt in no time with super-easy strip piecing.

Before You Begin

With the exception of a few simple shapes that require templates, pieces for this quilt can be rotary cut. An easy strip-piecing technique is used to make the Nine-Patch blocks, the pieced sashing, and parts of the Schoolhouse block.

Choosing Fabrics

The red-and-white scheme enhances this quilt's strong visual appeal, but a similar graphic impact can be created with any high-contrast two-color scheme. Replace the red with navy or spruce for a totally different look. Or substitute a variety of prints in a single color family for more visual texture. This quilt would also look terrific with scrap fabrics—choose country colors or brights for a twist on tradition.

To develop your own color scheme, photocopy the **Color Plan** on page 212, and use colored pencils to experiment with different color arrangements.

CUTTING

All of the measurements include ¼-inch seam allowances. Refer to the Cutting Chart on page 132 and cut the required number of strips in the sizes needed. Cut border strips first, cutting them on the lengthwise grain (parallel to the selvage). The balance of the strips may be cut on the crosswise grain of the fabric.

Referring to the directions on page 186, make templates for pieces A, B, C, and D, using the full-size pattern pieces on page 136. The Cutting Chart lists how many of each piece to cut with each template. Place the templates wrong side up on the wrong side of the fabric to cut the pieces. Turn the D template over to cut the D reverse pieces.

Quilt Sizes

	Lap (shown)	Queen
Finished Quilt Size	56½" × 71¼"	86" × 100¾"
Finished Block Size		
Schoolhouse	11"	11"
Nine-Patch	3¾"	3¾"
Number of Blocks		
Schoolhouse	12	30
Nine-Patch	20	42

Materials

Fabric	Lap	Queen
Red solid	2½ yards	4 yards
Muslin	2⅜ yards	4⅞ yards
Assorted red plaids	½ yard	1 yard
Backing	3½ yards	7⅞ yards
Batting	63" × 78"	92" × 107"
Binding	¾ yard	⅞ yard

NOTE: *Yardages are based on 44/45-inch-wide fabrics that are at least 42 inches wide after preshrinking.*

Cutting Chart

Fabric	Used For	Strip Width	Number to Cut Lap	Number to Cut Queen
Red solid	Borders	4½"	4	4
	Sashing	1¾"	15	28
	Strip Set 1	2"	2	4
	Strip Set 2	1½"	2	4
	Strip Set 2	1¾"	2	4
	Strip Set 3	1¼"	1	2
	Strip Set 3	1¾"	2	4
	E	1¾"	2	4
	G	1¾"	4	10
	A	Template A	12	30
Muslin	Sashing	1¾"	26	52
	Strip Set 1	2½"	2	4
	Strip Set 1	4½"	1	2
	Strip Set 2	2¼"	2	4
	Strip Set 3	1¾"	2	4
	F	1¾"	2	5
	G	1¾"	2	5
	B	Template B	12	30
	D	Template D	12	30
	D reverse	Template D	12	30
Red plaids	C	Template C	12	30

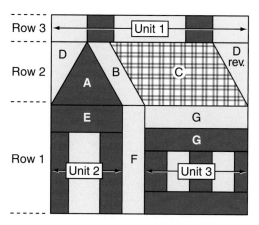

Cut sizes

E = 1¾" × 4½"
F = 1¾" × 6½"
G = 1¾" × 6¼"

Block Diagram

You will need to cut some of the strips into shorter lengths before assembling the Schoolhouse blocks, as follows:

• From the 1¾-inch red E strips, cut one 4½-inch-long E segment for each Schoolhouse block.

• From the 1¾-inch muslin F strips, cut one 6½-inch-long F segment for each Schoolhouse block.

• From the 1¾-inch red and muslin G strips, cut 6¼-inch-long G segments. You'll need two red and one muslin G piece for each Schoolhouse block.

Note: Cut and piece one sample block before cutting all the fabric for the quilt.

Piecing the Schoolhouse Blocks

Refer to the **Block Diagram** as you assemble the blocks. Rows 1 and 3 are pieced from rotary-cut strips and segments, which are labeled with letters and unit labels for easy reference. Row 2 pieces are cut from templates. Refer to the Quilt Sizes chart on page 131 to determine how many blocks you will need for the size quilt you are making.

Step 1. To make Row 3, sew a 2-inch red strip to either side of a 4½-inch muslin strip. Then add a 2½-inch muslin strip to either side of the red strips to complete Strip Set 1. See **Diagram 1.** Press the seams toward the red strips. Square up one end of the strip set and cut 2-inch segments from it, as shown. For the lap quilt, cut twelve segments. For the queen-size quilt, make two strip sets and cut a total of thirty segments.

Row 3

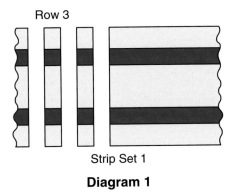

Strip Set 1

Diagram 1

Step 2. Sew a red A, a muslin B, a red plaid C, and muslin D and D reverse pieces together, as shown in **Diagram 2**, to complete Row 2 of the Schoolhouse block. Press the seams as desired and set aside. Make one Row 2 for each house.

Row 2

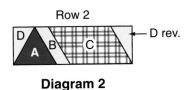

← D rev.

Diagram 2

Step 3. The house fronts are cut from Strip Set 2. To make the strip set, sew a 1½-inch red strip, a 2¼-inch muslin strip, and a 1¾-inch red strip together; see **Diagram 3.** Press seams toward the red strips. Square up one end of the strip set and cut 5-inch segments from it, as shown. Continue to make strip sets and cut segments until you have one unit for each house.

5"

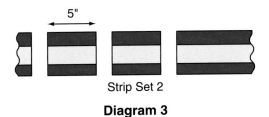

Strip Set 2

Diagram 3

Step 4. Referring to **Diagram 4**, sew a red E rectangle to the top edge of each unit. Add a muslin F segment to the right edge of each unit. Press the seams toward the red fabric.

Diagram 4

Step 5. To make the house sides, first make Strip Set 3. Sew together two red and two muslin 1¾-inch strips, alternating colors. To complete the strip set, add a 1¼-inch red strip to the outer muslin strip. See **Diagram 5.** Press the seams toward the red strips. Square up one end of the strip set and cut 2¾-inch segments from it, as shown. Continue making strip sets and cutting them into segments until you have one segment for each Schoolhouse block.

2¾"

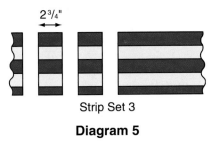

Strip Set 3

Diagram 5

Step 6. Referring to **Diagram 6**, sew a red G strip along the top and bottom edges of each segment. Add a muslin G strip along the top edge of each unit, as shown. Press the seams toward the red strip.

Step 7. Join the house fronts and sides in pairs, as shown in **Diagram 7**, to complete Row 1. Press the seams toward the house side.

Row 1

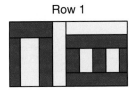

Diagram 6   **Diagram 7**

Step 8. Join Rows 1, 2, and 3 of each Schoolhouse block, as shown in the **Block Diagram** on page 132, carefully matching appropriate seams. Press the seams as desired.

Making the Sashing

Sashing Strips

Step 1. Sew a 1¾-inch muslin strip to each side of a 1¾-inch red strip, as shown in **Diagram 8**, to form Strip Set A. Press seams toward the red strip.

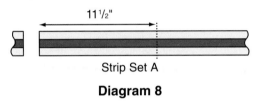

Diagram 8

Step 2. Square up one end of the strip set, then cut as many 11½-inch segments from it as possible. Save the leftover strip set pieces for the Nine-Patch sashing blocks. Make thirty-one sashing strips for the lap quilt or seventy-one for the queen size.

Nine-Patch Blocks

Step 1. From the leftover ends of the sashing strips, cut one 1¾-inch A segment for each Nine-Patch sashing square.

Step 2. Sew a 1¾-inch red strip to each side of a 1¾-inch muslin strip to make Strip Set B, as shown in **Diagram 9**. Press the seams toward the red strips. Square up one end of the strip set and cut as many 1¾-inch segments as possible. You will need two segments for each Nine-Patch sashing block.

Step 3. Sew a B segment to the top and bottom of an A segment, as shown in **Diagram 10**. Press as desired. Repeat to make twenty Nine-Patch blocks for the lap quilt or forty-two for the queen-size quilt.

Diagram 9   **Diagram 10**

Assembling the Quilt Top

Step 1. Lay out the Schoolhouse blocks, the Nine-Patch blocks, and the sashing strips, referring to the **Partial Lap Assembly Diagram** for placement. The queen-size quilt is laid out in the same manner; however, you will have seven sashing rows and six block rows. The queen-size quilt is five blocks wide.

Partial Lap Assembly Diagram

Step 2. Sew the Nine-Patch blocks and horizontal sashing strips together into rows. Sew the Schoolhouse blocks and the vertical sashing strips together into rows. In both types of rows, press the seams toward the sashing strips. Sew the rows together. Press.

Adding the Borders

Step 1. For either size quilt, measure the quilt top vertically, taking the measurement through the center of the quilt rather than along the sides. Trim two red borders to this length.

Step 2. Fold one strip in half crosswise and crease. Unfold it and position it along one side of the quilt top, with right sides together and the crease at the quilt's horizontal midpoint. Pin at the midpoint and ends first, then along the length of the entire side, easing in fullness if necessary. Sew the border to the quilt top, using a ¼-inch seam. Press the seam toward the border. Repeat, sewing the other border to the opposite side.

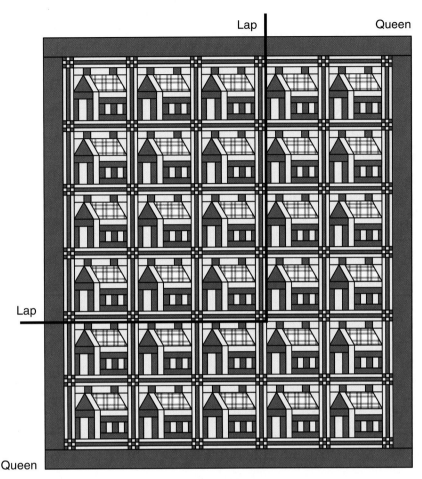

Quilt Diagram

Step 3. Measure the width of the quilt through the horizontal center, including the side borders. Trim the remaining red border strips to this length. In the same manner as for the side borders, pin the strips along one end of the quilt top, easing in fullness if necessary. Stitch the borders to the quilt top and press the seams toward the borders. See the **Quilt Diagram.**

Quilting and Finishing

Step 1. Mark the quilt top for quilting. The quilt shown is quilted in pairs of diagonal lines stitched ¼ inch apart. The pairs are spaced at 2-inch intervals across the inner portion of the quilt top. The red border is quilted in a series of math equations, such as 2 + 2 = 4. A miniature Schoolhouse is quilted in each corner.

Step 2. Regardless of which size quilt you're making, the backing will have to be pieced. For the lap quilt, cut the backing fabric in half crosswise and trim the selvages. Join the two pieces along the long edges and press the seam open. For the queen-size quilt, cut the backing fabric crosswise into three equal pieces, and trim the selvages. Sew the pieces together along the long edges, and press the seams away from the center panel. For more information on pieced quilt backs, see page 205.

Step 3. Layer the backing, batting, and quilt top; baste. Quilt as desired.

Step 4. Referring to the directions on page 206, make and attach double-fold bias binding using the red plaid fabric. You will need approximately 264 inches for the lap quilt and 380 inches for the queen size.

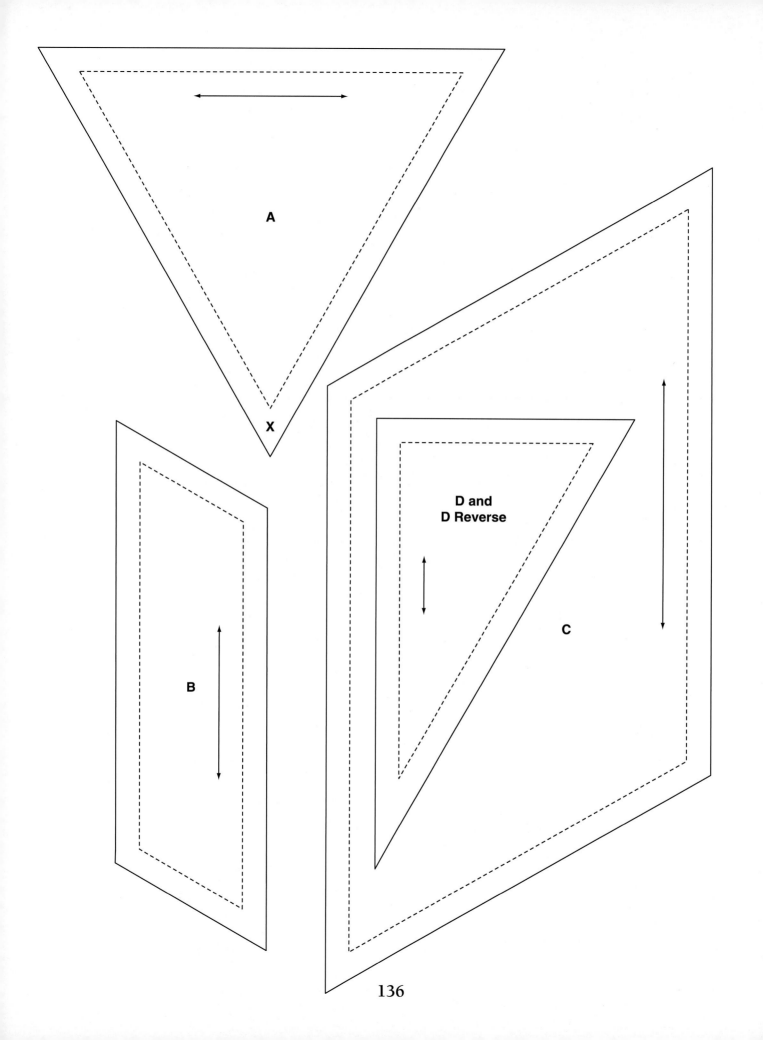

A

X

B

D and
D Reverse

C

136

One-Block Wonders

*D*o you love the look of a bed-size quilt but don't want to tackle something quite that large? There are lots of things you can make from just one block that can give you that same warm feeling of accomplishment. Use any of the quilt blocks in this book as inspiration to make something small and different the next time you're looking for a project without a lot of commitment. Reduce or enlarge the blocks as needed to suit the project.

• Make a block, bind it, and frame it under glass. Use acid-free framing supplies, and hang the block out of direct sunlight, just like you would any other quilted item. Or mount a block and frame it without glass. Framed blocks make a quick gift for a quilting friend, and they're also a great accessory to match a bed-size quilt if you decide to make one someday.

• Enlarge your favorite block and make a wall hanging. The larger pieces go together just as quickly as the smaller ones, but you'll have something really noticeable when you're done.

• Reduce the block pattern, and make a small pin for a wardrobe accessory.

• Need a name tag for your guild meetings? One block will do it. Quilt and bind the block like a small quilt, adding a large ribbon loop at the top of the block for hanging around your neck.

• Ornaments come in all sizes. Make several for your holiday tree, reducing the blocks as needed so they're not too overwhelming. Stitch a few extra to give as gifts.

• Soak up the compliments and drink drips with quilted coasters. Be sure to check the fabrics before you begin, to make sure the colors don't run. Make a matching table topper by enlarging the same block.

• If you've got to cook, you might as well have your quilting nearby. Use one block as the bib on an apron or several different blocks for quilted hot pads and trivets. Special heat-resistant fabric should be used with the batting when making projects that will be subjected to excessive heat.

• Fill a basket with lots of little stuffed pillows made from blocks that reflect the theme of the room.

Pickled Watermelon

Skill Level: Advanced

The Pickle Dish is a popular variation of the Wedding Ring quilt, with arcs made of triangles. Julee Prose of Iowa further adapted the pattern to create her unique double-size quilt. In Julee's quilt, the rings are not intertwined as in Double Wedding Ring quilts, and only one side of each melon shape has an arc of triangles. This allows the melon itself to be larger and take on the whimsical look of a watermelon wedge.

Before You Begin

The arcs of the quilt shown were hand pieced to ensure accuracy of placement of the vine motif in the green print. The directions given here are for machine piecing on paper foundations. The paper gets pulled away from the arcs before they are sewn to the melons.

Paper piecing is fast and fun, and it will give you accurate results. If you aren't familiar with sewing on a foundation, read through the project instructions carefully before beginning. For paper piecing, you will need to trace the C pattern sixteen times for the wallhanging or eighty times for the double-size quilt. For a quicker and easier way to prepare your paper foundations, see the "Sew Easy" box on page 141.

In addition to the foundation papers, you will need to make templates for the other pieces in the quilt. Patterns for pieces A, B, C, and D are on pages 145–147. If you prefer to hand piece or machine piece without using foundation papers, you will need to make a template for the triangles and square in the C arc.

Quilt Sizes

	Wallhanging	Double (shown)
Finished Quilt Size	45½" × 45½"	79½" × 96½"
Finished Ring Diameter	17"	17"
Number of Rings	4	20
Number of Pieced Arcs	16	80

Materials

Fabric	Wallhanging	Double
White-on-white print	2⅛ yards	9⅝ yards
Rose print	1½ yards	4½ yards
White-and-rose print	¾ yard	2½ yards
Green print	½ yard	2 yards
Assorted dark green prints	¼ yard	⅞ yard
Black solid	⅛ yard	¼ yard
Backing	3⅛ yards	7½ yards
Batting	53" × 53"	87" × 104"
Binding	½ yard	¾ yard

NOTE: *Yardages are based on 44/45-inch-wide fabrics that are at least 42 inches wide after preshrinking.*

This quilt is assembled with complete background A pieces, as well as with half-A and quarter-A pieces. Folding the A pattern piece, which is given as one-quarter of its full size, along the two straight edges will yield a full-size A template. To make templates for the half-A and quarter-A pieces that will go around the outer edges of the quilt, you will need to adapt the A pattern piece slightly.

To make a half-A template,

Cutting Chart

Fabric	Used For	Piece	Number of Pieces	
			Wallhanging	Double
White-on-white print	Background	A	5	32
	Background	Half-A	4	14
	Background	Quarter-A	4	4
Rose print	Melons	B	16	80
Black	Seeds	D	48	240

Fabric	Used For	Strip Width	Number of Strips	
			Wallhanging	Double
White-and-rose print	Arcs	2¼"	1 to start	1 to start
	Outer border	1½"	5	9
Green print	Arcs	2¼"	1 to start	1 to start
Assorted dark greens	Arcs	2¼"	1 to start	1 to start
Rose print	Inner border	5"	5	9

trace the pattern once, then flip it along one fold line and trace again. You then need to add a ¼-inch seam allowance along the long straight edge before cutting. To make the quarter-A template, trace the pattern as shown, then add a ¼-inch seam allowance along both straight edges before cutting.

For information on making and using templates, see page 186 in "Quiltmaking Basics."

Choosing Fabrics

The quiltmaker chose fabrics to enhance the watermelon theme. Rosy pink melons are dotted with black seeds and surrounded by green and white triangle rinds. All triangles in the pieced arcs repeat the same two prints. The squares at the ends of the arcs are sewn from an assortment of four dark green prints that closely match each other in color and value. Although the quiltmaker used a vine-striped fabric for her green rinds, we suggest that you avoid using fabrics with direc-

tional prints with the paper-piecing method.

If you prefer to use a directional print, we recommend that you make traditional see-through templates from the shapes in the C arc. You can then lay the templates over the fabric as you trace and cut to make sure your directional print is placed correctly. With this method, you would be more successful with hand piecing than with machine piecing.

To make pickled watermelons, you'll probably want to select similar colors to those used in the quilt shown. However, if you would like a completely different look, photocopy the **Color Plan** on page 215 and use colored pencils or crayons to create a color scheme that is uniquely yours.

Cutting

All measurements include ¼-inch seam allowances. Referring to the Cutting Chart, cut the required number of pieces for your quilt size. For the foundation piecing technique, cut individual pieces from the strips as you go along. We recommend cutting only one strip of each fabric to start, as you may find that you would like a slightly wider or narrower strip to work with.

Note: Cut and piece one sample ring before cutting all of the fabric for the quilt.

Piecing the Arcs

The arcs are pieced on paper foundations. With this method, an entire arc, represented by pattern piece C, is drawn full size on paper. The only seam allowance included is the one around the outer perimeter of the pattern piece. You will stitch your pieces directly to the paper, then remove the paper before sewing the arcs to the melon unit.

Sew Easy

You can trace templates with a hot-iron transfer pen or pencil, then use a medium-hot iron to transfer the image to paper foundations. You can usually get five or six prints from each tracing. Blank newsprint is a good choice for foundation piecing since it is sturdy enough to remain intact while you sew yet easy to tear away when you are finished with the quilt. Pads of newsprint in a variety of sizes are usually available at office- or school-supply stores.

Step 1. Template C consists of two halves—the left half and the right half. Trace one of each, then connect the halves, matching the dots. You will need one complete arc foundation for each pieced arc used in your quilt. If you have access to a photocopier that will make exact duplicates, it can be used to make copies. Trace the image as close to the center of your page as possible to help eliminate the distortion that sometimes takes place around the outer edges of photocopies. Make sure the page is perfectly flat against the

Sew Quick

Layer several sheets of tracing paper beneath your original tracing. Slip the stack under your sewing machine needle, and carefully stitch on all traced lines without thread in your machine. The punched holes are easy to see from either side of the tracing paper, and the additional perforations make the paper especially easy to tear away later. You can stitch about eight to ten sheets at a time.

copier's glass before beginning. Always compare copied images to the original templates before using them.

If you don't have access to a photocopier, trace each template individually. Use a fine-tip pen or a pencil sharpened often to keep lines narrow and uniform. This will help to ensure consistent seam lines and accurate piecing. This is the least desirable transfer method, however, since variations are more likely to occur when you make a large number of hand-drawn copies. See the "Sew Easy" and "Sew Quick" boxes for other transfer methods.

Step 2. Position a 2¼-inch strip of assorted dark green fabrics right side up at one end of the back side of the foundation, as shown in **Diagram 1.**

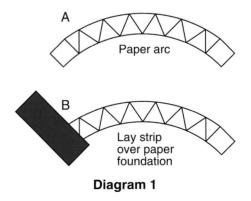

Diagram 1

Be sure that the fabric completely covers the end square on the pattern and that it also extends approximately ¼ inch past the line separating the square from the first triangle. If you are new to foundation piecing, you may find it easier at first to pin your first fabric in place. Do not sew yet.

Step 3. Position a 2¼-inch strip of assorted dark green fabric for the first triangle right side down on the foundation, as shown in **Diagram 2,** matching edges with the first dark green fabric where it overlaps the stitching line separating the two pieces. Hold or pin the two fabrics in place, flip the foundation over, and stitch directly on the line separating the square from the first triangle. Use a slightly shorter than normal stitch length, and begin and end the seam a few stitches past the drawn line.

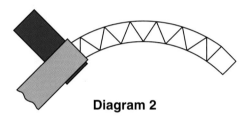

Diagram 2

Step 4. Turn to the reverse of the foundation and flip the second green strip right side up. Trim the seam allowance a bit if necessary to reduce bulk. Finger press the piece in place, or press with a warm iron. Cut away the excess tails from your fabric strips, but be sure to leave enough fabric to overlap the outer edges of the template. You must also leave enough of the second strip so that approximately ¼ inch of fabric overlaps all points of the line between the first and second triangles.

Step 5. Position a 2¼-inch white-and-rose print strip right side down on the foundation, as shown in **Diagram 3.** Holding the fabric in place, flip the foundation over, and sew along the line separating the first triangle from the second. Remove the foundation from your sewing machine, flip the foundation over, trim the seam allowance to a scant ¼ inch, and finger press. Continue adding green and white-and-rose pieces in the same manner until you have completed the arc.

Don't get confused about which direction your

fabric should be facing. The first piece of fabric is the *only* one placed right side up. All other pieces are positioned right side down for sewing. Also, remember that all fabric gets positioned on the back of the foundation paper, but all sewing takes place on the top, or right side, of the paper.

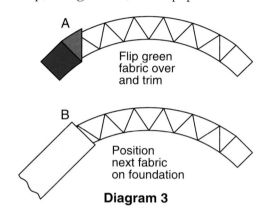

Diagram 3

Step 6. When all pieces have been sewn to the foundation, press with a warm iron. Using scissors or rotary-cutting equipment, cut on the outermost line of the foundation. Tear away the paper, taking care not to stretch the fabric.

Step 7. Repeat Steps 2 through 6 to construct the remaining pieced arcs required for your quilt.

Sew Easy

Paper piecing is a lot easier if you roughly trace the pattern from the right side of the paper to the back side. You will be stitching from the exact lines on the right side but positioning your fabrics from the wrong side. A rough tracing will help you align your fabrics so you won't come up short in the seam allowances. A light box or window is a big help for easier tracing.

Assembling the Rings

Step 1. Matching centers, sew a rose print B melon to each pieced arc, as shown in **Diagram 4.**

Press the seams toward the melons. Refer to page 191 in "Quiltmaking Basics" for more information about sewing curved seams.

Diagram 4

Step 2. Sew four melon/arc units to each full-size white-on-white background A piece, as shown in **Diagram 5.** Press the seams toward the melons. Again, refer to page 191 if you need more details on assembling these pieces. You will have leftover A pieces, which will be used to assemble the quilt top.

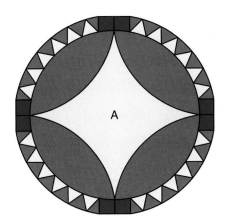

Diagram 5

Assembling the Quilt Top

Step 1. Using a design wall or other flat surface, lay out the completed rings in horizontal rows, along with the half-A and quarter-A pieces, as shown in the **Partial Assembly Diagram.**

Step 2. Beginning with the top row, connect the white background pieces to the first row of rings. Add the next row of background pieces, then the next row of rings. Continue sewing rows together until the quilt top is assembled. Press all seams away from the white background pieces.

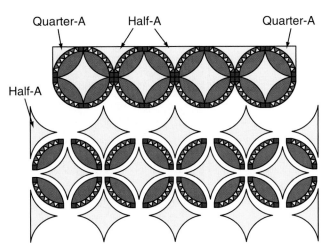

Partial Assembly Diagram

Remember to start and stop each seam ¼ inch from the ends of the white background pieces. Refer to page 191 for additional information about sewing curved seams.

Step 3. Using the appliqué technique of your choice, stitch three black seeds to each rose melon. Refer to the photograph on page 138 for placement. For information about appliqué techniques, refer to page 200.

Adding the Mitered Borders

The inner rose and outer white-and-rose print borders will be joined together first, then the two will be sewn to the quilt top as one unit.

Step 1. To determine the length of the side borders, measure the quilt top vertically through the center. To this measurement, add two times the finished width of the inner and outer borders (5½ inches × 2) plus approximately 5 inches. This is the length you need for each side border. In the same manner, measure the quilt top horizontally through the center, and calculate the length of the top and bottom borders.

Step 2. Sew the rose border strips together end to end to make a top, bottom, and two side borders in the sizes you've calculated. Sew the white-and-rose outer border strips together in the same

Double-Size Quilt Diagram

manner. Be sure to keep the side border strips separate from the top and bottom border strips.

Step 3. Pin and sew the rose border strips to the corresponding white-and-rose print strips. Press the seams toward the rose borders.

Step 4. Pin and sew the four borders to the quilt top, with the wide rose border on the inside. Refer to page 204 in "Quiltmaking Basics" for instructions on adding borders with mitered corners.

When preparing the miters, be sure to carefully match the two strips in adjacent borders. See the **Double-Size Quilt Diagram.**

Quilting and Finishing

Step 1. Mark the quilt top for quilting. The quilt shown has a floral motif in the center of each ring and in the borders. Outline quilting highlights the rings.

Step 2. Regardless of which quilt size you've chosen to make, the backing will have to be pieced. To make the backing for the wallhanging, cut the backing fabric crosswise into two equal lengths, and trim the selvages. From one length, cut a 13-inch-wide panel. Sew this narrow panel to one side of the full-width panel, as shown in **Diagram 6.** Press the seam open.

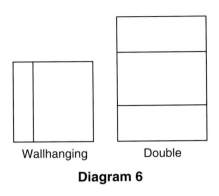

Wallhanging   Double

Diagram 6

Step 3. For the double-size quilt, cut the backing fabric crosswise into three equal lengths, and trim the selvages. Cut a 32-inch-wide panel from two of the segments, then sew one of these to each side of the full-width piece, as shown. Press the seams open.

Step 4. Layer the backing, batting, and quilt top, and baste. Quilt as desired.

Step 5. Make and attach double-fold binding, referring to the directions on page 206 in "Quilt-making Basics" for information. To calculate the amount of binding needed for your quilt size, add the length of the four sides of the quilt plus 9 inches. The total is the approximate number of inches of binding you will need.

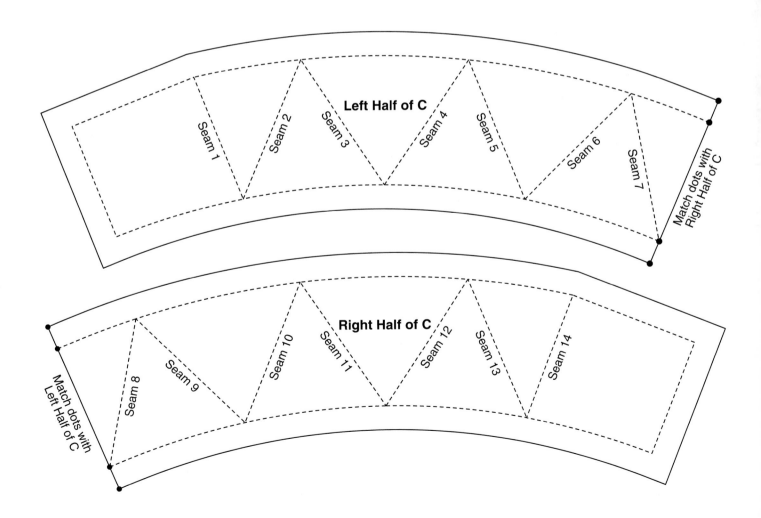

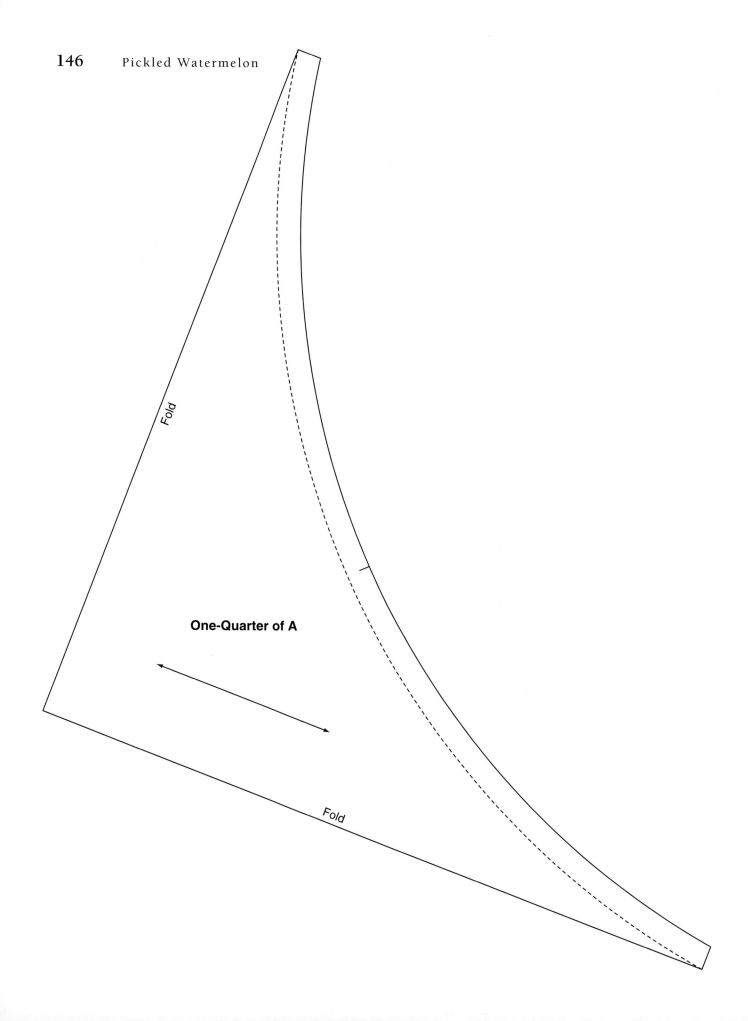

Fold

One-Quarter of A

Fold

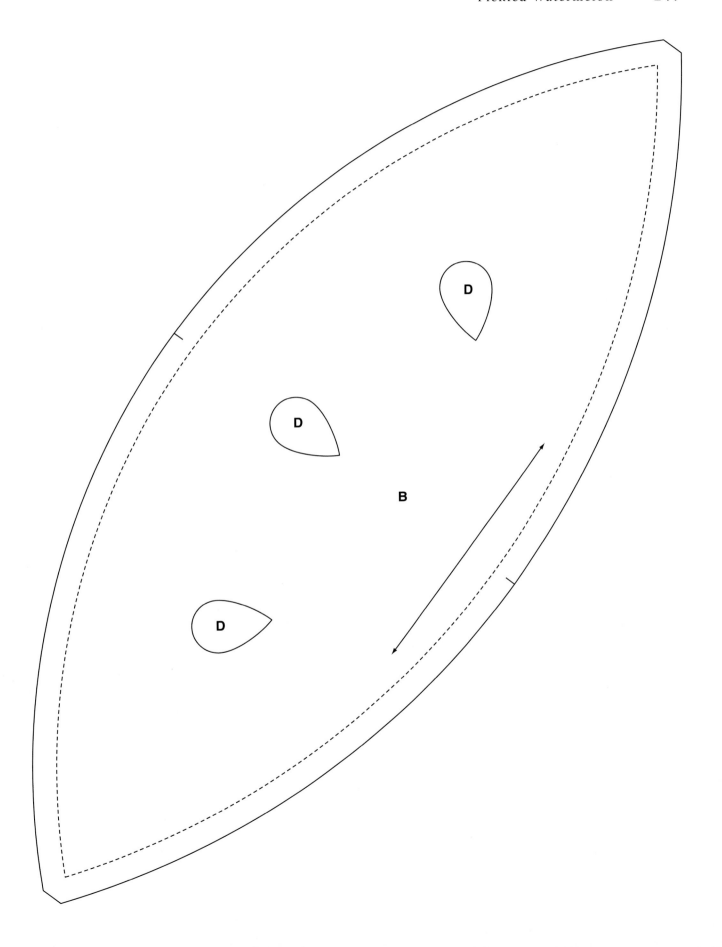

Amish Log Cabin

Skill Level: Challenging

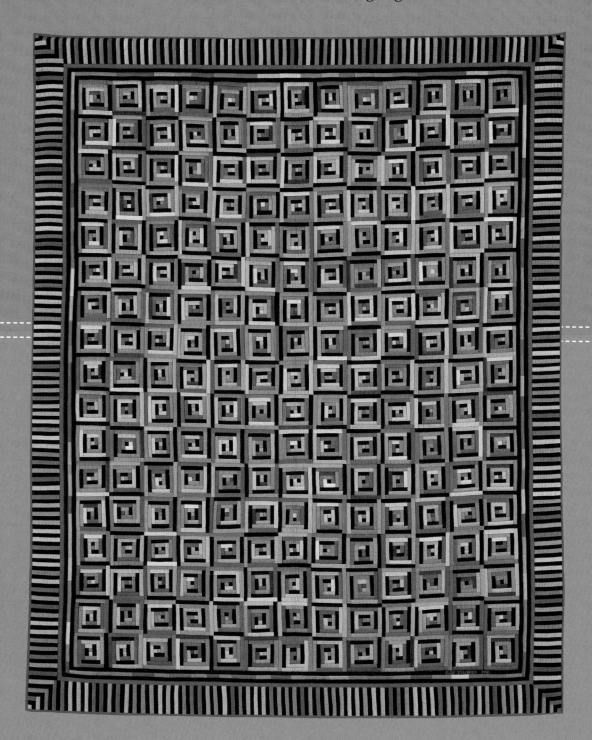

*T*his sparkling quilt is an explosion of color and movement. While
the deep, rich colors are traditional, the way they're used is not:
Instead of making all the blocks half dark and half light, quiltmaker
Elsie Schlabach mixed the colors and values in each block of this
twin-size quilt. The creative use of Off-Center Log Cabin blocks
creates the appearance of mitered corners on the pieced outer border.

Before You Begin

The directions for this quilt are written based on using the foundation method, which will make piecing the small blocks much easier. Read through the general construction directions in "Quiltmaking Basics," beginning on page 194, to become familiar with the foundation technique. Prepare a foundation for each block and corner block using the patterns on page 156. If you prefer to use the chain-piecing technique, see page 187 for details.

Choosing Fabrics

This quilt is comprised of only solid-color fabrics in what are generally thought of as Amish colors: blues, purples, greens, and reds, along with black. While the fabrics range in value from light to dark, the blocks are not strictly divided into light and dark halves, as with most Log Cabin blocks. Rather, the light and dark fabrics are sprinkled across the surface of the quilt, giving it a more spontaneous feeling.

Quilt Sizes

	Twin (shown)	Double	Queen
Finished Quilt Size	69½" × 87½"	83" × 101"	92" × 105½"
Finished Block Size	4½"	4½"	4½"
Number of Blocks	221	320	378

Materials

Fabric	Twin	Double	Queen
Assorted solids	10⅛ yards	14½ yards	17⅛ yards
Black	1¼ yards	1⅜ yards	1⅝ yards
Backing	5½ yards	7⅞ yards	8⅝ yards
Batting (optional)	76" × 94"	90" × 108"	98" × 112"
Binding	⅝ yard	¾ yard	¾ yard
Foundation material	4½ yards	5⅝ yards	6⅝ yards

NOTE: Yardages are based on 44/45-inch-wide fabrics that are at least 42 inches wide after preshrinking.

Don't worry about choosing fabrics that necessarily go together. Instead, select groups of solids based on their light, medium, and dark values.

The yardage requirements are generous estimates of the amounts actually used in the quilt. For a successful scrap quilt, variety is important, so you will likely start out with more yardage than indi-cated, but not all of it will be used. In addition to the pieced outer border, there are four narrow inner borders: two are black, one is pieced, and one is made from one of the fabrics used in the blocks. Decide on a color for this fourth border, and make sure you have at least ½ yard of it on hand—more if you also wish to use it extensively in the blocks.

149

Cutting Chart

Fabric	Strip Width	Number of Strips		
		Twin	Double	Queen
Assorted solids	1¼"	308	404	479
Border 4 fabric	1"	7	9	10
Black	1"	43	53	57

To help develop your own unique color scheme for the quilt, photocopy the **Color Plan** on page 216, and use crayons or colored pencils to experiment with different color arrangements.

Cutting

Referring to the Cutting Chart, cut the strips and borders needed for the quilt size you are making. Measurements for the borders include ¼-inch seam allowances. Cut all strips across the fabric width (crosswise grain). **Note:** Cut and piece one sample block before cutting all the pieces for the quilt.

The pieces in the block have a finished width of ½ inch. If you were piecing traditionally, you would cut 1-inch-wide strips. For the foundation method, begin by cutting 1¼-inch-wide strips from the fabrics. You may wish to decrease that width in ⅛-inch increments as you become more familiar with the technique, but don't cut pieces less than 1 inch wide.

The number of strips needed for logs is estimated based on using full-width yardage. If you are using scraps, the number of strips needed will vary.

To make sure that all the colors used in the inner quilt are also represented in the two pieced borders, cut one or two long strips of every color and set them aside. Cut additional strips as needed when assembling the borders.

Making the Foundations

Step 1. Make a template by enlarging the block pattern on page 156. Make a second template by tracing the full-size corner block pattern on page 156.

Step 2. Following the instructions on page 196 in "Quiltmaking Basics," transfer the pattern to your chosen foundation material. Make sure the marked lines are visible from the back side when you hold the foundation up to the light. Use the **Block Diagrams** as a reference for piecing order. Cut out the foundations, leaving a bit of extra material on all sides. Set the corner block foundations aside for now.

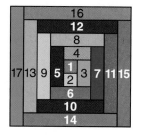 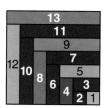

Corner Block

Block Diagrams

Piecing the Blocks

Make a sample block before cutting fabric for the entire quilt. If you experience problems while assembling the block, increase the strip width. Using strips slightly wider than necessary can be a real time-saver since not as much precision is required when positioning them for sewing. Reevaluate your work often. You may find that strip width can be decreased again once you are more familiar with the method.

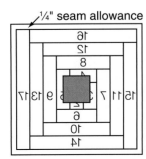

Sew Easy

If you have chosen to use the chain piecing method without a foundation, you'll need to cut the logs to length before sewing them. Refer to the list below to cut the strips into logs. The dimensions include ¼-inch seam allowances.

Log Number	Log Size
1, 2	1" × 1"
3, 4	1" × 1½"
5, 6	1" × 2"
7, 8	1" × 2½"
9, 10	1" × 3"
11, 12	1" × 3½"
13, 14	1" × 4"
15, 16	1" × 4½"
17	1" × 5"

The blocks in this quilt are not all clearly divided into dark and light halves. For best results, cut several strips of fabric in different colors and values and use them randomly to piece the sample block.

Step 1. Cut a 1¼-inch square of fabric for the block center, and place it right side up on the back side of a foundation, covering the area of piece 1, as shown in **Diagram 1.** Secure with tape, a bit of glue, or a pin. Hold the foundation up to the light with the back side away from you. You should be able to see a shadow of the square through the foundation. Check to make sure it extends past all lines surrounding piece 1.

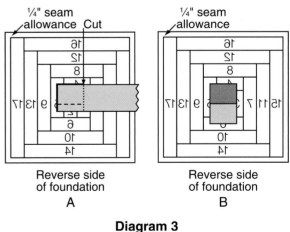

Reverse side of foundation

Diagram 1

Step 2. Select a strip of fabric for piece 2 and position it right side down on piece 1, as shown in **Diagram 2A.** Holding the fabric in position, flip the foundation to its front side and sew on the line separating pieces 1 and 2, as shown in **2B.** Begin and end the line of stitches approximately ⅛ inch on either side of the line.

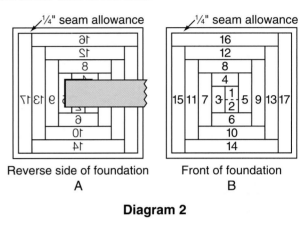

Reverse side of foundation
A

Front of foundation
B

Diagram 2

Step 3. Remove the foundation from the machine and flip it to the back side. If you used tape to secure the center piece, remove it now. Cut away the excess tail of fabric (cut just past the end of stitches, as shown in **Diagram 3A**). Flip piece 2 into a right-side-up position, finger pressing it into place. See **3B.**

Reverse side of foundation
A

Reverse side of foundation
B

Diagram 3

Step 4. Position the next strip right side down, as shown in **Diagram 4A** on page 152. Holding the strip in place, turn the foundation over and sew on the vertical line separating pieces 1 and 2 from piece 3, again beginning and ending approximately ⅛ inch on either side of the line. Remove from the machine, trim the tail, and flip piece 3 into a right-side-up position, finger pressing it into place, as shown in **4B**. Check to make sure all unsewn edges of piece 3 overlap seam lines around the piece's border.

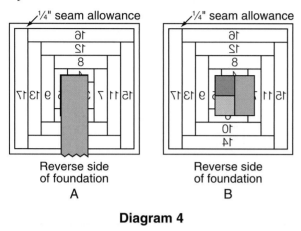

Diagram 4

Step 5. Continue to add pieces in numerical order. Remember to trim excess bulk from seam allowances, finger press each piece into place, and check to make sure the new piece overlaps all unsewn seam lines before stitching the next strip. After you have added the last piece, press with a warm iron, then cut on the outer line of the seam allowance.

Assembling the Quilt Top

Step 1. Lay out your blocks, rearranging them as necessary until you are satisfied with the color placement. Use the photo on page 148, the **Twin-Size Quilt Diagram,** or your own shaded drawing as a guide to block placement. Don't hesitate to flip blocks upside down or side to side if doing so improves the overall look of your quilt. As illustrated in **Diagram 5,** the blocks in the quilt shown don't all share the same orientation.

The **Twin-Size Quilt Diagram** illustrates the layout of the twin-size quilt, which has seventeen rows of thirteen blocks each. The layout for the

other two quilts is essentially the same: The double is made up of twenty rows with sixteen blocks in each, and the queen size has twenty-one rows with eighteen blocks in each.

Step 2. When you are satisfied with the layout, sew your blocks into rows, pressing the seams in opposite directions from row to row. If you are using removable foundations, tear away the portion surrounding the seam allowances where blocks were joined.

Note: Permanent foundations create additional bulk in the seam allowance. If seams are too bulky to press to one side, it may be necessary to press them open. Be sure to match and pin pressed-open seams carefully when rows are joined.

Step 3. Sew the rows together, carefully matching seams. Tear away all remaining portions of removable foundations. Press the seam allowances where rows were joined.

Making and Adding the Narrow Borders

This quilt has four narrow borders, each with a finished width of ½ inch. The first border is plain, the second is pieced, and the third and fourth are plain. There is also a wider pieced border that finishes at 3½ inches. **Diagram 6** is a detail of one corner of the quilt, showing how the borders and corner blocks work together.

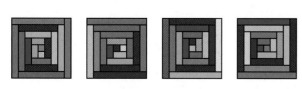

Diagram 5

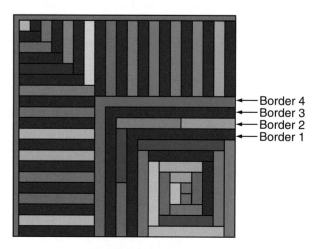

Diagram 6

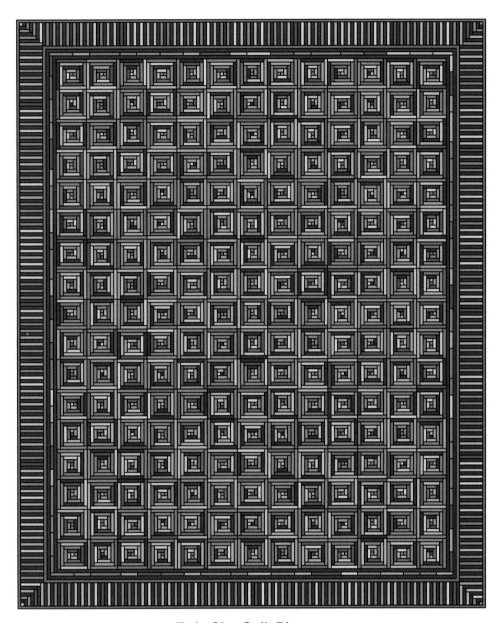

Twin-Size Quilt Diagram

Step 1. To make the three plain borders long enough, the 1-inch-wide strips must be sewn together end to end. Make all the side borders and all the top and bottom borders the same length to begin with, then trim them to the exact length later. For the twin-size quilt, sew two strips together for each side border, and sew one and a half strips together for each top and bottom border. For the double quilt, sew two and a half strips together for each side border, and sew two strips together for each top and bottom border. For the queen-size quilt, sew two and a half strips together for each of the four borders.

Step 2. To add the first border, measure the quilt from top to bottom, taking the measurement through the vertical center of the quilt, not at the sides. Cut two of the black side border strips to this length.

Step 3. Fold one strip in half crosswise and crease. Unfold it and position it right side down along one side of the quilt top, with the crease at the horizontal midpoint. Pin at the midpoint and ends first, then along the length of the entire side, easing in fullness if necessary. Sew the border to the quilt using a ¼-inch seam allowance.

Step 4. Repeat on the opposite side of the quilt.

Step 5. Measure the quilt from side to side, taking the measurement through the horizontal center of the quilt, not at the sides. Trim two of the black top and bottom border strips to this length. Add them to the quilt in the same manner as for the side borders.

Step 6. The next border is pieced from 1-inch-wide segments of various lengths cut from the same fabrics used in the blocks. Gather together all log segments left over from assembling the blocks. If necessary, trim them to 1 inch wide. Without sewing them together yet, arrange the segments into four long strips. As a general guideline for figuring the length of the strips, add 1 or 2 inches to the measurements you took for the first border. You will cut the strips to the exact length later. Cut additional 1-inch-wide segments if necessary, varying their length and color to create a pleasing design. As you lay out the segments, overlap the ends by 1/4 inch to compensate for seam allowances. When you are pleased with the appearance, begin sewing the segments together end to end, as shown in **Diagram 7**. Continue sewing until the strip length is slightly longer than required. Press the seams in one direction.

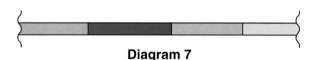

Diagram 7

Step 7. Measure and add the pieced border to the quilt top in the same manner as the black border, trimming each strip to the exact length required before sewing it to the quilt top.

Step 8. The third and fourth borders are plain and are added in the same manner as the first narrow black border. Use black strips for the third border and strips from one of the other colors for the fourth border. (The remaining black strips will be used in the pieced outer border.) Measure and trim the strips to length, and add them to the quilt sides first, then to the top and bottom.

Sew Easy

If color placement is not critical, the border strips can be strip pieced, then cut apart. Sew segments of varying lengths together end to end as described in Steps 6 and 7, but change the segment width to 2½ inches (the extra ½ inch will allow you to square up the strip if necessary). Make a 2½-inch-wide strip of calculated length (plus a bit extra) for side borders and another for top and bottom borders. After pressing, cut two 1-inch-wide strips from each pieced unit. Be sure to square up one side of the pieced unit before cutting the strips. Measure and trim each side strip to correct length. Flip the strips in opposite directions before sewing them to the quilt. Repeat for the top and bottom borders.

The same technique can be used to piece the wide outer borders. Cut the strips so they measure 1 × 8½ inches, and sew them together along the long edges. Make a strip set for the side borders and one for the top and bottom borders. After sewing the strips together and pressing them, square up one edge of each segment, then cut two 4-inch-wide pieces from each.

Making and Adding the Wide Border

The wide outer border is pieced from 1 × 4-inch strips of solid-color fabrics alternating with black. The alternating color scheme is continued in the corner blocks, giving the corners a mitered appearance.

Step 1. Measure the side border length as you did for the narrow borders. Divide the length by ½ inch, the finished size of each strip, and subtract 1 to allow for the seam allowance at each end. The result is the number of strips needed for the side border. For example, the side border on the twin quilt should measure approximately 81 inches. Divide by ½ (0.5) to get 162, then subtract 1. You will need 161 strips for each side border. If the actual length is not evenly divisible by ½, it may be necessary to ease in fullness as you pin the border to the sides of quilt.

Each border on the quilt shown begins and ends with a black strip. If you choose to follow the same layout, it may again be necessary to ease in fullness as you sew since actual seam allowances vary from quilter to quilter.

Step 2. Cut the black and color strips into 1 × 4¼-inch segments. (The extra ¼ inch allows for slight inaccuracies in aligning strips.) Lay out the strips, rearranging them until you are satisfied with the color placement. Sew the strips together, as shown in **Diagram 8**. Be very careful to match the strips exactly. Press all seams in the same direction. Measure the strip to be sure length is correct, then trim it to the correct 4-inch width. Make a second side border the same way.

Diagram 8

Step 3. Measure for the top and bottom borders now, before sewing the side borders to the quilt, and piece the top and bottom borders in the same way you did the side borders.

Step 4. Sew a pieced border to one side of the quilt, using the same method as for the narrow borders. Repeat on the opposite side.

Step 5. Referring to the **Block Diagrams** on page 150, make four corner blocks using the foundations prepared earlier.

Step 6. Sew a block to each end of the top and bottom borders, positioning the blocks so that piece 1 is always at the outermost corner of the quilt. Refer to the photo on page 148 and the **Twin-Size Quilt Diagram** on page 153 for correct positioning. Sew the top and bottom borders to the quilt.

Quilting and Finishing

Step 1. Mark the quilt top for quilting, if desired. The quilt shown is quilted along each seam line.

Step 2. Regardless of which quilt size you've chosen to make, the backing will have to be pieced. To make the most efficient use of the backing yardage, piece the back for the double and queen-size quilts with the seams running horizontally. For the twin-size quilt, piece the back with the seams running vertically. **Diagram 9** illustrates the three quilt backs. Begin by trimming the selvages from the fabric.

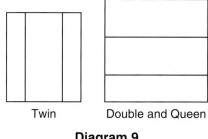

Twin   Double and Queen

Diagram 9

Step 3. For the twin-size quilt, divide the fabric crosswise into two equal pieces. Divide one of the pieces in half lengthwise, and sew one half to each side of the full-width piece. Press the seams open.

Step 4. For the double quilt, the backing should measure approximately 95 × 113 inches. Divide the yardage crosswise into three equal pieces, and sew two of the pieces together along the long edge. Measure the width of the joined pieces, and subtract the result from 113. This is the width of the strip you must cut from the third piece of fabric. Add the strip to the joined piece and press the seam open.

Step 5. For the queen-size quilt, the backing should measure approximately 104 × 118 inches. Divide the yardage crosswise into three equal pieces, and sew two of the pieces together along the long edge. Measure the width of the joined pieces, and subtract the result from 118 to find the width of the strip that must be cut from the remaining piece. Sew the strip to the joined piece and press the seam open.

Step 6. Layer the backing, batting if used, and quilt top, and baste. Quilt as desired.

Step 7. Referring to the directions on page 206 in "Quiltmaking Basics," make and attach double-fold binding. To calculate the amount of binding needed for the quilt size you are making, add up the length of the four sides of the quilt and add 9 inches. The total is the approximate number of inches of binding you will need.

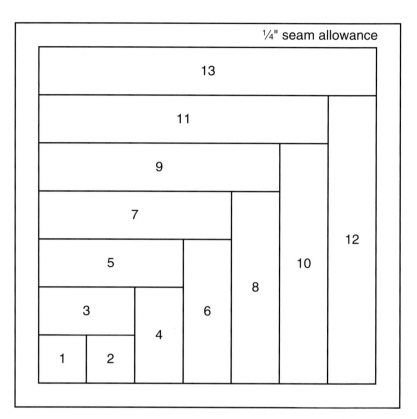

Corner Block Pattern

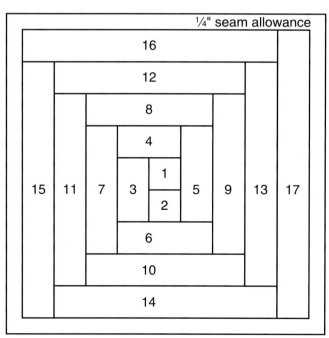

Block Pattern

Pattern shown is the mirror image of the finished block.
Note: Pattern is reduced. Enlarge it 150 percent before tracing.

Patch as Patch Can

Worn or damaged fabric in individual patches of a favorite and well-loved quilt needn't be cause for alarm. They *can* be repaired with just a few simple steps. Before you attempt any repairs, be sure the quilt does not have historical value or the repair could actual decrease the quilt's worth. Rare or historical quilts should only be handled by a professional conservator.

Here's how to replace a single patch:

1. Find or create a piece of replacement fabric slightly larger than the damaged area. If the quilt is fairly new, you may still be able to find the fabric. Older quilts present a greater challenge. Search vintage fabric sources for similar fabric or use a reproduction fabric from the same time period. Use a scanner to make creating your own fabric a breeze. Just scan the needed fabric and print it out onto a sheet of prepared photo transfer fabric. Be sure to create a piece larger than the damaged patch to allow for seams.

2. Photocopy the damaged patch onto a sheet of self-adhesive label paper to create a template. Cut out the template, peel off the backing, and adhere it to the replacement fabric, matching the grain. Cut the replacement patch ¼ inch larger than the template on all sides.

3. With the template still adhered, pin the replacement patch over the damaged area, placing the pins in the seam allowance. Pin only through the top layer of the quilt.

4. Appliqué the patch in place, avoiding the batting and backing layers. Remove the template.

5. Mimicking the original thread and stitch length as closely as possible, requilt the patch. Do not use a hoop.

Homespun Houses

Skill Level: Easy

An abundant collection of country plaids, checks, and stripes lends a "welcome home" feeling to Gerry Sweem's rendition of this old-time favorite design. Take the chill off a cold winter evening with this cozy king-size charmer, or scale it down in size for a special child.

Before You Begin

With the exception of a few simple shapes that require templates, most of the pieces are strips that can be rotary cut. Fabrics can be layered for even more efficient cutting.

You'll find general information and special tips to help you in constructing the basic Schoolhouse block in "Quiltmaking Basics," beginning on page 189.

Choosing Fabrics

While the set of this quilt is simple and straightforward, the choice of fabric makes it something truly special. Except for the borders, where specific yardages are required, each block is a scrap-happy combination that utilizes small bits and pieces of various plaid, checked, and striped fabrics in rich country shades.

It may take a little while to collect the variety of fabrics needed, but the end result is definitely worth it. You may want to substitute an occasional floral, paisley, or other print fabric to help you reach your goal.

The **Block Diagram** on page 161 is shaded to indicate placement of the key fabrics. There are two main fabrics in each block:

the "schoolhouse" fabric and the "background" fabric. The other fabrics can match each other or not, according to your preference. In some blocks, you may select the same fabric for the door, windows, and chimneys. In another block, you may experiment with a different fabric for each. The ultimate decision will be made by the number and size of the fabrics in your collection

and how scrappy a look you'd like in the finished quilt.

You'll notice there is no specific light/dark formula for the blocks in this quilt. Sometimes, the house is dark while the background is light. In other blocks, the opposite is true. The key is to maintain some contrast in value so the house stands out against the sky, and the door and windows are distinguishable from the rest of the

Quilt Sizes

	Twin	King (shown)
Finished Quilt Size	65" × 88"	99½" × 99½"
Finished Block Size	11½"	11½"
Number of Blocks	24	49

Materials

Fabric	Twin	King
Dark brown check	2⅛ yards	2½ yards
Tan plaid	2¼ yards	2¾ yards
Black-and-brown plaid	2⅜ yards	2⅞ yards
Assorted plaids, checks, and stripes	3¾ yards	6 yards
Backing	5¼ yards	9 yards
Batting	73" × 96"	108" × 108"
Binding (red plaid)	¾ yard	⅞ yard

NOTE: *Yardages are based on 44/45-inch-wide fabrics that are at least 42 inches wide after preshrinking.*

Cutting Chart

Fabric	Used For	*Lengthwise* Strip Width	Number to Cut Twin	Number to Cut King
Dark brown check	Border 1	2"	4	4
Tan plaid	Border 2	3½"	4	4
Black-and-brown plaid	Border 3	5½"	4	4
Red plaid	Binding	27" × 27"	1	
		31" × 31"		1

Fabric	Used For	Dimensions	Number to Cut per Block
Each Schoolhouse plaid	L	1¾" × 6¼"	1
	G	1¾" × 5½"	1
	I	1¾" × 3¾"	1
	M	1½" × 6¼"	1
	K	1½" × 3¾"	2
	C	Template C	1
Each block background	H	1¼" × 6¾"	1
	N	1¼" × 6¼"	1
	B	Template B	1
	O	2½" × 4"	1
	Q	2½" × 3"	2
	D and D reverse	Template D	1 each
Each window plaid	J	1¾" × 3¾"	2
Each door plaid	E	2" × 5½"	1
Each chimney plaid	P	2" × 2½"	2
Each roof plaid	A	Template A	1

house. The contrast can be as strong or as subtle as you wish, but a mix of light and dark houses and high and low contrast blocks makes for the most visually exciting quilt. Don't be afraid to experiment!

Cutting

All measurements include ¼-inch seam allowances. Referring to the Cutting Chart, cut the required number of strips in the sizes needed. Cut border strips along the *lengthwise* grain (parallel to the selvage). Strips for the Schoolhouse blocks may be cut either lengthwise or crosswise.

For ease of construction, rotary cutting dimensions are given with the **Block Diagram**. For example, the piece labeled G does not require a template to cut. The letter label is given for easy

reference. Because some of the pieces are similar but not identical, it is helpful to label your stacks of pieces by their letters.

Make templates for pieces A, B, C, and D using the full-size pattern pieces on page 164. See page 186 for complete details on making and using templates. Cut one piece A, B, C, D, and D reverse for each block, as directed in the Cutting Chart. Place templates A and D wrong side up on the wrong side of the fabric to trace your pieces. Then turn template D over to trace D reverse pieces.

In the quilt shown, the block in the top left corner is facing the opposite direction from all of the other houses. To make a similar block for your quilt, you will need to cut the A and B pieces for that block with the template right side up on the wrong side of the fabric.

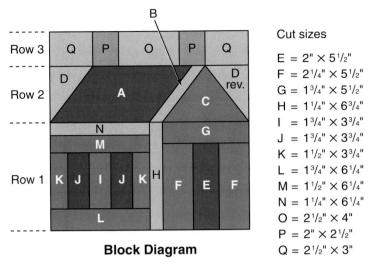

Block Diagram

Cut sizes

E = 2" × 5½"
F = 2¼" × 5½"
G = 1¾" × 5½"
H = 1¼" × 6¾"
I = 1¾" × 3¾"
J = 1¾" × 3¾"
K = 1½" × 3¾"
L = 1¾" × 6¼"
M = 1½" × 6¼"
N = 1¼" × 6¼"
O = 2½" × 4"
P = 2" × 2½"
Q = 2½" × 3"

Note: Cut and piece one sample block before cutting all the fabric for the quilt.

Piecing the Schoolhouse Blocks

Refer to the **Block Diagram** as you assemble each block. Before stitching any units together, lay out all the pieces for one block to ensure that you're happy with your fabric choices.

Step 1. To make the front of the house, sew an F house fabric piece to either side of an E door fabric piece along the long sides, as shown in **Diagram 1**. Press seams toward the darker fabric. Add a G house fabric strip above the door, then sew an H background fabric strip to the left of the unit, referring to the diagram. In each case, press the seam toward the newly added piece.

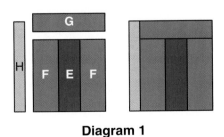

Diagram 1

Step 2. Sew a J window fabric piece to either side of an I house fabric piece along the long sides. Add K house fabric strips to each end of the unit, referring to **Diagram 2**. Press all seams toward the darker fabric. Add an L house fabric piece to the

bottom of the window unit and an M house fabric piece along the top edge. Then sew an N background fabric strip to the top of the window unit, as shown. In each case, press the seam toward the newly added piece.

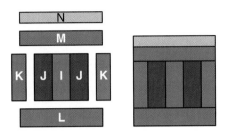

Diagram 2

Step 3. Join the house front to the window unit, as shown in **Diagram 3**, to complete Row 1. Press the seam toward the house front and set aside.

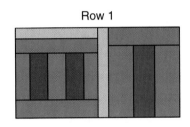

Diagram 3

Step 4. Sew an A, B, C, D, and D reverse piece together to form Row 2, as shown in **Diagram 4**. The C house peak should be cut from your house fabric, and the D and D reverse pieces should match the background fabric in Row 1. Choose any contrasting fabric for the A roof piece. Press the seams so they are in the opposite direction of the seams they will meet in Row 1, then set aside.

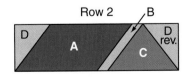

Diagram 4

Step 5. For Row 3, sew a P chimney fabric piece to either side of an O background fabric piece. Sew a Q background fabric piece to each end of the row. See **Diagram 5.** Press the seams to one side.

Row 3

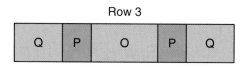

Diagram 5

Step 6. Join Rows 1, 2, and 3, referring to the **Block Diagram** on page 161. Carefully match any appropriate seams. Press the seams as desired.

Step 7. Repeat Steps 1 through 6, making twenty-four blocks for the twin or forty-nine blocks for the king.

Step 8. To make an opposite facing block, as in the top left corner of the quilt shown, piece one of your blocks with the house front unit sewn to the left of the window unit. Then piece Row 2 in reverse order, using the A and B pieces cut with the template right side up on the fabric. Row 3 is constructed in the same manner as for all other blocks.

Assembling the Quilt Top

Step 1. Referring to the **Quilt Diagram,** lay out the Schoolhouse blocks for a pleasing visual balance of lights and darks and occasional brights.

Step 2. Sew the blocks together in horizontal rows. Press the seams in opposite directions from row to row. Sew the rows together, carefully matching seams where the blocks meet. Press.

Adding the Borders

This quilt is surrounded by three borders, and each is added in the same sequence: the two side strips are attached first, followed by the top and bottom strip of the same fabric. Piece together border strips as necessary. Then, following the directions for Steps 1–4, trim them to the necessary length when they are added to the quilt top.

The procedure for adding borders is the same whether you are making the twin-size or the king-size quilt. Only the length of the strips will vary.

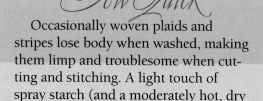

Occasionally woven plaids and stripes lose body when washed, making them limp and troublesome when cutting and stitching. A light touch of spray starch (and a moderately hot, dry iron) will restore crispness.

Step 1. Measure the quilt from top to bottom, taking the measurement through the center of the quilt, not the sides. Cut two dark brown check side borders to this length.

Step 2. Fold one strip in half crosswise and crease. Unfold it and position it right side down along one side of the quilt top, with the crease at the quilt's center. Pin at the center and ends first, then along the entire side, easing in fullness if necessary. Sew the border to the quilt top. Press the seam toward the border. Repeat on the opposite side.

Step 3. Measure the width of the quilt through the horizontal center of the quilt and including the side borders. Cut two dark brown check border strips to this length. In the same manner as for the side borders, position, pin, and stitch the border to the quilt top. Press the seam toward the border. Repeat on the opposite end.

Step 4. In the same manner, add the tan plaid borders to the sides, then the top and bottom of the quilt top, followed by the black-and-brown plaid border strips.

Quilting and Finishing

Step 1. Mark the quilt top for quilting. The quilt shown is quilted in an overall Baptist Fan pattern, as shown in **Diagram 6.**

Diagram 6

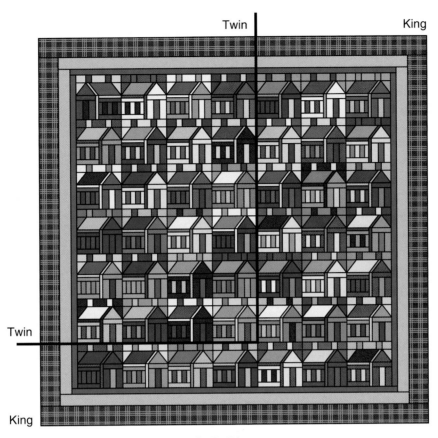

Twin

King

Twin

King

Quilt Diagram

Step 2. Regardless of which size quilt you're making, you'll need to piece the backing. For the twin-size quilt, cut the backing fabric in half crosswise, and trim the selvages. Cut one piece in half lengthwise, and sew one half to each side of the full-width piece. Press seams away from the center.

For the king-size quilt, cut the backing fabric crosswise into three equal pieces. Trim the selvages and sew the pieces together along the long edges. Press the seams away from the center panel. See page 205 for more information on making quilt backings.

Step 3. Layer the backing, batting, and quilt top; baste the layers together.

Step 4. Quilt all marked designs, adding any additional quilting as desired.

Step 5. Referring to the directions on page 206, make and attach double-fold bias binding. Use the square of red plaid fabric that has been set aside for this purpose. For the twin-size quilt, you will need approximately 316 inches; for the king-size quilt, you will need approximately 408 inches.

Sew Easy

The yardage requirements for this quilt include enough fabric to cut the border strips lengthwise from the fabric so you can take advantage of the stability of the lengthwise grain and eliminate the need for seaming.

Use the leftovers creatively—in some of the house blocks, to make a hanging sleeve, or for a quilt label. Or, like the maker of this quilt, plan a special design for a completely reversible quilt!

**D and
D Reverse**

A

C

B

Key:

C

A

Adding the Antique Look

You don't have to wait decades for your quilts to achieve the same vintage look as Grandma's. Use any or all of the following approaches to create an heirloom for tomorrow that looks like it came from yesteryear.

• Search out vintage fabrics from antique dealers. They can be expensive, but these fabrics are as authentic as it gets. Create an entire quilt if you're lucky enough to find enough fabric or incorporate a few pieces of antique yard goods with current fabrics. A less expensive alternative is to salvage useable pieces of fabric from old garments.

• Fabric manufacturers go to great lengths to research prints from the past and reproduce them for today's quilters. You can find fabrics representative of nearly every increment of time from the mid-1700s to the 1950s. Pair your fabric selection with a pattern from that same era for a truly authentic look.

• Soften your color palette by using cream or tan fabrics in place of white. White fabrics used in quilts from the past rarely stay white over a long period of time.

• Quilts from the late nineteenth century often included a maverick block. Mavericks are blocks that are slightly different than the rest of the blocks used in the quilt.

• If you are using new fabrics, soak them in strong tea to give them a consistent, old look. You can also use tea or coffee to create stains like those often found on older quilts.

• Overdyeing some or all of your fabrics can also create an older look. Overdyeing is a technique used to change the color of a fabric by dyeing over it with another color.

• Age your fabrics in a diluted bleach solution or leave them in the sun to fade. You can also buy fabric fading kits to help you achieve the same result.

• Prewash your fabrics but not your batting. If you've used a cotton or cotton-blend batting, the batting will shrink slightly when the completed quilt is washed and give you the look and feel of a much-loved older quilt.

Plaid Double Wedding Ring

Skill Level: Intermediate

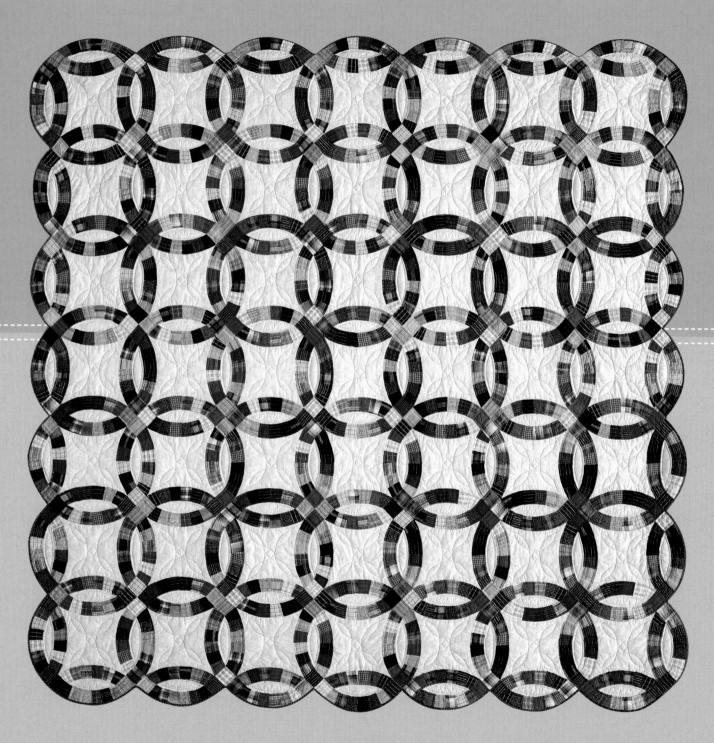

The straight lines of woven plaids and stripes may not seem like an obvious match with the graceful curves of the Wedding Ring pattern, yet they work together very well in this cozy rendition of the classic Double Wedding Ring. Cleo Snuggerud stitched this double-size quilt using a technique developed by John Flynn. The directions that follow are for traditional template construction.

Before You Begin

If this is your first Double Wedding Ring quilt, be sure to read "Quiltmaking Basics," beginning on page 191, before starting the project. Although each pattern in this book contains specific information for its own unique assembly, many aspects of construction are similar from quilt to quilt.

You will need to make templates from pattern pieces A, B, C, D, and E on page 171. For information about making and using templates, see page 186 in "Quiltmaking Basics."

Choosing Fabrics

The rings of this quilt are pieced from an assortment of plaids and stripes in mostly subdued colors, but don't be afraid to mix in a few bright colors for pizzazz, as this quiltmaker did. The yardages for the plaids and stripes listed in the Materials chart are an estimate of the total amount required. For best results, buy small cuts of many plaid and striped fabrics until you've accumulated the total number of yards required for your quilt size.

Quilt Sizes

	Wallhanging	Double (shown)
Finished Quilt Size	52" × 52"	86½" × 86½"
Finished Ring Diameter	17"	17"
Number of Rings	16	49
Number of Pieced Arcs	80	224

Materials

Fabric	Wallhanging	Double
Assorted plaids and stripes	3 yards	8½ yards
Muslin	1⅞ yards	4⅞ yards
Backing	3¼ yards	8⅛ yards
Batting	60" × 60"	95" × 95"
Binding	¾ yard	1 yard

NOTE: *Yardages are based on 44/45-inch-wide fabrics that are at least 42 inches wide after preshrinking.*

The quilt shown was made entirely from woven plaids and stripes, not printed fabrics. The woven designs give the quilt a homespun feel, one that is softer than what would have been achieved with printed plaids.

If you've never worked with woven plaids, you should note that the weave is usually a little looser than that of printed cot-tons, which means they can fray and shift more easily. Don't let that word of caution prevent you from using woven plaids, however. The result is definitely worth the effort.

To develop your own color scheme for the quilt, photocopy the **Color Plan** on page 213, and use crayons or colored pencils to experiment with different color arrangements.

Cutting Chart

Fabric	Used For	Piece	Number of Pieces	
			Wallhanging	Double
Muslin	Background	A	16	49
	Melons	B	40	112
Assorted plaids and stripes	Connecting wedges	C	80	224
	Outer wedges of arcs	D	80	224
	Outer wedges of arcs	D reverse	80	224
	Inner wedges of arcs	E	320	896

Cutting

All measurements include ¼-inch seam allowances. Referring to the Cutting Chart, cut the required number of pieces for your quilt size. Each piece was cut with the straight of grain running through its vertical center rather than with the grain aligned with its straight side edge.

Note: Cut and piece one sample ring before cutting all of the fabric for the quilt.

Sew Easy

Because woven plaids and stripes may shift, especially when handling small pieces, try misting your pieces with spray starch. This added bit of stiffness will enable you to line up the edges of the fabric pieces and use an assembly line piecing technique.

Piecing the Arcs

Step 1. Stack the D, D reverse, and E pieces in separate piles. For a scrappy look, mix the plaids and stripes within each pile, then simply pull a piece off the stack when sewing. Begin each pieced arc with a D piece. To the right of it, sew a succession of four E pieces, as shown in **Diagram 1**. End with a D reverse piece. As you sew, be sure pieces

are oriented so that curves arch in the same direction, as shown. Gently press seams to one side, taking care not to stretch the unit. Repeat until you have assembled all the arcs required for your quilt.

Diagram 1

Step 2. Center and sew a pieced arc to one side of each muslin B melon, as shown in **Diagram 2**. Refer to page 191 in "Quiltmaking Basics" for specific information and advice on assembling the pieces common to most Wedding Ring quilts. Press seams toward the melons. You will use half of the pieced arcs for this step.

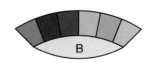

Diagram 2

Step 3. Sew a plaid C piece to each end of the remaining arcs, as shown in **Diagram 3**.

Diagram 3

Step 4. Center and sew these longer pieced arcs to the arc/melon units already assembled. See **Diagram 4**. Press all seams toward the melons. Again, refer to page 191 for more detailed information about sewing curved seams.

Diagram 4

Assembling the Quilt Top

Step 1. Referring to **Diagram 5**, sew the completed arc/melon units to the background A pieces. Be sure to start and stop your seams ¼ inch from each end.

Make 1 for either size.

Make 6 for wallhanging. Make 12 for double.

Make 9 for wallhanging. Make 36 for double.

Diagram 5

Then use a design wall or other flat surface to lay out the units in rows, as shown in the **Partial Assembly Diagram.** The double-size quilt will have seven rows of seven rings each. The wallhanging will have four rows of four rings each.

Step 2. Sew the units together into rows. Sew the rows together to complete the quilt top, as shown in the **Double-Size Quilt Diagram** on page 170 When you sew the units and rows together, you will need to start and stop stitching ¼ inch from each end of the arc. See page 193 for detailed information about assembling the rows.

Quilting and Finishing

Step 1. Mark the quilt top for quilting. In the quilt shown, the rings were outline quilted and have a floral motif in the center.

Step 2. Regardless of which quilt size you have chosen to make, the backing fabric will have to be pieced. **Diagram 6** on page 170 shows the layout for both quilt backs. For the wallhanging, cut the backing fabric in half crosswise, and trim the selvages. Cut one piece in half vertically. Cut a 21-inch-wide panel from the remaining piece. Sew a half-segment to each side of the 21-inch panel.

Step 3. For the double-size quilt, cut the backing fabric crosswise into three equal lengths, and trim the selvages. Cut a 28-inch-wide panel

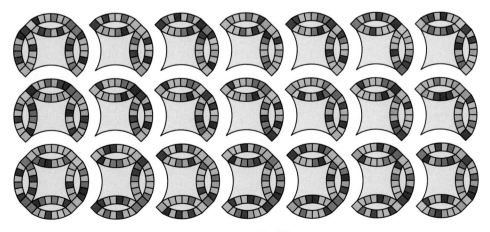

Partial Assembly Diagram

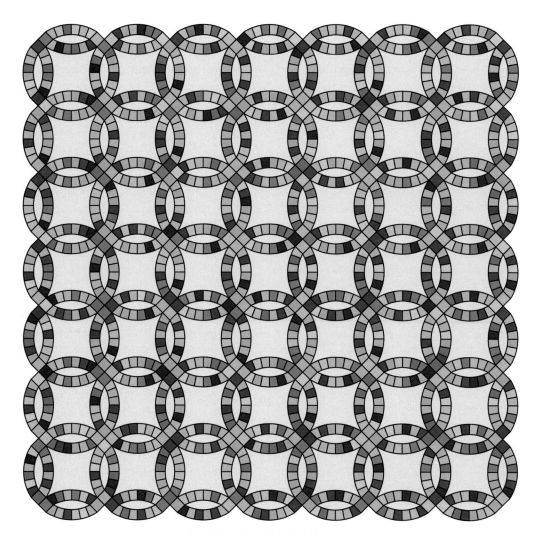

Double-Size Quilt Diagram

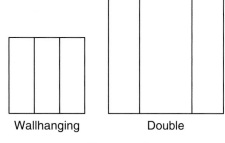

Wallhanging   Double

Diagram 6

from two of the pieces. Sew a 28-inch-wide panel to each side of the full-width panel, as shown. Press the seams open.

Step 4. Layer the backing, batting, and quilt top, and baste. Quilt as desired.

Step 5. Use narrow bias binding to bind the quilt. See page 208 for information about making bias binding and applying it around curves.

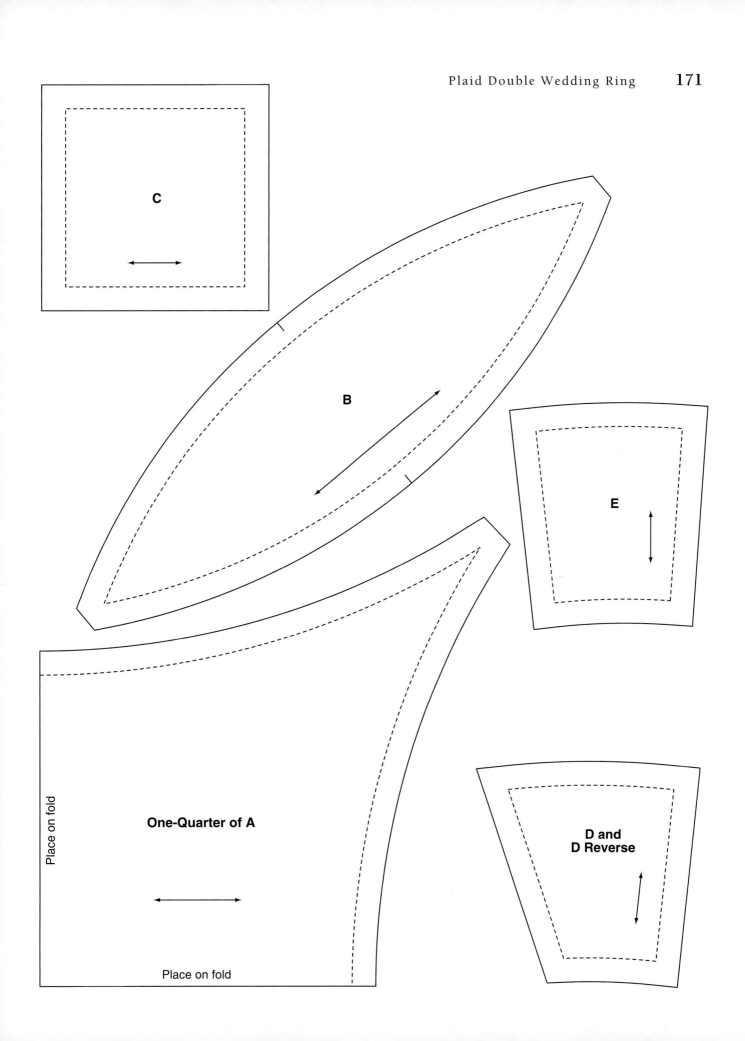

C

B

E

One-Quarter of A

Place on fold

Place on fold

D and
D Reverse

Teacher of the Year

Skill Level: Easy

$\mathcal{T}$his twin-size quilt, with its strong colors, clever quilting motifs, and creative set, was designed for a favorite schoolteacher, who just happened to be quiltmaker Miriam Dean's daughter! Large, simple shapes and easy strip piecing make sewing a snap, while the manageable size is perfect for that special teacher or young scholar in your life.

Before You Begin

With the exception of a few simple shapes that require templates, all of the pieces are strips and squares that can be rotary cut. In addition, an easy strip-piecing technique is used to assemble large portions of each Schoolhouse block. These blocks go together very quickly and easily since there are no set-in seams.

Beginning on page 189 in "Quiltmaking Basics," there is more general information about constructing the Schoolhouse block, as well as more specific details on strip-piecing techniques.

Choosing Fabrics

This is a quilt that lends itself equally well to subtle prints, splashy textures, crayon-bright solids—or any combination!

Making the blocks from the same fabrics, as this quiltmaker has done, enables you to use quick-cutting and strip-piecing techniques. The result is a crisp, visually striking design. If you don't mind sacrificing speed for variety, however, you might enjoy raiding your scrap bag to give each house its own fabric twist.

Quilt Size

Finished Quilt Size	60½" × 80½"
Finished Block Size	10"
Number of Blocks	
Schoolhouse	18
Apple	1
Block 1	12
Block 2	4

NOTE: *Because the specific block arrangement is critical to the overall design of the quilt, no variations in size or layout are provided.*

Materials

Fabric	Amount
Navy print	2 yards
Muslin	2⅞ yards
Red print	1⅔ yards
Dark green print	⅓ yard
Black subtle print	½ yard
Gray subtle print	⅛ yard
Backing	3¾ yards
Batting	66" × 86"
Binding	¾ yard

NOTE: *Yardages are based on 44/45-inch-wide fabrics that are at least 42 inches wide after preshrinking.*

To develop a unique color scheme for the quilt, photocopy the **Color Plan** on page 212, and use colored pencils to experiment with different color arrangements.

Cutting

All of the measurements include ¼-inch seam allowances. Refer to the Cutting Chart on page 174 and cut the required number of strips in the sizes

Cutting Chart

Fabric	Used For	Strip Width	Number of Strips	Second Cut Dimensions	Number to Cut
Navy print	Borders*	5½"	4		
	Block 1	10⅞"	1	10⅞" squares	6
	Block 2	11¼"	1	11¼" square	1
Muslin	Unit 1	2¾"	1		
	Unit 1	5¾"	1		
	Unit 2	3"	1		
	Units 3 and 5	1¼"	5		
	Unit 4	1¾"	2		
	A	Template A			18
	C	Template C			18
	E	Template E			18
	G	Template G			18
	G reverse	Template G			18
	J	1¼"	6	1¼" × 6¾"	36
	Block 1	10⅞"	3	10⅞" squares	8
	Block 2	11¼"	1	11¼" square	1
	Center square			10½" square	1
Red print	D	Template D			18
	H	1¼"	2	1¼" × 4½"	18
	I	1¼"	3	1¼" × 5¼"	18
	Unit 2	1¼"	2		
	Units 3 and 5	1¼"	5		
	Unit 4	1¼"	3		
	Apple	Apple template	1		
	Corner squares	5½"	1	5½" squares	4
Dark green	K	2"	5	2" × 10½"	18
	Leaf	Leaf template			1
Black print	B	Template B			18
	F	Template F			18
	Stem	Stem template			1
Gray print	Unit 1	3"	1		

Cut border strips on the lengthwise grain.

needed. Cut the navy print fabric first, cutting the border strips and strips for the large navy triangles along the lengthwise grain (parallel to the selvage). Cut the balance of the strips across the fabric width (crosswise grain).

Make templates for pieces A, B, C, D, E, F, and G, as well as for the apple, stem, and leaf appliqués, using the full-size pattern pieces on page 180. The templates, with the exception of the ap-

pliqué pieces, include ¼-inch seam allowances. Refer to page 186 for complete details on making and using templates.

The Cutting Chart indicates how many of each piece to cut with each template. Place the A, C, E, F, G, and apple, leaf, and stem templates wrong side up on the wrong side of the fabric to cut those pieces.

Turn the G template over to cut G reverse. The

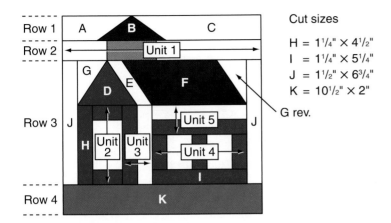

Cut sizes

H = 1¼" × 4½"
I = 1¼" × 5¼"
J = 1½" × 6¾"
K = 10½" × 2"

Schoolhouse Block Diagram

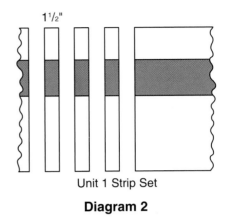

Unit 1 Strip Set

Diagram 2

B and D patterns are symmetrical, so they can be placed faceup or facedown.

Note: Cut and piece one sample block before cutting all the fabric for the quilt.

Piecing the Schoolhouse Blocks

Refer to the **Schoolhouse Block Diagram** as you assemble each block. For ease of construction, each pattern piece is identified by letter, and strip-pieced units are numbered. You will need 18 Schoolhouse blocks for this quilt.

Step 1. Sew an A, B, and C piece together in sequence, as shown in **Diagram 1**, to complete Row 1 of the Schoolhouse block. Press the seams toward A and C. Repeat to make 18 rows, then set them aside.

Diagram 1

Step 2. To make Row 2, sew a 2¾-inch muslin strip, a 3-inch gray print strip, and a 5¾-inch muslin strip together side by side to form a Unit 1 strip set, as shown in **Diagram 2**. Press the seams toward the gray strip. Square up one end of the strip set and cut eighteen 1½-inch segments from it, as shown. Label these segments Row 2 and set them aside.

Step 3. Row 3 is assembled in sections that are joined together before being attached to the other rows in the block. To make the house front section, sew a 1¼-inch red print strip to either side of a 3-inch muslin strip to form a Unit 2 strip set, as shown in **Diagram 3**. Press the seams toward the red strips. Using a rotary cutter and ruler, square up one end of the strip set and cut eighteen Unit 2 segments, each 2 inches wide, as shown.

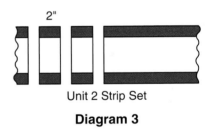

Unit 2 Strip Set

Diagram 3

Step 4. Sew together the 1¼-inch red print strips and the 1¼-inch muslin strips in pairs to form strip sets, as shown in **Diagram 4**. Press the seams toward the red strips. Square up one end of each strip set and cut eighteen Unit 3 segments, each 4½ inches wide, as shown. Save the remaining strip sets for use in Step 7.

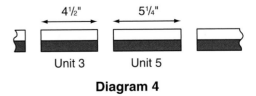

Diagram 4

Step 5. Referring to **Diagram 5** on page 176, sew a Unit 3 segment to the right edge of each

Unit 2 segment, so that the red strip in Unit 3 is attached to the edge of Unit 2 and the muslin strip is on the outer edge of the new unit. Sew a red print H along the left edge of Unit 2, as shown, to complete each house front. Press the seam allowances toward the red strips and set the units aside.

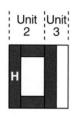

Diagram 5

Step 6. For the house side, pin then sew together three 1¼-inch red print strips and two 1¾-inch muslin strips, beginning with a red strip and alternating colors. See **Diagram 6**. Press the seams toward the red strips. Square up one end of the strip set and cut eighteen Unit 4 segments, each 2¼ inches wide, as shown.

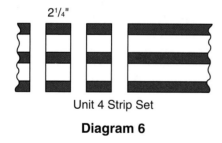

Unit 4 Strip Set

Diagram 6

Step 7. From the remaining red and muslin strip sets made in Step 4, cut eighteen 5¼-inch Unit 5 segments, as shown in **Diagram 4** on page 175.

Step 8. Sew the red edges of Unit 5 to the top edges of Unit 4. See **Diagram 7**. Then sew a red I to the bottom edge of each Unit 4, as shown. In each case, press the seams toward the red strips.

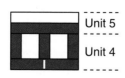

Diagram 7

Step 9. Sew together the house fronts and the house sides, as shown in **Diagram 8**. Press the seams toward the house front.

Diagram 8

Step 10. To make the roof of the house, sew D, E, F, G, and G reverse together in sequence, as shown in **Diagram 9**. Press the seams toward the darker pieces. Make eighteen roof units, then sew them to the top of the houses, as shown. Press.

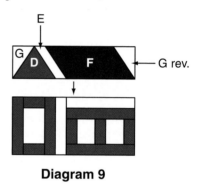

Diagram 9

Step 11. To complete Row 3, sew a muslin J to either side of the house units, as shown in **Diagram 10**. Then add a dark green K strip (Row 4) to the bottom edge of each house, as shown. Press all seams toward the new strips.

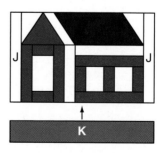

Diagram 10

Step 12. To complete the blocks, sew Rows 1 and 2 together, then sew them to the house tops. See the **Schoolhouse Block Diagram** on page 175.

Appliquéing the Center Block

Use the appliqué method of your choice for the center Apple block. If you need more information about appliqué methods, see "Sew Easy" for specific details on the simple freezer paper appliqué method. Or see page 200 for additional information on needle-turn appliqué.

Step 1. Prepare a fabric apple, leaf, and stem for appliqué. Then fold the 10½-inch muslin center square in half vertically, horizontally, and diagonally both ways and crease lightly. Using the crease marks as a guide, place the stem, then the apple and leaf in the center of the block, referring to the photograph on page 172. The apple will overlap the bottom raw edge of the stem. Pin or baste all pieces in place.

Step 2. Using thread to match the appliqués and your favorite invisible stitch, appliqué the stem, apple, and leaf in place.

The freezer paper appliqué method works especially well for shapes with lots of curves—such as the apple and leaf. The paper is a stabilizer, allowing you to turn seam allowances with ease.

Trace the *finished size* template onto the dull side of the freezer paper and cut out the paper shape directly on the pencil line. With a dry iron, press the freezer paper waxed side down on the wrong side of the appliqué fabric. Cut the fabric, adding a ³/₁₆-inch seam allowance around the paper shape. Roll the seam allowance over the dull side of the paper and baste it down, stitching through the paper.

Pin the shape to the background fabric and appliqué in place. Remove the basting stitches, make a small slit in the background fabric behind the appliquéd shape, and remove the freezer paper with tweezers.

Add interest to your quilt with a bit of embroidery. Use two or three strands of dark brown or black embroidery thread and a simple stem or chain stitch to replace the appliqué apple stem. You'll add a touch of texture—and save time, too!

Piecing the Setting Blocks

There are two setting blocks that combine with the Schoolhouse and Apple blocks to give the quilt top its barn raising setting. Block 1 consists of a navy and muslin half-square triangle. Block 2 consists of a navy and muslin quarter-square triangle plus a muslin half-square triangle. Refer to the **Setting Blocks Diagram** as you work.

Block 1   Block 2

Setting Blocks Diagram

Block 1

Step 1. Cut six 10⅞-inch muslin squares in half diagonally, as shown in **Diagram 11A**, to make twelve triangles. Repeat with the six 10⅞-inch navy print squares.

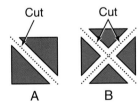

Diagram 11

Step 2. Sew a navy print triangle and a muslin triangle together along the diagonal edge to form a square, as shown in the **Setting Blocks Diagram**. Press the seams toward the navy triangle. Make twelve of these navy/muslin squares.

Block 2

Step 1. Cut the muslin and the navy 11¼-inch squares diagonally into quarters, as shown in **11B** on page 177. Sew a navy triangle to a muslin triangle along a short edge, as shown in the **Setting Blocks Diagram** on page 177. Repeat to make four sets of navy/muslin triangles. Press the seams toward the navy triangles.

Step 2. Cut the remaining two 10⅞-inch muslin squares in half diagonally, as you did for Block 1, to make four triangles.

Stitch the navy/muslin triangle to the large muslin triangle along the long edge to form a square. Press the seams toward the muslin triangle. Repeat to make four Block 2 setting blocks.

Assembling the Quilt Top

Step 1. Use a design wall or other flat surface to lay out the Apple block, the Schoolhouse blocks, and the Block 1 and Block 2 setting blocks in seven horizontal rows of five blocks each, referring to the **Assembly Diagram** for directional placement of Blocks 1 and 2.

Step 2. Sew the blocks together in horizontal rows, as shown. Press the seams in opposite directions from row to row.

Step 3. Sew the rows together, carefully matching seams where the blocks meet.

Adding the Border

Step 1. Measure the quilt from top to bottom, taking the measurement through the center of the quilt, not along the sides. Trim two of the borders to this length for side borders.

Step 2. Fold one side border in half crosswise and crease. Unfold it and position it right side down along one side of the quilt top, with the crease at the quilt's horizontal midpoint. Pin at the midpoint and ends first, then along the length of the entire side, easing in fullness if necessary. Sew the border to the quilt top, using a ¼-inch seam

Assembly Diagram

allowance. Press the seams toward the border. Repeat on the opposite side.

Step 3. Measure the width of the quilt, taking the measurement through the horizontal center of the quilt. Do not include the side borders in your measurement, but add ½ inch to your measurement for seam allowances. Trim the remaining two navy borders to this length. Sew a 5½-inch red print corner square to each end of both navy borders. Press the seams toward the navy borders.

Step 4. In the same manner as for the side borders, position and pin a border strip along the top edge of the quilt, matching seams and easing in fullness if necessary. Stitch the border to the quilt top. Repeat, adding the remaining border to the bottom edge of the quilt. Press the seams toward the borders. See the **Quilt Diagram.**

Quilt Diagram

Quilting and Finishing

Step 1. Mark the quilt top for quilting. The Schoolhouse blocks in the quilt shown are quilted in the ditch, with a sun quilted in each upper right-hand corner. The Apple block is outline quilted and has a crosshatched background. The navy triangles in Blocks 1 and 2 are quilted in concentric triangles. The muslin triangles are quilted with the letters of the alphabet, large numerals, paper doll–style children holding hands, and other whimsical motifs. The paper doll motif repeats in the borders, and each corner square has a quilted apple. Crayon-colored quilting thread (red, yellow, green, and blue) is used throughout.

Step 2. Cut the backing fabric in half crosswise, and trim the selvages. Cut one piece in half lengthwise and sew one half to each side of the full-width piece. The seams will run parallel to the top and bottom of the quilt top. Press the seams away from the center panel. For more information on pieced quilt backs, see page 205.

Step 3. Layer the backing, batting, and quilt top; baste. Quilt all marked designs, adding any additional quilting as desired.

Step 4. Referring to the directions on page 206, make and attach double-fold binding from the red print fabric. You will need approximately 290 inches of binding.

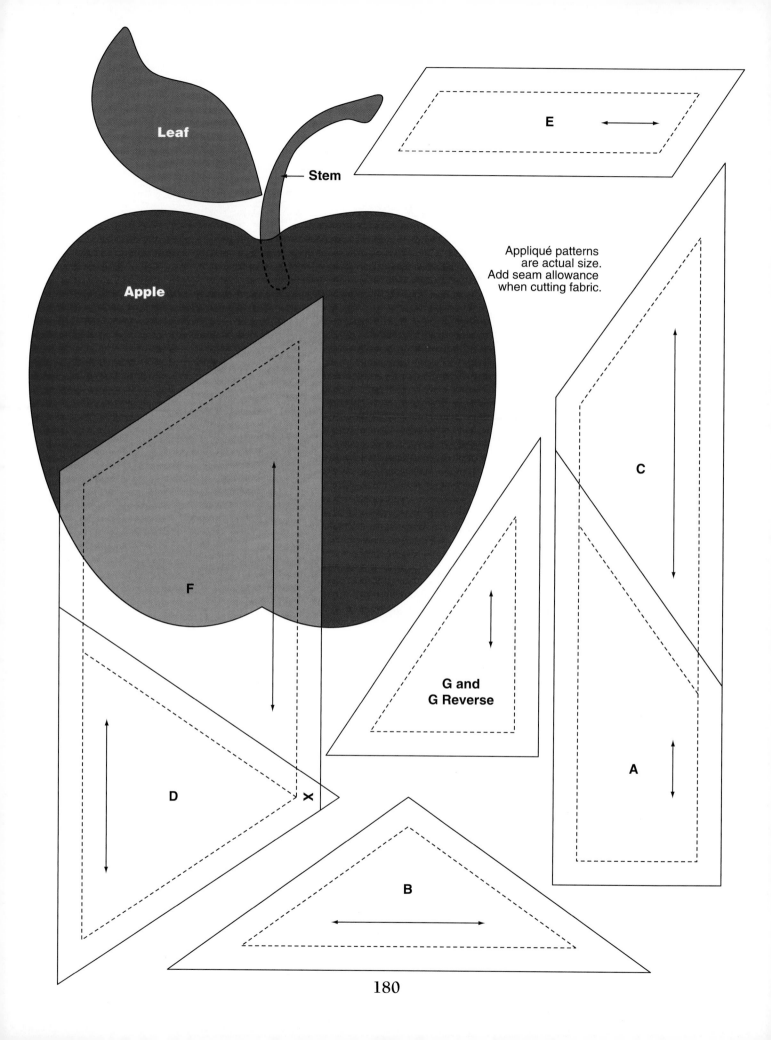

Leaf

Stem

Apple

F

Appliqué patterns
are actual size.
Add seam allowance
when cutting fabric.

E

C

A

G and
G Reverse

D

X

B

180

Quilting at the Hardware Store

Face it—quilters are pushovers when it comes to tools and gadgets, and we'll use anything we can get our hands on if it gets the job done. Don't overlook your neighborhood hardware store or home center as a great source for nifty notions. And who knows? You may even find yourself with some extra company and great advice the next time you venture out.

• Mylar washers make great templates for round appliqué shapes. Because they are thin and hold up well to heat, you can iron the fabric directly onto them, much like you would a freezer paper template. The result is a perfect circle every time. Metal washers are great for using to draw an exact circle, and if you're one of those quilters who thinks outside the box, you'll discover that washers make great embellishments, too.

• A carpenter's motto is "Measure twice, cut once," so you'll find rulers in all kinds of shapes and sizes.

• Toolboxes make great sewing baskets. Their covered and open compartments are useful for holding all kinds of objects. Multiple trays means there's lots of room for all your stuff.

• Storage bins sold to hold nails, screws, and other assorted small objects are just as handy for the quilter to hold pins, needles, buttons, and so much more. Label each compartment to make finding what you need easy.

• Clamps can hold your quilt sandwich onto the table and act as an extra hand when fabric needs to be stretched back into alignment.

• Retrieve pins and needles from the floor with a magnet. Attach one to the end of a yardstick, which can also be found at the hardware store, and you won't even have to bend over.

• Sandpaper is great for keeping templates from slipping while you're cutting out your pieces. Use a sandpaper-covered board as a surface for arranging multiple layers of appliqués—they'll never slip or move around.

• Dowel rods and tubing come in many sizes and are great for holding everything from spools of thread to ribbon.

• Count on being able to find masking tape in a multitude of widths for machine quilting.

• Automotive paste wax comes in handy if you're a machine quilter. Using a circular motion, apply a small amount of wax to the bed of the machine to make a smooth surface; it helps the quilt slide easily during machine quilting sessions.

• Latex gloves, disposable paint/stain gloves, and bead-bottomed gardening gloves all make great grippers for guiding a large quilt when you machine quilt. These gloves are all lightweight and flexible, so you can pick up pins while wearing them, yet their rubbery texture lets you grip fabric easily.

Once you've shopped yourself out at the hardware store, you'll have to head for the party store (for cardboard cake boards—great templates!), the art store (lots of fabric paint!), the dollar store (tissue paper for foundation piecing!), and the health food store (for nutritious snacks for marathon sewing sessions!). Shop 'til you drop!

Quiltmaking
Basics

This section provides a refresher course in basic quiltmaking techniques. Refer to it as needed; it will help not only with the projects in this book but also with all your quiltmaking.

Quiltmaker's Basic Supply List

Here's a list of items you should have on hand before beginning a project.

• **Iron and ironing board:** Make sure these are set up near your sewing machine. Careful pressing leads to accurate piecing.

• **Needles:** The two types of needles commonly used by quilters are *betweens,* short needles used for hand quilting, and *sharps,* long, very thin needles used for appliqué and hand piecing. The thickness of hand-sewing needles decreases as their size designation increases. For instance, a size 12 needle is smaller than a size 10.

• **Rotary cutter, plastic ruler, and cutting mat:** Fabric can be cut quickly and accurately with rotary-cutting equipment. There are a variety of cutters available, all with slightly different handle styles and safety latches. Rigid, see-through acrylic rulers are used with rotary cutters. A 6 × 24-inch ruler is a good size; for the most versatility, be sure it has 45- and 60-degree angle markings. A 14-inch square ruler will also be helpful for making sure blocks are square. Always use a special mat with a rotary cutter. The mat protects the work surface and helps to grip the fabric. Purchase the largest mat practical for your sewing area. A good all-purpose size is 18 × 24 inches.

• **Safety pins:** These are generally used to baste quilts for machine quilting. Use rustproof nickel-plated brass safety pins, preferably in size #0.

• **Scissors:** You'll need several pairs of scissors—shears for cutting fabric, general scissors for cutting paper and template plastic, and small, sharp embroidery scissors for trimming threads.

• **Seam ripper:** A seam ripper with a small, extra-fine blade slips easily under any stitch length.

• **Sewing machine:** Any machine with a straight stitch is suitable for piecing quilt blocks. Follow the manufacturer's recommendations for cleaning and servicing your sewing machine.

• **Straight pins:** Choose long, thin pins with glass or plastic heads that are easy to see against fabric so that you don't forget to remove one.

• **Template material:** Sheets of clear and opaque template plastic can be purchased at most quilt or craft shops. Gridded plastic is also available and may help you to draw shapes more easily. Various weights of cardboard can also be used for templates, including common household items like cereal boxes, poster board, and manila file folders.

• **Thimbles:** For hand quilting, a thimble is almost essential. Look for one that fits the finger you use to push the needle. The thimble should be snug enough to stay put when you shake your hand. There should be a bit of space between the end of your finger and the inside of the thimble.

• **Thread:** For hand or machine piecing, 100 percent cotton thread is a traditional favorite. Cotton-covered polyester is also acceptable. For hand quilting, use 100 percent cotton quilting thread. For machine quilting, you may want to try clear nylon thread as the top thread, with cotton thread in the bobbin.

• **Tweezers:** Keep a pair of tweezers handy for removing bits of thread from ripped-out seams and for pulling away scraps of removable foundations. Regular cosmetic tweezers will work fine.

Selecting and Preparing Fabrics

The traditional fabric choice for quilts is 100 percent cotton. It handles well, is easy to care for, presses easily, and frays less than synthetic blends.

The yardages in this book are generous estimates based on 44/45-inch-wide fabrics. It's a good idea to always purchase a bit more fabric than necessary to compensate for shrinkage and occasional cutting errors.

Prewash your fabrics using warm water and a mild soap or detergent. Test for colorfastness by first soaking a scrap in warm water. If colors bleed, set the dye by soaking the whole piece of fabric in a solution of 3 parts cold water to 1 part vinegar. Rinse the fabric several times in warm water. If it still bleeds, don't use it in a quilt that will need laundering—save it for a wallhanging that won't get a lot of use.

After washing, preshrink your fabric by drying it in a dryer on the medium setting. To keep wrinkles under control, remove the fabric from the dryer while it's still slightly damp and press it immediately with a hot iron.

Cutting Fabric

The cutting instructions for each project follow the list of materials. Whenever possible, the instructions are written to take advantage of quick rotary-cutting techniques. In addition, some projects include patterns for those who prefer to make templates and scissor cut individual pieces.

Although rotary cutting can be faster and more accurate than cutting with scissors, it has one disadvantage: It does not always result in the most efficient use of fabric. In some cases, the method results in long strips of leftover fabric. Don't think of these as waste; just add them to your scrap bag for future projects.

Rotary-Cutting Basics

Follow these two safety rules every time you use a rotary cutter: Always cut *away* from yourself, and always slide the blade guard into place as soon as you stop cutting.

Step 1: You can cut several layers of fabric at a time with a rotary cutter. Fold the fabric with the selvage edges together. You can fold it again if you want, doubling the number of layers to be cut.

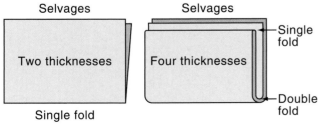

Diagram 1

Step 2: To square up the end of the fabric, place a ruled square on the fold and slide a 6 × 24-inch ruler against the side of the square. Hold the ruler in place, remove the square, and cut along the edge of the ruler. If you are left-handed, work from the other end of the fabric.

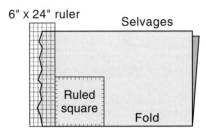

Diagram 2

Step 3: For patchwork, cut strips or rectangles on the crosswise grain, then subcut them into smaller pieces as needed. The diagram shows a strip cut into squares.

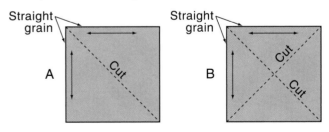

Diagram 3

Step 4: A square can be subcut into two triangles by making one diagonal cut (A). Two diagonal cuts yield four triangles (B).

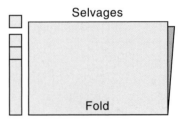

Diagram 4

Step 5: Check strips periodically to make sure they're straight and not angled. If they are angled, refold the fabric and square up the edges again.

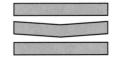

Diagram 5

Enlarging Patterns

Every effort has been made to provide full-size pattern pieces. But in some cases, where the pattern piece is too large to fit on the page, a partial pattern is given or the pattern runs at a reduced size. Take the book to a photocopier and enlarge the pattern by the percentage indicated on the pattern piece.

Making and Using Templates

To make a plastic template, place template plastic over the book page, trace the pattern onto the plastic, and cut out the template. To make a cardboard template, copy the pattern onto tracing paper, glue the paper to the cardboard, and cut out the template. With a permanent marker, record on every template any identification letters and grain lines, as well as the size and name of the block and the number of pieces needed. Always check your templates against the printed pattern for accuracy.

The patchwork patterns in this book are printed with double lines. The inner dashed line is the finished size of the piece, while the outer solid line includes the seam allowance.

For hand piecing: Trace the inner line to make finished-size templates. Cut out the templates on the traced line. Draw around the templates on the wrong side of the fabric, leaving ½ inch between pieces. Then mark ¼-inch seam allowances before you cut out the pieces.

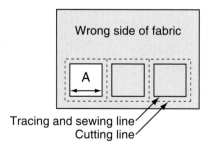

Diagram 6

For machine piecing: Trace the outer solid line on the printed pattern to make templates with seam allowance included. Draw around the templates on the wrong side of the fabric and cut out the pieces on this line.

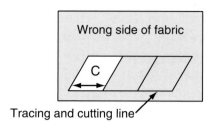

Diagram 7

For appliqué: Appliqué patterns in this book have only a single line and are finished size. Draw around the templates on the right side of the fabric, leaving ½ inch between pieces. Add ⅛- to ¼-inch seam allowances by eye as you cut the pieces.

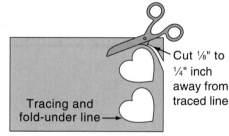

Diagram 8

Piecing Basics

Standard seam allowance for machine piecing is ¼ inch. For hand piecing, the sewing line is marked on the fabric.

Hand Piecing

Cut fabric pieces using finished-size templates. Place the pieces right sides together, match marked seam lines, and pin. Use a running stitch along the marked line, backstitching every four or five stitches and at the beginning and end of the seam.

When you cross seam allowances of previously joined units, leave the seam allowances free. Backstitch just before and after you cross, then resume stitching the seam.

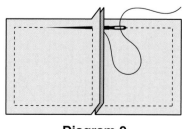

Diagram 9

Machine Piecing

Cut the fabric pieces using templates with seam allowances included or using a rotary cutter and ruler without templates. Set the stitch length at 10 to 12 stitches per inch.

Place the fabric pieces right sides together, then sew from raw edge to raw edge. Press seams before crossing them with other seams, pressing toward the darker fabric whenever possible.

Chain piecing: Some of the quilts in this book were assembled using a technique called chain piecing, or assembly line piecing, in which like segments are fed through the sewing machine one after another, without lifting the presser foot or clipping threads on individual segments. The end result is a chain of sewn segments connected to one another by a short length of thread, as shown in **Diagram 10.**

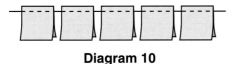

Diagram 10

Chain piecing is a good choice if pieces have a finished width of 1 inch or more. Wider strips are easier to handle than very narrow ones, and if slight variations do occur, they won't be as noticeable in a wider strip. Another benefit of chain piecing is its speed. Since it is assembly line sewing, chain piecing usually makes block construction faster. You can perform the same step on all the blocks before moving on to the next step.

Quick-Pieced Triangle Squares

Many Amish quilts, including a handful featured in this book, use triangle squares. A triangle square is made of two right triangles sewn together along their longest sides to make a square, as shown in **Diagram 11.**

Diagram 11

Both of the techniques described here will help you assemble accurate triangle squares more quickly than you could using the traditional method of sewing individual triangles together. Examples for both methods produce finished triangle squares that are 2¾ inches. However, if you need triangle squares in a different size, follow the directions below.

Method 1: Grids

The grid method is a good choice if you plan to make many identical triangle squares. Two pieces of fabric are cut oversize, placed together with right sides facing, then marked, sewn, and cut apart into individual triangle squares. This technique requires careful marking and sewing, but it produces multiples of identical triangle squares quickly and allows you to avoid working with bias edges. It is an especially useful method when working with very small triangle squares because your results may be more accurate than with other piecing methods.

To make a scrap quilt that's full of visual texture, variety is important and can be achieved by using grids with fewer squares. Adjust the number of squares in the grid to suit the design you are trying to achieve.

Step 1. To determine the correct size to cut the fabric, you must first determine the number of triangle squares you wish to make and the dimensions of the squares in the grid. Each square drawn in the grid will result in two triangle squares and is equal to the finished size of the triangle square, plus ⅞ inch.

In this example, the finished size of the triangle square is 2¾ inches. The number of identical triangle squares required is 60, so:

60 triangle squares required ÷ 2 completed triangle squares in each grid square = a grid of 30 squares

Grid size = finished size of 2¾ inches + ⅞ inch = 3⅝-inch grid required

A grid of 5 squares by 6 squares produces 60 triangle squares and measures 18⅛ × 21¾ inches.

To allow a bit of extra fabric on all sides, choose two pieces of fabric that are at least 19½ × 22¾ inches.

Note: If your fabric cuts are narrow, adjust the grid layout. For instance, a grid of 3 squares by 10 squares will yield the same number of triangle squares but can be drawn on a piece of fabric that measures approximately 11½ × 37 inches.

Step 2. On the wrong side of the lighter fabric, use a pencil or permanent marker to draw a grid of squares, as shown in **Diagram 12A.** Begin approximately ½ inch from the edge of the fabric. Referring to **12B,** carefully draw a diagonal line through each square in the grid; these lines will be cutting lines.

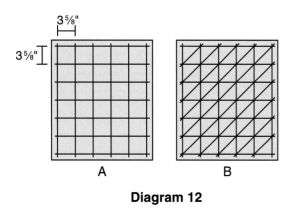

Diagram 12

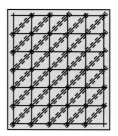

To help you distinguish sewing lines from cutting lines, use a different color ink to mark each line.

Step 4. Use a rotary cutter and ruler to cut the grid apart. Cut on all the grid and diagonal lines, as shown in **Diagram 14A.** Carefully press the triangle squares open, pressing each seam toward the darker fabric. Trim off the triangle points at the seam ends, as shown in **14B.** Continue marking and cutting triangle squares until you have made the number required for the quilt you are making.

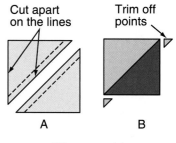

Diagram 14

Sew Quick

To eliminate the need to draw lines directly on fabric, use a hot-iron transfer pen to draw the grid on a sheet of paper, then iron the image onto the wrong side of your lightest fabric.

along both sides of the diagonal lines, as shown in **Diagram 13.** Use the edge of your presser foot as a ¼-inch guide, or draw a line ¼ inch from each side of the diagonal line to indicate sewing lines.

Step 3. Position the marked fabric and the second piece of fabric with their right sides together. Press to help the two pieces adhere to each other and use a few straight pins to secure the layers. Using a ¼-inch seam allowance, stitch

Method 2: Single Squares from Squares

If you prefer a scrappier look or if you would like to make use of small pieces of fabric, the individual square method may be useful. Squares of different fabrics are sandwiched and sewn together, then cut apart diagonally to yield two identical triangle squares.

Step 1. Determine the required size of fabric squares by adding ⅞ inch to the desired finished size of your triangle squares. For a 2¾-inch triangle square, you must cut 3⅝-inch squares of fabric.

Sew Easy

To make the finished size of your squares as accurate as possible, cut fabric squares slightly larger than necessary, then trim back the completed triangle squares after assembly.

Step 2. Select two fabrics for a triangle square and cut a 3⅝-inch square from each. Draw a diagonal line from one corner to the other on the wrong side of the lightest square. Position the squares with their right sides together, taking care to align all edges. Sew a seam ¼ inch from each side of the drawn line. After sewing the seams, cut the squares in half on the drawn line. Press the seam in each triangle square toward the darkest fabric (see **Diagram 15**).

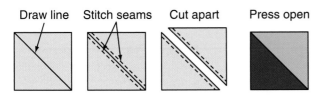

| Draw line | Stitch seams | Cut apart | Press open |

Diagram 15

Step 3. Continue making triangle squares until you have completed the total number required for your quilt. If you are sewing many triangle squares, chain piecing will help speed up the process. Draw diagonal lines and pair each square with its counterpart. Feed the units through the sewing machine one after another in a continuous chain, without breaking the threads.

Set-In Seams

For Schoolhouse and other blocks: While many of the Schoolhouse blocks in this book call for simple, straight seam sewing, occasionally the design of a block will require that you sew a set-in seam. A set-in seam is one that requires you to fit a piece (or pieces) into the quilt block by pivoting at a key point. Although this is not especially difficult, it does call for some advance planning.

The need for a set-in seam can be seen in the roof and skyline of House 2 in **Diagram 16**. While House 1 can be completed by adding Rows 2 and 3 with simple, straight seam sewing, the A and A reverse pieces cannot be added to House 2 quite so simply. Because of the angled seams, you will need to turn a corner to get the pieces to fit.

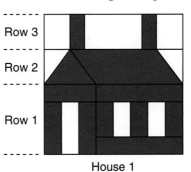

House 1

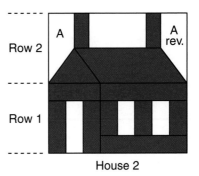

House 2

Diagram 16

Step 1. Sew the roof unit to the top of the house, as shown in **Diagram 17**.

Diagram 17

Step 2. Place a fabric A piece along the chimney edge, with right sides together and top edges aligned. Use a pencil to mark a dot ¼ inch from the bottom edge of A, as shown in **Diagram 18A**. Pin, then begin sewing at the dot, taking a ¼-inch seam allowance. Start with a backstitch and stitch outward in the direction indicated by the arrow. Wait to press.

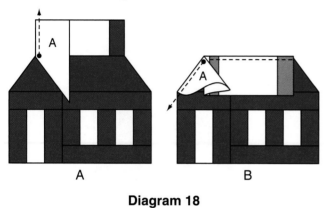

A   B

Diagram 18

Step 3. Maneuver the A piece so that its angled bottom edge is aligned with the angled edge of the large pieced unit, as shown in **18B**. Pin, taking care that the marked dot is secured at the pivot point. Once again, begin sewing at the dot, taking a ¼-inch seam allowance. Backstitch, then stitch outward in the direction indicated by the arrow. Finish by pressing both seams away from A.

Step 4. Repeat Steps 1 through 3 to attach the A reverse piece to the opposite side of the block.

While it is generally easier to stitch outward from a pivot point, this is not always possible. In quilts with complex designs, you may need to complete a series of long seams, turning corners as you go.

To do this, begin by marking all of the ¼-inch pivot points before you start to sew. Work from pivot point to pivot point, pinning and taking the standard ¼-inch seam allowance. Adjust your stitching so that you finish with the sewing machine needle in the down position as you reach each pivot point. Pin to the next pivot point, turn the quilt top under the machine needle, and continue sewing. Work your way from point to point until the rows are completely joined.

While it is advisable to press seam allowances toward the darker of the two sewn fabrics, this is not always possible, especially when set-in seams are involved. You can eliminate the problem of darker seam allowances shadowing through lighter fabrics by carefully grading the seam allowances. Trim the darker allowance to a *scant* ¼ inch (or ³⁄₁₆ inch) so that it hides behind the lighter—and wider—seam allowance.

For 8-Pointed Star blocks: Pattern pieces must sometimes be set into angles created by other pieces, as shown in the diagram. In **Diagram 19**, pieces A, B, and C are set into the angles created by the four joined diamond pieces.

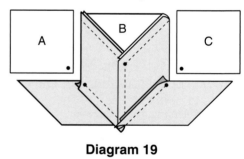

Diagram 19

Step 1. Keep the seam allowances open where the piece is to be set in. Begin by sewing the first seam in the usual manner, beginning and ending the seam ¼ inch from the edge of the fabric and back-stitching at each end, as shown in **Diagram 20**.

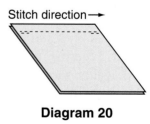

Stitch direction →

Diagram 20

Step 2. Open up the pattern pieces and place the piece to be set in right sides together with one of the first two pieces. Begin the seam ¼ inch from the edge of the fabric and sew to the exact point where the first seam ended, backstitching at the beginning and end of the seam, as shown in **Diagram 21.**

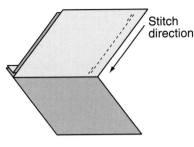

Diagram 21

Step 3. Rotate the pattern pieces so that you are ready to sew the final seam. Keeping the seam allowances free, sew from the point where the last seam ended to ¼ inch from the edge of the piece, as shown in **Diagram 22.**

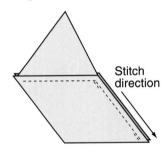

Diagram 22

Step 4. Press the seams so that as many of them as possible lie flat. The finished unit should look like the one shown in **Diagram 23.**

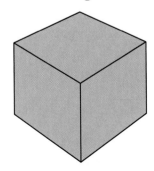

Diagram 23

Sewing Curved Seams

Most of the assembly procedures you'll encounter in Wedding Ring quilts involve matching curved seams. Center points are marked on the pattern pieces, so be sure to copy the points to your templates for easier matching. Also, to help you align pieces accurately, templates have been drawn to eliminate excess seam allowances at the points. The step-by-step directions below give information about successfully sewing the different types of curved seams you'll encounter. With a little practice, you'll be able to sew curves with confidence and ease.

Sewing Arcs to Melons

Step 1. Mark the center of each side of the melon and background pieces. If your quilt is made with solid rather than pieced arcs, mark the centers of the arcs, too. You may make a small mark with a pencil or fine-tip permanent pen. Or simply make a small snip at the center point with the tip of your scissors. Be careful not to cut deeper than ⅛ inch into the seam allowance. See **Diagram 24.**

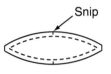

Diagram 24

Step 2. With right sides together, match the center of a melon to the center seam of a pieced arc, then pin at this point. See **Diagram 25A.** Match and pin the ends of the arc and melon. Place more pins along the seam if you like. See **25B.**

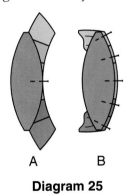

A   B

Diagram 25

Step 3. With the melon on top, sew the two pieces together using a ¼-inch seam allowance. If you haven't pinned along the seam, manipulate the fabric with your fingers to fit the curve. Remove the pins as the needle approaches them. Press the seams toward the arc unless directed otherwise in the project instructions. Open out the melon piece, pressing the seam toward the arc unless directed otherwise. See **Diagram 26**.

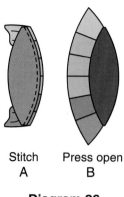

Stitch
A

Press open
B

Diagram 26

Step 4. Sew the pieced arcs with connecting wedges to the opposite or unsewn side of the melon. Match the center of the melon with the center seam of the longer arc and pin at that point. Then pin at each end. It is also helpful to place pins at the seam intersections at each end of the melon, matching the seams where the ends of the arc are sewn to the melon with the seams of the connecting wedges on the arc. See **Diagram 27A**.

Use a few more pins along the side, or simply manipulate the fabric with your fingers as you sew. Again, sew with the melon on top, using a ¼-inch seam allowance. It may be necessary to stop occasionally and reposition the fabric. If you do, be sure to stop with the needle down. Stitch all the way to the end of the arc. Open out the melon piece, pressing the seams toward the arcs unless directed otherwise. See **27B**.

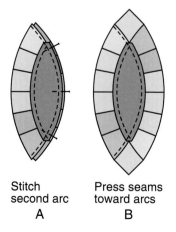

Stitch
second arc
A

Press seams
toward arcs
B

Diagram 27

Sewing Arcs to the Background

With right sides together, pin the center of one side of a background piece to the center of an arc/melon unit, with the background piece on top. Stick a pin in the background piece, ¼ inch from one end. Match that point with the seam on the arc between the connecting wedge and the next inner wedge of the arc. Repeat on the opposite end of the background piece. Add more pins along the length of the curve if you like. Sew the pieces together with a ¼-inch seam allowance. See **Diagram 28**.

Important: Start and stop your seams ¼ inch from each end, and backstitch. If you don't leave the ¼-inch seam allowance open, you won't be able to attach the arc/melon unit on the adjacent side.

Press the seams away from the arcs unless directed otherwise in the project instructions.

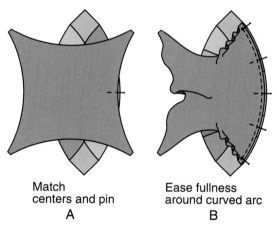

Match
centers and pin
A

Ease fullness
around curved arc
B

Diagram 28

Sew Easy

To help ease your fabric along the curves, try clipping into the seam allowances on the concave curves. By making several small snips (no deeper than ⅛ inch) into the seam allowance, you'll give your fabric the flexibility to bend and manipulate around the convex curve of the melon to which you are attaching it.

Sewing Rings into Rows

Step 1. Sew additional arc/melon units to the quilt top following the project instructions. **Important:** When adding remaining arc/melon units, remember to match the seams where connecting wedges meet the rest of the arc, with the point ¼ inch from the tip of the background piece. Be sure to keep the ¼-inch seam allowance unsewn at the beginning and end of each curved seam.

Step 2. Once you have four arc/melon units coming together where four circles interconnect (see **Diagram 29**), you will need to stitch the connecting wedges together. To do so, match the raw edges of two adjacent connecting wedges and stitch from the edge to ¼ inch from the inner point where the wedges are connected to the arcs. Backstitch. Repeat for the other pair of wedges. Finger press the two seams you've just sewn in opposite directions, pin the remaining raw edges of the wedges together, and stitch, backstitching ¼ inch from each end.

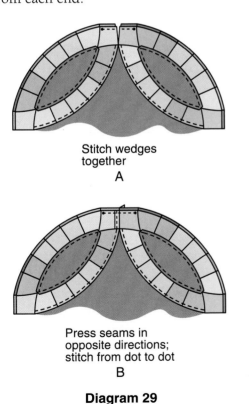

Stitch wedges
together
A

Press seams in
opposite directions;
stitch from dot to dot
B

Diagram 29

Step 3. Sew the quilt top together as illustrated for your project, using the same techniques de-scribed here for aligning curves and finishing the connecting wedge seams.

Appliquéing Rings to a Border

In a few projects in this book, the Wedding Ring quilt tops are appliquéd to a border unit or background. Any appliqué method will work for this step, but a freezer paper technique (see page 201) may help seam allowances stay in place easily.

Step 1. To make a stabilizing template for appliqué, connect the individual template pieces for the pieced arc, including the connecting wedges on opposite ends. Be sure you don't include seam allowances when constructing the shape of the complete arc. See **Diagram 30**.

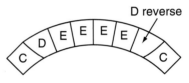

Diagram 30

Step 2. Trace the shape onto the nonwaxy side of freezer paper and cut it out. Make a freezer paper template for each outer arc to be appliquéd.

Step 3. Align a freezer paper arc, waxy side up, to the wrong side of an outer pieced arc. The freezer paper should fit snugly against the inner seam allowance where the arc connects to the background piece. Use the tip of a medium-hot iron to press the outer seam allowance of the ring onto the freezer paper. See **Diagram 31**. This eliminates the need for basting or turning under edges as you work and holds the seam allowance securely as you appliqué the rings to the border.

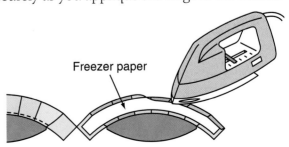

Freezer paper

Diagram 31

Sew Easy

The tip of a clean hot-glue gun makes a convenient "iron" for adhering freezer paper to the fabric seam allowance. The small tip can help you manipulate fabric more easily and will help avoid burned fingertips that sometimes come from using an iron.

Repeat, ironing a new freezer paper template onto each outer arc in your quilt. Construct the border and center the top on it, as described in the project directions. Appliqué the ring edges to the borders. Remove all freezer paper templates when the appliqué is complete.

Foundation Piecing

Many Log Cabin designs are perfect candidates for the foundation method of piecing. Nineteenth-century quilters used this technique to construct their quilts, sewing fabric pieces to either the front or back side of a foundation onto which a copy of the block had been drafted. Foundation piecing is enjoying a strong revival today, with more and more quilters designing blocks specifically for use with this method.

Foundations help ensure that your quilt will be square. Log Cabin and Pineapple blocks won't pucker up in the middle when they are pieced on a foundation. In addition, foundation piecing is often the best choice for blocks with narrow logs. It's much easier to construct a perfect block full of ½-inch logs when those logs are sewn to a rigid foundation with premarked lines. Sewing individual narrow strips together with an exact ¼-inch seam allowance is possible, of course, but accurate results are more difficult to achieve.

One disadvantage of the foundation method is the fact that a separate foundation must be prepared for each individual block. This requires additional preparation time as well as added materials. But there are benefits that help offset this extra preparation: You save cutting time by not having to cut individual logs to exact sizes. Working with long strips that are trimmed as you go means the actual sewing moves along quickly.

Foundation Basics

With the foundation method, an entire block is first drawn to scale on the chosen foundation material. The only seam allowance included is the one around the outer perimeter of the design. **Diagram 32** illustrates a typical template for the foundation method.

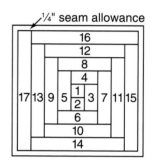

Diagram 32

The foundation technique used in this book involves positioning the fabric on one side of the foundation (the reverse side) and sewing on the opposite side (the front, marked side). Seams are stitched directly onto one of the marked lines of the template. If you are unfamiliar with this technique, it may at first seem awkward. But if you position the fabric correctly and are careful to sew on the lines, every log will be perfect, no matter how narrow its finished width.

Some quilters choose to piece on the front of a foundation, but that method requires that you use exact seam allowances. One advantage to choosing foundation piecing in the first place is its simplicity and speed, so it seems awkward to slow the process down by including a step that requires more precision.

There is one thing you must keep in mind as you work: Since the fabric will be sewn to the back of the foundation, the finished block will always be a *mirror image* of the template. For some blocks, this does not create a problem—the light and dark areas are clearly defined. For others, getting the fabrics in the right place can sometimes be confusing. Where color or value may change from block to block, or where blocks are not symmetrical, misplaced fabric can alter your entire design.

It may be helpful to premark all or part of the logs of your foundation, on either the front or back side, as shown in **Diagram 33.** Jotting down simple designations such as light, dark, or the actual color of a log will save time and keep frustrating seam-ripping sessions to a minimum.

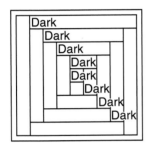

Diagram 33

Foundation Materials

There are two types of foundations—permanent and removable—and both are exactly what their names imply. Several types of materials fall into each category, all with advantages and disadvantages. Though the following list is by no means exhaustive, the descriptions may help you decide which type will be best for your project.

Permanent Foundations

Muslin is the most common example of a permanent foundation material. Some advantages include the following:

• The foundation will remain in the finished quilt permanently. The extra layer of fabric makes hand quilting more difficult, but since it adds more depth to the finished top, extensive quilting may not be necessary or desired. Many Log Cabin quilts with permanent foundations are tied rather than quilted.

• The extra fabric often eliminates the need for batting.

• The foundation will permanently stabilize the fabric, making careful placement of fabric grain less of a consideration.

• The foundation will help reinforce stitching, so seam allowances can be trimmed back a little more. This may help make outline quilting somewhat easier.

Some disadvantages of this type of foundation include:

• The material can stretch as it's handled. Be careful not to tug on the foundation too much as you work, or the block may become distorted. Tightly woven muslin will minimize the problem.

• The block sometimes seems to shrink as you add pieces. This is caused by the slight loft created by each new seam. The amount of shrinkage is usually very small but should be considered if you plan to use a pieced border that must fit the quilt top exactly.

Two other options in the permanent foundation category include flannel and sheer interfacing. Flannel may be a bit harder to hold on to as you work, but it adds more depth and body than muslin. Spray-on starch or sizing will stiffen the flannel slightly, making it easier to handle. As for the interfacing, the additional layer it adds is easier to hand quilt through than muslin. Sheer interfacing is a good choice for those who intend to hand piece on a foundation.

Removable Foundations

Paper is the most commonly used removable foundation. Among its advantages are the following:

• The foundation will be removed after the top is assembled and, thus, will not add an extra layer of fabric to your quilt.

• The paper will remain rigid as you work. There is no need to worry about distorting or shrinking the block.

• The cost of materials is very low.

Some of the disadvantages of paper as a foundation include:

• It can sometimes be time-consuming to remove, especially if pieces are very small.

• It will not remain in place to permanently stabilize the fabric, so cutting and positioning pieces on grain is more of a consideration.

Many types of paper can be used as foundation material. For example, blank newsprint is a good choice. It is sturdy enough to remain intact while handling but pulls away easily when your top is complete. Newsprint is available in pads from 9 × 12 inches up to poster size, so it works well for blocks that are too large to draft onto a piece of 8½ × 11-inch paper.

Inexpensive copier paper, onion skin, and tracing papers are options for small blocks. Other foundation choices in the removable category include vanishing muslin, a loosely woven fabric that deteriorates and falls away when ironed, and tear-away paper, which is designed to be used as a stabilizer during machine embroidery.

Transferring the Image

There are several ways to transfer the template onto your foundation material.

Transfer Pens

Use a hot-iron transfer pen to draw the full-size block onto tracing paper. The image can usually be ironed onto a foundation material five or six times. Retrace over the original transfer for additional ironings, being careful to mark over the existing lines exactly. A transfer pen can be used on both fabric and paper foundations, but do a test first to be sure it will work on your chosen material.

Photocopies

Photocopies are an option for smaller blocks. The major disadvantage of photocopying is the slight distortion that's almost certain to occur. To minimize that distortion, make sure the page being copied is completely flat against the glass screen of the copier. Always check your copies to make sure blocks are square. Copiers can alter size slightly, too, so measure your copies carefully if a slight variation in block size will affect the finished quilt top. Always use the same generation of copies in your project, since copies of copies will usually be a slightly different size.

Computer Printouts

Those of you who use a computer to design quilt blocks can print the images directly onto paper. Most drawing programs have a "tile" feature that allows you to print large designs in segments, then tape the segments together to make a whole. For small blocks, some quilters feed freezer paper–backed muslin through their printers—but check with your printer's manufacturer before attempting that! In general, if a printer will accept card stock, it will probably process fabric. Printer ink should be tested for permanency on a piece of scrap fabric.

Light Box

A simple light box, or a lamp placed underneath a glass table, can be used to help you see the template clearly enough to trace it directly onto a foundation. However, with this method only one block can be drawn at a time. Blocks may be different due to slight tracing variations.

Other Considerations

Pens and other markers can be used to mark foundations. If you are using permanent foundations, be sure the markings on them are permanent, too, or that they will wash out completely without staining. You don't want your finished quilt to be ruined by bleeding ink during its first bath. Always check a new marker on scrap fabric before using it in a project, even if it's a brand you have used before. If the ink bleeds, try to heat set it by ironing a marked scrap for a few minutes with a medium-hot iron. Check again for colorfastness. If the ink still bleeds, do not use it on permanent foundations.

Permanent inks are not necessary for removable foundations. Just be sure to choose a marking system that won't wear off onto fabric as you work.

Fabric Grain

For maximum strength and stability and minimum distortion, fabric should be cut along its lengthwise or crosswise grain. Ideally, the straight of grain should be parallel with the outer perimeter of your block. For most pieces in Log Cabin quilts, this means positioning the grain line parallel to the seam. The rectangles, squares, and occasional triangles used to assemble quilt blocks in this book are simple shapes that will be easy to cut on grain. Grain placement is most important if you are using removable foundations that won't remain in the quilt as permanent stabilizers.

Stitch Length

Most foundation piecing is done with a slightly shorter than normal stitch length. Twelve to fourteen stitches per inch will produce good results. Be sure not to make your stitches too small, or they could cause unnecessary wear to the fabric. Also, very small stitches will be more difficult to remove if an error occurs.

Smaller stitches will "punch" your paper foundations, making them easier to remove. And smaller stitches are less likely to be distorted when foundations are pulled away.

Foundation Piecing a Log Cabin Block

This section takes you step by step through the construction of one sample Log Cabin block. You may want to make a sample block here to learn the technique, or you may decide to select a particular project and jump right in. Even if you don't make a sample block, it's a good idea to read through all of the steps in this section so that you

understand the process thoroughly before beginning any of the projects.

All of the foundation piecing instructions in this book contain recommended sizes for strip widths. It's easiest to cut long strips of fabric, then trim the logs to length as the block is assembled.

The strip width is based on the finished size of the log. The finished width of each log in this sample block is ¼ inch. If we add ¼ inch to each side to allow for seam allowances, the cut size becomes ¾ inch. When you first learn to piece on a foundation, it's usually best to add an additional ⅛ to ¼ inch to the calculated size. The extra bit of fabric will give you more flexibility as you position your strips onto the back of the foundation, and the excess will be trimmed away after sewing.

The Cutting Chart in each project takes this into consideration, calling for wider than necessary strips. However, since it will only take a practice block or two for you to become a foundation piecing pro, you may not want to cut extra-wide strips for the entire quilt. Cut just enough to construct one or two blocks to start with, then reevaluate the strip width, reducing it when you feel comfortable doing so. Never cut the strips narrower than the finished width plus ¼-inch seam allowance on each side.

For the sample block, make a foundation from the block pattern on page 26. Start by cutting 1¼- to 1½-inch-wide strips across the width of your fabrics. Since the extra width will be trimmed away after sewing, the method may at first seem wasteful, but remember that you'll probably decrease the width after one or two blocks. Even if you prefer to continue using wider than necessary strips, the time you'll save and the perfect results you'll achieve by piecing on a foundation will likely make the use of additional fabric an unimportant consideration.

Step 1. Pieces are sewn to the foundation in numerical order. Cut a 1¼-inch square from the fabric you set aside for the center piece, log 1. Place it right side up on the back side of your foundation, centering it over the lines surrounding the area for log 1, as shown in **Diagram 34**. Use tape, a dab of glue stick, or a pin to hold the fabric in place.

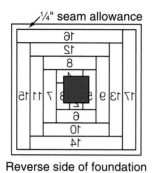

Reverse side of foundation

Diagram 34

Step 2. Hold the foundation up to the light with the back side away from you. You should be able to see the shadow of log 1. Does the shadow overlap all drawn lines for log 1? Is the overlap sufficient to create a stable seam allowance when those lines are sewn? If not, reposition the piece and check again before continuing.

Step 3. Find the strip of fabric set aside for log 2 and position it on the back side of your foundation, right side down. Align the strip along the left and lower edges of log 1, as shown in Diagram 35A. The strip will entirely cover log 1.

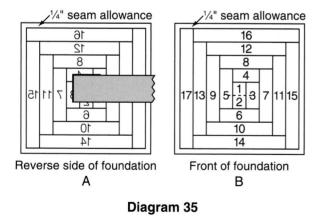

Reverse side of foundation
A

Front of foundation
B

Diagram 35

Step 4. Holding the strip in place, flip the foundation over. Sew on the line separating log 1 from log 2, beginning and ending approximately ⅛ inch

on either side of the line, as shown in **35B** in the previous step. Remove the foundation from the machine.

Step 5. Flip again to the back side of your foundation. Trim away the excess tail of fabric from log 2 just past the end of the seam line, as shown in **Diagram 36A**. If necessary, trim away excess fabric from the seam allowance you've created. If you used tape to secure the first piece, remove it now.

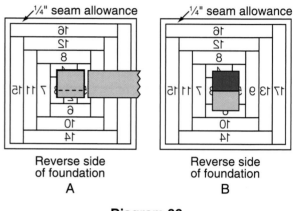

Reverse side
of foundation
A

Reverse side
of foundation
B

Diagram 36

Step 6. Flip log 2 into a right-side-up position, finger pressing it firmly into place. If you prefer, keep an iron near your work area to press pieces as you go. The back side of your foundation should now resemble **36B**.

Step 7. Hold the foundation up to the light with the back side away from you. You will now be able to see the shadow created by the fabric for log 2. Its raw edges should overlap all unsewn seam lines for log 2. This assures you there will be sufficient seam allowance on all sides when you add the adjacent logs.

One way to judge whether your strip has been placed correctly is to take a look at your seam allowance before trimming away the excess. Is it overly wide? If so, the piece you've just sewn may have been positioned incorrectly on the foundation. **Diagram 37** shows two examples of log 2 placement; here log 2 appears transparent to make the differences easier to see. In **37A**, the strip is aligned against the left and lower edges of log 1, as directed in Step 3. In **37B,** the strip is aligned lower on log 1.

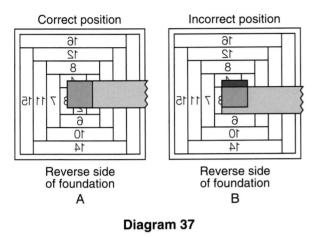

Diagram 37

When the seam in **37B** is stitched, it will have a larger than necessary seam allowance, stealing width from the log 2 fabric. The remaining width may not be adequate to cover the area for log 2 and create a stable seam allowance on its remaining sides when the fabric is flipped into place. **Diagram 38** shows the result: This strip is now too narrow to have an adequate seam along its lower edge.

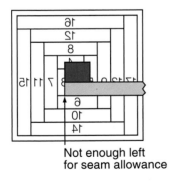

Diagram 38

Step 8. Log 3 is added in exactly the same way as log 2. Position a strip of fabric right side down on the foundation, aligning its top with log 1 and its left edge with the left edges of logs 1 and 2, as shown in **Diagram 39A.** The strip will completely cover the sewn pieces.

Flip the foundation over, and sew on the vertical line separating log 3 from logs 1 and 2, be-

ginning and ending approximately ⅛ inch on either side of the line. Remove the foundation from the machine.

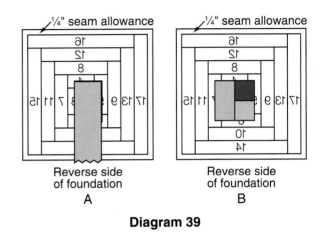

Diagram 39

Step 9. Trim the excess tail from log 3. Trim excess seam allowance if necessary. Flip log 3 into a right-side-up position, finger pressing it firmly into place. The reverse side of your foundation should now resemble **39B.**

Step 10. Position log 4 right side down on the foundation, as shown in **Diagram 40A.** Holding the fabric in place, flip the foundation over and sew on the horizontal line separating log 4 from logs 1 and 3. Remember to begin and end the seam approximately ⅛ inch on either side of the line. Remove the foundation from the machine.

Step 11. Turn the foundation over to the back side, and trim the excess tail of fabric from log 4,

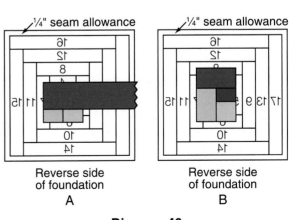

Diagram 40

just as you did with the previous logs. Trim excess seam allowance if necessary, then finger press log 4 into a right-side-up position. The back side of your foundation should now resemble **40B** on page 199.

Step 12. Sew all remaining logs to the foundation in exactly the same way. After adding log 7, the back of your foundation should resemble **Diagram 41A** and the front side should resemble **41B**. Notice that each new seam acts as a stabilizer for those it intersects.

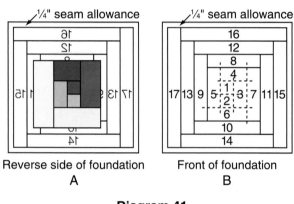

Diagram 41

Step 13. Log 17 is the final piece for this block. After it has been added, press the entire block lightly. Align your plastic ruler with an *outer* line of the seam allowance, and cut directly on the line with your rotary cutter. Be careful not to cut off the seam allowance. Repeat for the remaining outer lines. Leave removable foundations in place until your quilt top is assembled.

Sew Easy

Although you can use scissors to trim your blocks, rotary-cutting equipment is more accurate. The ruler holds the unstitched outside edges of the logs firmly in place as you cut with the rotary cutter.

Appliqué Basics

Review "Making and Using Templates" on page 186 to learn how to prepare templates for appliqué. Lightly draw around each template on the right side of the fabric using a pencil or other nonpermanent marker. These are the fold-under lines. Cut out the pieces ⅛ to ¼ inch to the outside of the marked lines.

In this section, we include a number of additional techniques to assist you with the specific projects in this book. You may find that a combination of methods will work best within the same quilt, depending on the individual shapes involved. We suggest that you experiment with each of these techniques to see which best suits your sewing style.

The Needle-Turn Method

Pin the pieces in position on the background fabric, always working in order from the background to the foreground. For best results, don't turn under or appliqué edges that will be covered by other appliqué pieces. Use a thread color that matches the fabric of the appliqué piece.

Step 1. Bring the needle up from under the appliqué patch exactly on the drawn line, as shown in **Diagram 42**. Fold under the seam allowance on the line to neatly encase the knot.

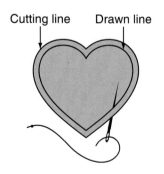

Diagram 42

Step 2. Insert the tip of the needle into the background fabric right next to where the thread comes out of the appliqué piece. Bring the needle out of the background fabric approximately ¹⁄₁₆ inch away from and up through the very edge of the fold, completing the first stitch, as shown in **Diagram 43**.

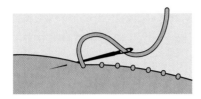

Diagram 43

Step 3. Repeat this process for each stitch, using the shank of your needle to turn under ½-inch-long sections of seam allowance at a time. As you turn under a section, press it flat with your thumb and then stitch it in place, as shown in **Diagram 44.**

Diagram 44

Sow Easy

Here are a few extra pointers for needle-turn appliqué.

• For a neater finished edge, clip inner points and curves before sewing. Make a perpendicular cut into an inner point, almost to the turn line. Make small V-shaped cuts on inner curves, again almost to the turn line. Make as many cuts as necessary to help you achieve a smooth fold. Take a few extra appliqué stitches at cuts to reinforce fabric. Use a drop of Fray Check as necessary to prevent raveling.

• Turn under points by cutting off the tip slightly. Fold the remaining seam allowance under to the turn line. Next, turn the seam allowance on one side of the point, then the other. To achieve a sharp point, it may be necessary to trim excess fabric at the folds as you work.

Freezer Paper Appliqué

Freezer paper can help make many appliqué projects easier. The paper acts as a stabilizer, allowing crisper points and smoother curves.

You can purchase plain white freezer paper at most grocery stores. Gridded freezer paper is available at many quilt shops.

Two different methods of freezer paper appliqué are explained here. Read through the directions for both, then choose the method that suits you best.

Method 1: Freezer Paper Appliqué

Step 1. Use a template to draw your patterns onto the dull (nonwaxy) side of the freezer paper.

Step 2. Cut out the shapes on the lines. Do not add a seam allowance.

Step 3. Use a medium to hot, *dry* iron to press the shiny (waxy) side of the shapes onto the right side of your fabric, as shown in **Diagram 45.** The iron will adhere the paper to the fabric.

Diagram 45

Step 4. Cut out the shape from the fabric, adding a ³⁄₁₆- to ¼-inch seam allowance around all edges of the paper template, as shown in **Diagram 46.**

Diagram 46

Step 5. Peel away the freezer paper and center it, waxy side up, on the reverse side of your fabric. Press the seam allowance over the template, as shown in **Diagram 47.** The waxy coating will soften and hold your seam in place. This method eliminates basting, but you will still need to clip the curves and points.

Diagram 47

Step 6. Appliqué the pieces to the block, then make a small slit in the background fabric and use a pair of tweezers to remove the freezer paper.

Method 2: Freezer Paper Appliqué

Follow Steps 1 through 4 under "Method 1: Freezer Paper Appliqué." Leaving the freezer paper adhered to the right side of your fabric, pin the piece to the background fabric. As you stitch the appliqué to the background, turn under the seam allowance on the edge of the freezer paper. Use the edge of the paper as a guide for the fold of your fabric. After your appliqué is stitched in place, gently peel off the freezer paper.

Making Bias Vines

Some of the projects in this book include sashing or borders with appliqué bias strips for vines. The directions specify the size fabric square required for the individual project, as well as the number of strips needed. The strip width given is the width you will need to cut the strips if you are using bias bars. If you are not using bias bars, the instructions here indicate the formula for determining the width to cut the bias strips.

Step 1. Mark and cut a 45 degree angle on the vine fabric, as shown in **Diagram 48A.**

Step 2. Cut bias strips parallel to the first 45 degree cut, as shown in **48B.** If you are using the fold method described in Step 3, multiply the desired finished width of the vine by 3, add ¼ inch to that figure, and cut. For example, if you want a vine to finish at ¾ inch wide, the bias strips should measure 2½ inches.

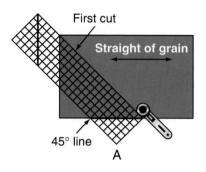

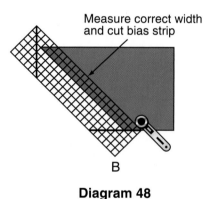

Diagram 48

Step 3. Fold each strip into thirds, as shown in **Diagram 49.** Make sure that the raw edges will be concealed by the folded edges. Press carefully. Position, pin or baste, then appliqué the vines in place, as instructed in the project directions.

Diagram 49

Using Bias Bars

Using bias bars is particularly helpful when you need long, narrow stems or vines. Bias bars, which are sold in sets of several widths, are made to withstand the heat of an iron.

Step 1. Cut a bias strip, as shown in **Diagram 48.** The chart below lists cut widths for three sizes of bias strips. **Note:** These widths apply only to strips cut for bias bars.

Finished Width	Cut Width
1/8 inch	7/8 inch
1/4 inch	1 1/8 inches
3/8 inch	1 3/8 inches

Step 2. Fold the strip in half lengthwise, with wrong sides together. Press lightly to hold the edges of the fabric together as you stitch. To avoid stretching, set the iron down to press one section, lift the iron, set it down and press a different section, and repeat until the entire strip has been pressed. Sew the raw edges together, using a 1/4-inch seam allowance. Trim the seam allowance to approximately 1/8 inch, as shown in **Diagram 50A.**

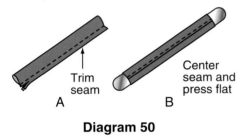

Diagram 50

Step 3. Insert the appropriate-size bias bar into the tube. Turn the tube slightly to center the seam along the flat edge of the bar, as shown in **50B.** Dampen the fabric with water or spray starch, and press the seam allowance to one side.

Step 4. Flip the tube over, and check to make sure the seam will be hidden when the strip is appliquéd to the quilt. When you are satisfied with the appearance, press the top side of the tube and remove the bias bar. If the vines are particularly long, you will need to slide the bias bar along the inside of the fabric tube to press the entire length before removing the bar.

Pressing Basics

Proper pressing can make a big difference in the appearance of a finished block or quilt top. It allows patchwork to open up to its full size, permits more precise matching of seams, and results in smooth, flat work. Quilters are divided on the issue of whether a steam or dry iron is best; experiment to see which works best for you. Keep these tips in mind:

• Press seam allowances to one side, not open. Whenever possible, press toward the darker fabric. If you find you must press toward a lighter fabric, trim the dark seam allowance slightly to prevent show-through.

• Press seams of adjacent rows of blocks, or rows within blocks, in opposite directions. The pressed seams will fit together snugly, producing precise intersections.

• Press, don't iron. Bring the iron down gently and firmly. This is especially important if you are using steam.

• To press appliqués, lay a towel on the ironing board, turn the piece right side down on the towel, and press very gently on the back side.

Assembling Quilt Tops

Lay out all the blocks for your quilt top using the quilt diagram or photo as a guide to placement. Pin and sew the blocks together in vertical or horizontal rows for straight-set quilts and in diagonal rows for diagonal-set quilts. Press the seam allowances in opposite directions from row to row so that the seams will fit together snugly when rows are joined.

To keep a large quilt top manageable, join rows into pairs first and then join the pairs. When pressing a completed quilt top, press on the back side first, carefully clipping and removing hanging threads; then press the front.

Mitering Borders

Step 1. Start by measuring the length of your finished quilt top through the center. Add to that figure two times the width of the border, plus 5 inches extra. This is the length you need to cut the two side borders. For example, if the quilt top is 48 inches long and the border is 4 inches wide, you need two borders that are each 61 inches long (48 + 4 + 4 + 5 = 61). In the same manner, calculate the length of the top and bottom borders, then cut the borders.

Step 2. Sew each of the borders to the quilt top, beginning and ending the seams ¼ inch from the edge of the quilt. Press the border seams flat from the right side of the quilt.

Step 3. Working at one corner of the quilt, place one border on top of the adjacent border. Fold the top border under so that it meets the edge of the other border and forms a 45 degree angle, as shown in **Diagram 51**. If you are working with a plaid or striped border, check to make sure the stripes match along this folded edge. Press the fold in place.

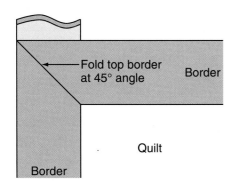

Diagram 51

Step 4. Fold the quilt top with right sides together and align the edges of the borders. With the pressed fold as the corner seam line and the body of the quilt out of the way, sew from the inner corner to the outer corner, as shown in **Diagram 52.**

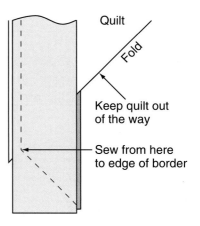

Diagram 52

Step 5. Unfold the quilt and check to make sure that all points match and the miter is flat. Trim the border seam allowance to ¼ inch and press the seam open.

Step 6. Repeat Steps 3 through 5 for the three remaining corners.

Marking Quilting Designs

To mark a quilting design, use a commercially made stencil, make your own stencil using a sheet of plastic, or trace the design from a book page. Use a nonpermanent marker—such as a silver or white pencil, chalk pencil—or chalk marker, that will be visible on the fabric. You can even mark with a 0.5 mm lead pencil, but be sure to mark lightly.

If you are using a quilt design from a book, either trace the design onto tracing paper or photocopy it. If the pattern will be used many times, glue it to cardboard to make it sturdy.

For light-color fabrics that you can see through, place the pattern under the quilt top and trace the quilting design directly onto the fabric. Mark in a thin, continuous line that will be covered by the quilting thread.

With dark fabrics, mark from the top by drawing around a hard-edged design template. To make a simple template, trace the design onto template plastic and cut it out around the outer edge. Trace around the template onto the fabric, then add inner lines by eye.

Piecing the Quilt Backing

Depending upon the size of your quilt, you may not have to piece the quilt back if you're making a small wallhanging, which is only 46¾ × 35 inches in size. However, if you are making a larger wallhanging or a bed-size quilt, piecing the backing is necessary. **Diagram 53** shows how quilt backings are generally pieced together for each quilt size. Refer to the project directions, however, for information on yardage, how to cut the backing fabric, how to seam it, and pressing suggestions.

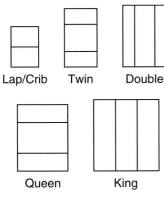

Diagram 53

Layering and Basting

Carefully preparing the quilt top, batting, and backing will ensure that the finished quilt will lie flat and smooth. Place the backing wrong side up on a large table or clean floor. Center the batting on the backing and smooth out any wrinkles. Center the quilt top right side up on the batting; smooth it out and remove any loose threads.

If you plan to hand quilt, baste the quilt with thread. Use a long darning needle and white thread. Baste outward from the center of the quilt in a grid of horizontal and vertical rows approximately 4 inches apart.

If you plan to machine quilt, baste with safety pins. Thread basting does not hold the layers securely enough during machine quilting, plus the thread is more difficult to remove when quilting is completed. Use rustproof nickel-plated brass safety pins in size #0, starting in the center of the quilt and pinning approximately every 3 inches.

Hand Quilting

For best results, use a hoop or a frame to hold the quilt layers taut and smooth during quilting. Work with one hand on top of the quilt and the other hand underneath, guiding the needle. Don't worry about the size of your stitches in the beginning; concentrate on making them even, and they will get smaller over time.

Getting started: Thread a needle with quilting thread and knot the end. Insert the needle through the quilt top and batting about 1 inch away from where you will begin stitching, as shown in **Diagram 54**. Bring the needle to the surface in position to make the first stitch. Gently tug on the thread to pop the knot through the quilt top and bury it in the batting.

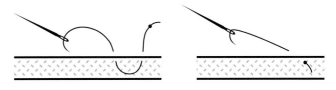

Diagram 54

Taking the stitches: Insert the needle through the three layers of the quilt. When you feel the tip of the needle with your underneath finger, gently guide it back up through the quilt. When the needle comes through the top of the quilt, press your thimble on the end with the eye to guide it down again through the quilt layers, as shown in **Diagram 55**. Continue to quilt in this manner, taking two or three small running stitches at a time.

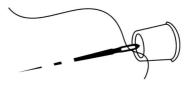

Diagram 55

Ending a line of stitching: Bring the needle to the top of the quilt just past the last stitch. Make a knot at the surface by bringing the needle under the thread where it comes out of the fabric and up through the loop of thread it creates. Repeat this knot and insert the needle into the hole where the thread comes out of the fabric. Run the needle inside the batting for an inch and bring it back to the surface, as shown in **Diagram 56.** Tug gently on the thread to pop the knot into the batting layer. Clip the thread.

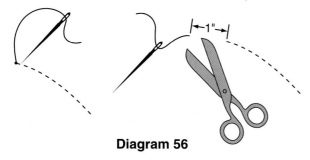

Diagram 56

Machine Quilting

For best results when doing machine-guided quilting, use a walking foot (also called an even feed foot) on your sewing machine. For free-motion quilting, use a darning or machine-embroidery foot.

Use thread to match the fabric colors, or use clear nylon thread in the top of the machine and a white or colored thread in the bobbin. To secure the thread at the beginning of a line of stitches, adjust the stitch length on your machine to make several very short stitches, then gradually increase to the regular stitch length. As you near the end of the line, gradually reduce the stitch length so that the last few stitches are very short.

For machine-guided quilting, keep the feed dogs up and move all three layers as smoothly as you can under the needle. To turn a corner in a quilting design, stop with the needle inserted in the fabric, raise the foot, pivot the quilt, lower the foot, and continue stitching.

For free-motion quilting, disengage the feed dogs so you can manipulate the quilt freely as you stitch. Guide the quilt under the needle with both hands, coordinating the speed of the needle with the movement of the quilt to create stitches of consistent length.

Making and Attaching Binding

Double-fold binding, which is also called French-fold binding, can be made from either straight-grain or bias strips. To make double-fold binding, cut strips of fabric four times the finished width of the binding, plus seam allowance. In general, cut strips 2 inches wide for quilts with thin batting or scalloped edges and 2¼ to 2½ inches wide for quilts with thicker batting.

Straight-Grain Binding

To make straight-grain binding, cut crosswise strips from the binding fabric in the desired width. Sew them together end to end with diagonal seams.

Place the strips with right sides together so that each strip is set in ¼ inch from the end of the other strip. Sew a diagonal seam, as shown in **Diagram 57,** then trim the excess fabric, leaving a ¼-inch seam allowance.

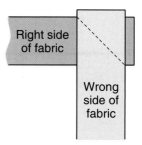

Diagram 57

Continuous Bias Binding

Bias binding can be cut in one long strip from a square of fabric that has been cut apart and resewn into a tube. To estimate the number of inches of binding a particular square will produce, use this formula: Multiply the length of one side by the length of another side, and divide the result by the width of binding you want. Using a 30-inch square and 2¼-inch binding as an example: $30 \times 30 = 900$; $900 \div 2\frac{1}{4} = 400$ inches of binding.

Step 1. To make bias binding, cut a square in half diagonally to get two triangles. Place the two triangles right sides together, as shown, and sew with a ¼-inch seam, as shown in **Diagram 58.** Open out the two pieces and press the seam open.

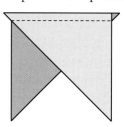

Diagram 58

Step 2. Using a pencil and a see-through ruler, mark cutting lines on the wrong side of the fabric in the desired binding width. Draw the lines parallel to the bias edges, as shown in **Diagram 59**.

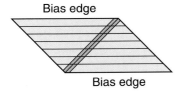

Bias edge

Bias edge

Diagram 59

Step 3. Fold the fabric with right sides together, bringing the two nonbias edges together and offsetting them by one strip width (as shown in **Diagram 60**). Pin the edges together, creating a tube, and sew with a ¼-inch seam. Press the seam open.

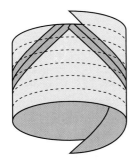

Diagram 60

Step 4. Cut on the marked lines, turning the tube to cut one long bias strip, as shown in **Diagram 61**.

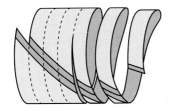

Diagram 61

Attaching the Binding

Trim excess batting and backing even with the quilt top. For double-fold binding, fold the long binding strip in half lengthwise, with wrong sides together, and press. Beginning in the middle of a side, not in a corner, place the strip right sides together with the quilt top, align raw edges, and pin.

Step 1. Fold over approximately 1 inch at the beginning of the strip and begin stitching ½ inch from the fold, as shown in **Diagram 62**. Sew the binding to the quilt, using a ¼-inch seam and stitching through all layers.

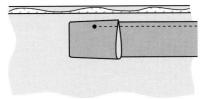

Diagram 62

Step 2. As you approach a corner, stop stitching ¼ inch from the raw edge of the corner. Backstitch and remove the quilt from the machine. Fold the binding strip up at a 45 degree angle, as shown in **Diagram 63A**. Fold the strip back down so there is a fold at the upper edge, as shown in **63B**. Begin sewing ¼ inch from the top edge of the quilt, continuing to the next corner. Miter all four corners in this manner.

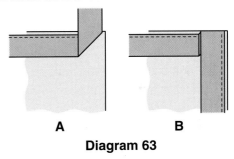

A   **B**

Diagram 63

Step 3. To finish the binding seam, overlap the folded-back beginning section with the ending section, as shown in **Diagram 64**. Stitch across the fold, allowing the end to extend approximately ½ inch beyond the beginning.

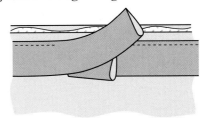

Diagram 64

Step 4. Turn the binding to the back of the quilt and blindstitch the folded edge in place, covering the machine stitches with the folded edge. Fold in the adjacent sides on the back and take several stitches in the miter. In the same way, add several stitches to the miters on the front, as shown in **Diagram 65.**

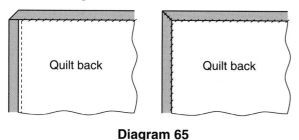

Diagram 65

Binding Curves

It is important that you use bias binding, which has more stretch, for quilts with curved outer edges. Refer to "Making and Attaching Binding" on page 206 for detailed information about making French-fold bias binding. You will need to make your bias binding 2 inches wide.

Step 1. To estimate the length of bias binding needed, measure around the perimeter of one outside arc. Multiply this measurement by the number of arcs around the outside of the quilt, then add 15 inches to the measurement. The calculation is the approximate number of inches of bias binding you will need.

Step 2. Begin sewing on the binding at the midpoint of a ring. With raw edges even, sew the binding around the curve, easing in the fullness. Do not stretch the binding to make it smooth.

Step 3. When you get to the inner point of two arcs, clip the seam allowance of the quilt for a flat fit, as shown in **Diagram 66.** Keep the needle down through all thicknesses of fabric, pivot at the inner point, and then continue stitching around the next curve, easing in the fullness of the binding.

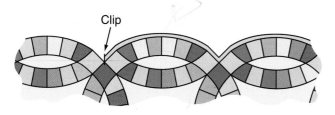

Diagram 66

Step 4. Continue sewing around each curve, clipping as necessary to help the binding turn at the corners. As you sew, make sure the portion of the quilt where binding has been attached is lying flat and is not buckled or puckered by binding that is pulled too tight.

When you have completed sewing the binding to the front of the quilt, fold the binding to the back of the quilt and stitch it in place by hand. Bury your thread tails as you go. As you near an inner point, fold the binding on one side of the point and stitch it to the inner corner. Then fold in the binding on the other side of the corner. The binding will automatically form a miter. Continue hand stitching in place.

Treat outer, pointed areas of connecting wedges as you would a quilt corner, mitering each outer point as described in Step 2 of "Attaching the Binding" on page 207.

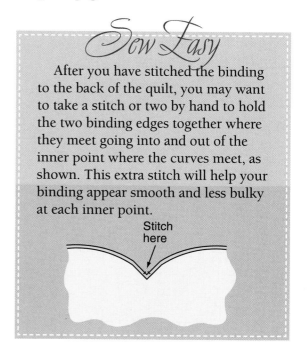

Sew Easy

After you have stitched the binding to the back of the quilt, you may want to take a stitch or two by hand to hold the two binding edges together where they meet going into and out of the inner point where the curves meet, as shown. This extra stitch will help your binding appear smooth and less bulky at each inner point.

Stitch here

Signing Your Quilt

Be sure to sign and date your finished quilt. Your finishing touch can be a simple signature in permanent ink or an elaborate inked or embroidered label. Add any other pertinent details that can help family members or quilt collectors 100 years from now understand what went into your labor of love.

Color Plans

Photocopy and enlarge these color plans and use them to experiment
with color schemes for your quilt.

Broken Star

Spiderwebs and Dewdrops

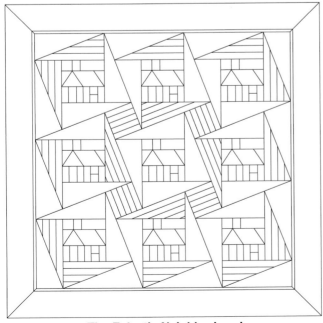

The Eclectic Neighborhood

Trade Secrets

Boredom with a project often leads to yet another UFO (UnFinished Object). Get together with another quilting friend and trade projects. It will be just like starting something new, which is probably what you would have done anyway. This theory also works for completing stages of the quilting process you don't like to do, like basting and binding. Swap jobs with someone else, or hire someone to do it for you.

Trailing Starflower

Reasons to Quilt

1. It's raining.

2. The cat purred.

3. There's a clean spot on the kitchen table.

4. The sun is shining.

5. You got a call from a credit card solicitor.

6. The mail came early.

7. Your doctor's appointment was canceled.

8. Your mother-in-law is coming for an extended visit.

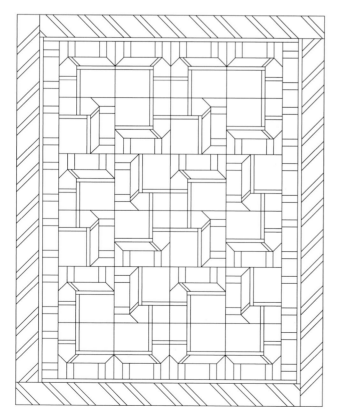

Row Houses

Barn Raising Pinwheels

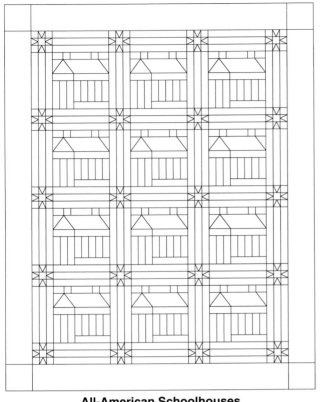

All-American Schoolhouses

Amish Easter Baskets

Colorful Scrap Baskets

*When life
hands you scraps,
make quilts.*

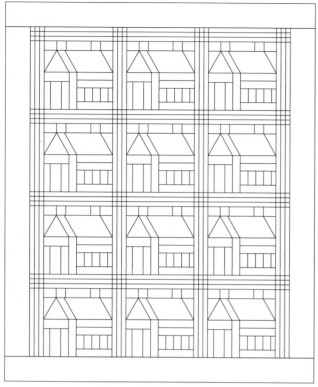

Little Red Schoolhouses

Timesaving Tip

Make one block before cutting

out the pieces for the entire quilt.

If there are any mistakes or you

don't like the color combination,

you can catch those problems

without wasting lots of time,

energy, and fabric.

WANTED: Candidates for Quilting Queen

Must be able to:

- Achieve a perfect ¼" seam

- Ignore large piles of laundry and dishes

- Create handmade works of art for all occasions

- Give away handmade works of art without regret

- Smuggle bags of fabric into house without being noticed

- Stash large amounts of fabric throughout the living quarters

- Juggle multiple projects without guilt

- Understand that fat quarters do not need to lose weight

- Attend monthly piece talks and be familiar with quilting lingo

- Consume a wide variety of chocolate-related goods

Teacher of the Year

Robbing Peter to Pay Paul

Absolutely free
stuff for quilters:

• Inspiration

• Creativity

• Warm Fuzzies

• Relaxation

Blessed
are the
Piecemakers

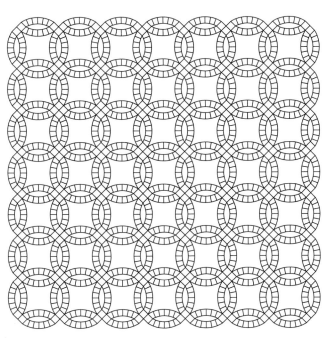

Plaid Double Wedding Ring

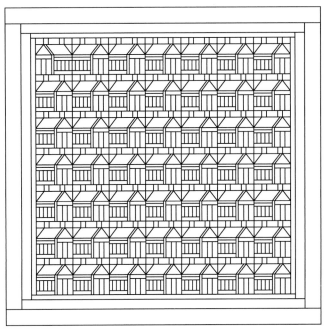

Homespun Houses

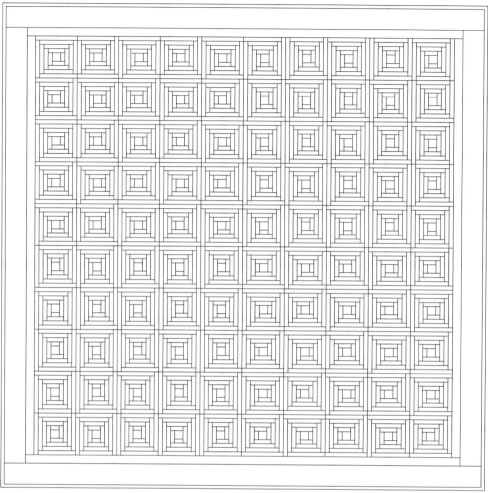

Barn Raising

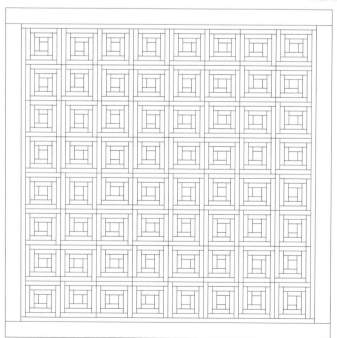

Paths to the Diamonds

Pass it on!

Keep the quilting bug alive and well by infecting someone else with your love of the art. Choose an easy block to begin with so that success is easily achieved. Instill good habits but be relaxed about the "rules" of quilting. Learning is sometimes achieved by making mistakes. Above all, have fun!

On the Road Again . . . Paducah Bound

Pickled Watermelon

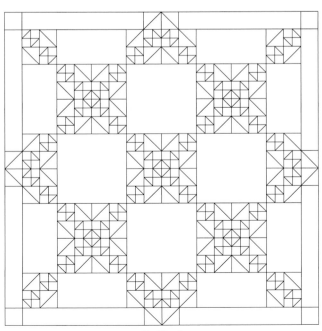

Solitude

*A Quilt
Fits Perfectly
Every Time*

Sports for Quilters

- Running to the quilt shop

- Hurdling over piles of books

- Lifting large quantities of fabric

- Racing to finish a project deadline

- Swimming through pages of quilt magazines

- Kicking around new ideas

- Spinning new yarns about quilting adventures

- Cycling through decades of quilting designs

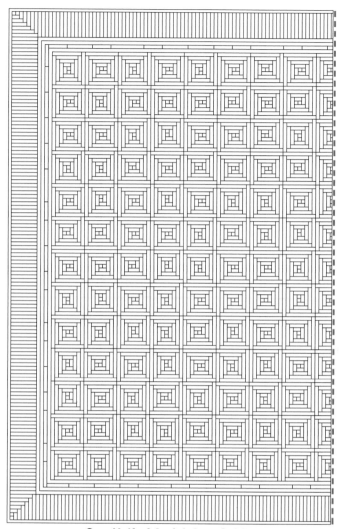

One-Half of Amish Log Cabin

Rose Rings

*Quilters Make
Great Comforters*

ACKNOWLEDGMENTS

Barn Raising Pinwheels, pieced by Barbara Berliner, Dexter, Michigan, and machine quilted by Cathy Sexton. Barbara made this quilt for her son, Matthew. She has been quilting for nearly 20 years and is a member of the Greater Ann Arbor Quilt Guild and the Booneslick Trail Quilters Guild. Her quilt design is a variation of a pattern called Give and Take that originally appeared in *Quiltmaker* magazine No. 23.

Rose Rings, made by Susan Stein, White Bear Township, Minnesota. Susan is a prolific quilter, having made hundreds of quilts, wallhangings, and garments since beginning quiltmaking in 1977. She is also the author of *Double Wedding Ring Quilts: Coming Full Circle* and has contributed to several books in the Singer Reference Library.

Barn Raising, made by Mark Stratton, Pasadena, California. Mark was introduced to quiltmaking by his mother, Carly Stratton, a former home-ec teacher who "let no one leave the house without learning to sew." Mark is inspired by images as diverse as traditional Amish quilts and the Navajo rugs he and his wife collect. This quilt is the result of what Mark calls "careful planning and considerable serendipity." Begun as a way to use up some teal fabric, the quilt grew to include navy and royal blue, pink, purple, and magenta. It was hand quilted by an Amish family.

Row Houses, made by Judy Spahn, who now resides in scenic Yellville, Arkansas. Quilting has taken a back seat to raising Boer goats and working to improve forests on land inherited from her parents. Judy's quiltmaking career, begun in the 1970s, has included 12 years on the Jinny Beyer Hilton Head Seminar staff, membership in the Virginia art quilt group New Image, and participation in the Fairfield Fashion Show. Many of her quilts have been published in Jinny Beyer's books and in various magazines. Judy's quilt Row Houses illustrates her early interest in experimenting with geometric design. Judy continues to create original geometric work and to share her love of design through occasional lectures and workshops in her new Arkansas location.

Trailing Starflower, made by Bethany S. Reynolds, Ellsworth, Maine. Bethany is the author of several quilt books, including *Magic Stack-n-Whack® Quilts*. She and her husband run a pattern and ruler business, BSR Design, Inc. Bethany lectures and teaches quilting across the United States and abroad.

Spiderwebs and Dewdrops, made by Susan Stein, White Bear Township, Minnesota. This wallhanging is an example of Susan's specialty Double Wedding Ring quilts, which combine a traditional pattern with unexpected contemporary embellishments. It also is made with Susan's favorite medium—hand-dyed cotton fabrics.

The Eclectic Neighborhood, made by Margaret Harrison, Charleston, South Carolina. Margaret began this unusual exploration of color and motion in Mary Golden's Housing Development class. She likes to experiment with new quilting techniques and uses the creative process as an exciting way to add a new dimension to her life. Margaret is a charter member of the Cobblestone Quilters Guild and the Quilters of South Carolina.

Solitude, made by Johanna Wilson, Plum Creek Patchwork, Walnut Grove, Minnesota, and machine quilted by Bonnie Erickson. Since she first quilted an antique quilt top in 1984, Johanna has become a nationally known quilting teacher and designer with nine published books, numerous patterns, and a wide assortment of articles in national quilt magazines. She has also designed several popular fabric lines, and her quilt retreats have brought many quilters to the Minnesota prairie to share her enthusiasm and expertise.

All-American Schoolhouses, made by Sharyn Craig, El Cajon, California. Sharyn is a nationally recognized quilting teacher and author. As a teacher, she admits that the Schoolhouse block is a sentimental favorite of hers. She combined traditional schoolhouses with pieced stars in this project to use as a class sample on quilt settings.

Robbing Peter to Pay Paul, made by Becky Herdle, North Branford, Connecticut. Becky enjoys making traditional quilts with a colorful twist, and she calls this quilt her Amish Orange Peel. Her book, *Time-Span Quilts: New Quilts from Old Tops*, was released in 1994.

Amish Easter Baskets, made by Elsie Vredenburg, Tustin, Michigan. Amish Easter Baskets has been judged at numerous quilt shows and has won awards totaling $2,700. Elsie donated this beauty to the Museum of the American Quilter's Society (MAQS) in Paducah, Kentucky. The quilt appears here courtesy of Elsie and MAQS. Elsie is an accomplished quilter who drafted the pattern for Amish Easter Baskets based on an antique quilt.

Broken Star, made by Kathryn L. England, Lewiston, Idaho. Kathryn first tried quilting in 1980, when her husband started medical school, and she's been "hooked" ever since. She made this quilt as a gift for her husband. It appeared in the Summer 1993 issue of *Old Fashioned Patchwork*. Kathryn is a member of the Seaport Quilters Guild in Lewiston.

Colorful Scrap Baskets, pieced by Naoko Anne Ito, Berkeley, California, and quilted by Betty Schoenhals. Naoko Anne drafted the pattern herself and machine-pieced the quilt top. It wasn't until eight years later that she found Betty, a quilter she trusted to do the fine hand quilting. Naoko Anne is a member of the East Bay Heritage Quilters, and she organized the first United States/Japan quilting symposium. She has also taken several groups of American quilters and teachers to Japan. She credits her quilting teacher, Roberta Horton, for inspiring her.

On the Road Again . . . Paducah Bound, made by Nancy Chizek, Ann Arbor, Michigan. Nancy found inspiration for this quilt from a design by quiltmaker and author Trudie Hughes, and created it for a challenge project in which the black and dark gray fabrics were provided. This was Nancy's first attempt at free-motion machine quilting. She's been quilting for about 14 years and says she enjoys all aspects of the process, "especially buying the fabric." Nancy uses both hand and machine techniques for piecing, appliqué, and quilting.

Paths to the Diamonds, made by Doris Heitman, Williamsburg, Iowa, and quilted by Alice Williamson. Doris created her contemporary-looking quilt after hearing a lecture by quiltmaker and teacher Mary Ellen Hopkins. She likes Log Cabins because of the many variations possible. A longtime quilter, Doris prefers wallhangings because she can finish them quickly and move on to the next project.

Little Red Schoolhouses, made by Mary Stori, Brodhead, Wisconsin. Mary is an internationally recognized lecturer, teacher, author, judge, and quilter whose work has appeared and won awards in numerous national shows. She has written extensively for sewing-related magazines and books. Mary has authored *The Wholecloth Garment Stori, The Stori Book of Embellishing,* and *The Stori of Beaded Embellishment.* Her newest book is *Beading Basics: 30 Embellishment Techniques for Quilters.* She's appeared on HGTV's *Simply Quilts* and *Sew Perfect* several times. Mary has also designed garments for four Fairfield Fashion Shows and has designed a line of fabric and her own line of trapunto quilting stencils for Quilting Creations. Mary says that traveling worldwide to present lectures, workshops, and fashion shows, and escorting quilting tours for Specialty Tours keep her motivated.

Pickled Watermelon, made by Julee Prose, Ottumwa, Iowa. Julee adapted the Pickle Dish variation of the Wedding Ring for her original Pickled Watermelon quilt for the 1989 American Quilter's Society show in Paducah, Kentucky. This quilt was also featured in the June 1994 issue of *Quilting Today* magazine.

Amish Log Cabin, made by Elsie Schlabach, Millersburg, Ohio. Elsie was inspired to create a quilt in the tradition of Amish scrap quilts of the 19th century. The quilt uses 47 different colors and combines hand and machine piecing and hand quilting. Elsie has been quilting since 1956 and has won numerous awards for her work. This quilt has won awards at the Quilter's Heritage show in Lancaster, Pennsylvania, and the American Quilter's Society show in Paducah, Kentucky.

Homespun Houses, made by Gerry Sweem, Reseda, California. Gerry is an award-winning quilter with ribbons from AIQA shows in Houston, the Lancaster Quilter's Heritage Celebration, and the American Quilter's Society in Paducah. Several of her quilts have also been published in quilting magazines. She is an avid hand quilter who, according to her husband, eats, sleeps, breathes, and quilts. Gerry is a member of the San Fernando Valley Quilt Guild.

Plaid Double Wedding Ring, made by Cleo Snuggerud, Sioux Falls, South Dakota. Cleo is the owner of Heirloom Creations, a retail shop that caters to the needs of quilters. She has been quilting for more than 30 years. Cleo is a first-generation quilter, but has taught her son to quilt and is currently working on teaching her mother.

Teacher of the Year, made by Miriam Dean, Winston-Salem, North Carolina. Miriam's inspiration for the quilt began with the bell tower on the small country church of which she was a member for many years. During the month that she finished the quilt, her schoolteacher daughter was named Teacher of the Year—a natural name for the quilt! Miriam's original block and quilting designs in this charming quilt have garnered several awards. In the Forsyth Piecers and Quilt Guild Show, it was named Judges' Choice and Viewers' Choice; in the Belle Chere Show in Asheville, North Carolina, it was also named Judges' Choice. Teacher of the Year was also featured in the Fall 1990 issue of *Quilt* magazine. Miriam has been quilting since 1981, and she primarily makes quilts for her family, friends, and charitable organizations, and for her own enjoyment.